AF521855

Through the Eyes of a Child

A Memoir

Kathleen Audrey James

Published 2019.

Printed in the United States of America.

ISBN 978-1-950647-19-4

Publisher's Cataloging-in-Publication data

Names: James, Kathleen Audrey. author.
Title: Through the eyes of a child : a memoir / Kathleen Audrey James.
Description: Parker [Colorado] : Bookcrafters, 2019. Hardcover.
Identifiers: ISBN: 978-1-950647-10-1
Subjects: LCSH: Autobiography. | Prep school students—Biography. |
World War, 1939-1945—Children—England—Biography.
BISAC: BIOGRAPHY & AUTOBIOGRAPHY / General
Classification: LCC DA566.9 | DDC 920 JAMES–dc22

Publishing assistance by
BookCrafters, Parker, Colorado.
www.bookcrafters.net

To my son Jeff
with all my love

1939 In the garden at "Holmfield"

Introduction

Mother always said it was the most beautiful day one could ever have imagined—cobalt blue skies, a slight breeze rustling through trees laden with fragrant blossoms and spring flowers blooming in the parks and gardens all over town. Music, emanating from the glass symphony hall in the Buxton Pavilion Gardens across St. John's Road, drifted through the open windows of the hospital room where she lay resting. It was the day of my birth, May 17, 1935.

Located about 165 miles northwest of London in the county of Derbyshire (pronounced "Darbyshire"), at the heart of England's "Peak District," Buxton has historically been hailed as "The Spa of Blue Waters," and the "Bath of the North," after the town in southwest Britain so famous for its own healing springs. Like Bath, Buxton too was an early Roman settlement, and, in its more recent history, a picturesque haven for visitors hailing from throughout Europe. It is tucked away in a basin encircled by mountain and moor *and* at one of the highest geographical spots in England. Axe Edge, just behind my childhood home, rises 1,760 feet above sea level, which, for the low-lying isle of England, is a high spot indeed.

Far away from the madding crowds of "the city," Buxton

has long meant the bucolic—fresh air, recreation, sport and cultural activity—its surrounding hamlets, villages, ancestral homes, parks and famous springs providing tales and histories enough to fill whole bookshelves. What follows is but one small history, a recollection of youth, a home, and a family. One that began, like everyone's does, I suppose, simply enough in a not-so-simple time.

The unrest that existed in Western Continental Europe at the time of my appearance that May, I learned soon enough, was overwhelmingly due to a man named Adolph Hitler. After the death of Germany's President Hindenburg in 1934, Hitler bullied himself into the roles of both Chancellor *and* Führer of Germany, and the words "Heil Hitler" became the salute demanded of every "loyal" German—foreshadowing his ultimate desire to wrest the same from the rest of Europe and the British Isles.

As news of his advancing army travelled from a Europe still haunted by the carnage of World War I, it seemed at first as implausible, as it would become so quickly and ultimately unavoidable, that if his will to global domination was to be thwarted, the task would fall to a nation of Britons intractable in their desire to make a stand. At the time of my birth, I think few of England's citizens were willing to concede the real possibility that our country could be affected so totally by the death, destruction, and deprivation it was about to experience; the growing storm a bit too far off and surely not the sort of thing one should stick one's nose into unless absolutely necessary.

Into this brewing turmoil I arrived, the second child of a Mummy and Daddy who, like so many others, were waiting and wondering what lay ahead.

Chapter 1

My father was a veteran of World War I who served on active duty in Germany after the war as part of the British Army of Occupation. The youngest of five children, his father had been perhaps the most popular official in Buxton—the much-revered and beloved Superintendent of Police. As a result, Dad grew up in a house attached to the police station, his family's lives much-governed by what went on within local law enforcement.

After being discharged from the army, Father returned home to resume his position at Buxton's local department of electricity—the Buxton branch office equivalent of America's Public Service Company during the twentieth century. His keen interest in mathematics and electrical engineering, coupled with an education acquired from a nearby college had led him to the job. A gentle man and a gentleman, a deep thinker with a great sense of adventure, Father was good at what he did and valued by his employer, but, he carried with him an underlying restlessness that spurred a great desire to travel to other parts of the world; one I have always largely put down to his travels while in the military.

My mother was third youngest in a family of twelve

children. She suffered an unhappy childhood, her mother's death occurring when Mum was but twelve years old and the final element in causing a family on the verge of collapse to split apart entirely, scattering them throughout the globe and leaving her, for all intents and purposes, alone. In her time, choices for unattached young women of no important social standing were definitely few and often bleak, if not disastrous. Mother, clear-headed, determined and a decidedly fortunate anomaly, successfully applied in her late teens for a position "in service" as companion to a titled "Lady" to whom, after some provided schooling, she remained employed for several years. It was only after the outbreak of World War I, when her ladyship's wish for her accompaniment abroad to play the tables at Monte Carlo filled Mother with such overwhelming dread of being trapped on the continent, she left her employ. A difficult decision—Mum loved her position and was fond of her ladyship—she simply could not acquiesce.

Armed with a newfound wealth of experience, she searched instead for another position, answering a newspaper ad for a companion and social secretary at the home of two "maiden ladies"—the Misses Shirt, Margaret and sister Emily—daughters of a late gentleman farmer whose estate provided for them the rest of their lives in the posh little Derbyshire spa town of Buxton. Understanding little more than the town's bucolic location just to the north of her birthplace in Halesowen, and its popularity among those with certain health concerns and retirees, mother travelled to meet them.

Upon her arrival and subsequent interview, each party was delighted with the other, and Mum was hired on the spot.

~~~
~~~

"I've brought you a nice cup of tea," said the vision in the doorway carrying a tray. Her voice was soft and appealing, her hair a cloud of spun gold. Her demeanour was gentle and ladylike and her eyes a deeply startling blue. The cup rattled as she handed it to him with unsteady hands, and, with equally unsteady hands he took it, thanking her for her thoughtfulness, and completely smitten by her breath-taking beauty and presence...

In the course of his regular duties for the Buxton Electricity Department, my father had been called in as an expert to troubleshoot a mysterious electrical problem at the home of two of Buxton's local maiden ladies... Electricity indeed! Chemistry too... My parents had met.

As they courted, my father eagerly shared all the possibilities he saw ahead and his dreams of all the places he wanted to go. At ease and surrounded by his family in a place he'd always known, he felt confident in whatever lay ahead. Mother, relatively new to her surroundings, her family and siblings uprooted, had, in my father, somewhat met her opposite. They shared a willingness to see where life would take them and a spirit of adventure and a love story that would span fifty years and three continents.

~~~

Dad had two older brothers who were grown and married. By the time he was in his teens, they were both living in one of England's larger cities, Birmingham, about sixty miles south of Buxton. My Uncle Sam, the eldest and named after my grandfather, shared many of my father's interests. An electrical engineer by profession, Sam wrote books on
~~~

engineering and taught at Birmingham University on occasion. He was a tall, well-built man like his father.

The second brother, Uncle Willy, was of slighter build and the middle one of the three boys. Quick-witted and analytical, Willy spent many years in India promoting linotype machines and printing products for a large British manufacturer. He was accompanied there by his wife, a prominent society figure and the daughter of the Commissioner of Roads for all of Great Britain. Upon their return to England, Willy became an editor at one of Birmingham's prominent daily newspapers. I remember him fondly and, although I did not have opportunity to be around him very much, we seemed to have a special rapport. He was always very warm in his manner, and I've never forgotten a piece of advice he shared. "Walk me to the bus station, Kath?" he asked on one of his visits, a drizzly day.

As we walked along, he said, "You're still just a young girl, but I'm going to tell you something very important—remember, you can do anything you want to in life if *you really want to do it.* And if you do, there'll be no stopping you... Never forget that." Such basic advice, I know, but so revolutionary at my young age. I truly never have forgotten it or just the way he said it. Each time throughout my life when convinced I couldn't do something, I have thought of our conversation and gone ahead and accomplished it anyway. As a rule, as well as a gift more valuable than any material one he could have ever given me, it has never worn out just as it has equally always stood me in good stead.

Father had a sister too, Evelyn (pronounced Eve-Lynn). Elegant and beautiful with shining auburn hair, everyone turned whenever Evelyn entered a room. The second eldest of the five children, she was self-sufficient and self-possessed, highly organized, and a true rarity for the time—a professionally licensed physical therapist and masseuse who received her professional training in London. The wild and overgrown moors surrounding Buxton were covered with heather that rotted down in the dampness to form layers of rich, black peat. Removed, this would be taken to the spa and mixed with Buxton's naturally sourced, eighty-two-degree Fahrenheit mineral waters. Evelyn would put patients on a regimen of therapy, massage, peat baths and compresses, which would be applied to the afflicted parts of the body to soothe joints and assist in the management of patients' aches and pains. She had her own "surgery" near Buxton's famous mineral baths and spa and worked with both the local doctors and doctors of patients who journeyed from all over the country to Buxton to address their health issues.

During my very early years, Evelyn was married to a photographer well-known for wedding and family portraits in town. The couple had two daughters who were grown and married by the time I approached my teens, by which time Evelyn and he had divorced. Evelyn then remarried to one of the town's leading doctors who was, somewhat unbelievably, also a Justice of the Peace and Magistrate with a grown family of his own—one of his sons was in fact our own family physician. There is actually a bit more to this story than I knew when I was young, but what's important is that Auntie Evelyn was ever-present during my young childhood, always wanting to take me under her wing to guide me to great accomplishments.

Being older than Daddy, Evelyn had also wanted in his earlier years to direct him in social life, as she, herself a socialite who loved to dance and throw parties, had a circle of friends many considered (not least according to her) among the "better society people one should know" in town. By my father and mother's estimations, they were "a very snobbish crowd." Every Saturday night there was a dance held in the glassed-in concert hall at the fashionable Pavilion Gardens in the centre of its beautiful park surrounded by tennis courts, bowling greens and tearooms. It even had its own resident symphony orchestra. It was certainly the place to see and be seen with friends of a "certain social standing," and Evelyn was always to be found near its centre on these very festive yet formal occasions for which the men wore black tie and pale yellow kid gloves, the ladies extravagant ball gowns.

As Daddy was young, single, and handsome, Evelyn absolutely insisted that he attend these soirees so that she might introduce him to suitable and eligible young ladies worthy of the family's respectable social position. Daddy, single-minded and a force to be reckoned with, was not so keen on this idea—neither of my parents could ever stand for nonsense or snobbery, perhaps another of the very qualities that attracted them to one another... However, Auntie Evelyn, a sheer force of her own, would not to be put off and, possessing a best friend who was both a young society woman and very attracted to Father, was absolutely driven to triumph in the discussion. It seemed to Evelyn a match made in heaven, and she was not taking no for an answer—determined he was going to marry this young lady.

Evelyn went to work on her scheme: arranging meetings, planning parties and further dances to attend—any excuse to put the two of them together as often as possible. Dad, needless to say, was neither impressed nor attracted to Evelyn's friend or any other woman in her circle. My mother, still a relatively new girl in town and definitely not a Buxtonian, much less a socialite, had simply come out of the blue and captured his heart. He was head over heels in love with a delicate rose whom he considered decidedly a cut above anyone else.

As far as Evelyn was concerned, it was war. My mother, while admittedly an incredibly sweet and lovely young lady, was an outsider and therefore definitely not good enough for her brother. At the mention of my father's preference for spending time with Mum, Evelyn would stamp her foot and carry on, refusing to include her in any plans just as she doggedly attempted to push my father more and more into the company of her friends and, especially, the suitable match she reckoned was for father's own good; whatever his obvious disinterest.

One day, just a little way into their courtship, my father arranged to have Mum meet him at his family home. She arrived before him and was met in the hallway by my Grandfather James, who, unlike Evelyn, both liked her very much and approved of her as my father's chosen companion. She adored him too, almost undoubtedly seeing in him a father figure she never had, and often telling me over the years how much she loved him for his fine character, gentleness, and wisdom—traits that all his sons indeed had inherited. Asking her into his study for a chat, Mum and Grandpa had spent a pleasant few minutes together when they heard someone in the hall. Thinking it was Dad, Mum excused herself and left Grandfather in the study. She walked down the hallway to look for him and, there, coming toward her in the other direction, was Evelyn.

As they passed, Evelyn gathered her skirts up in her fists and pulled them sharply to the side opposite Mother so they wouldn't touch as they passed, and then turning her head away as she did in a sharp gesture clearly meant to snub her.

Standing in the study doorway, Grandpa was a witness

to the whole thing and, startling both women, said in a booming voice: "*Evelyn!* In my study. *Now!*" Their raised voices came through the thick panelled door, and, shortly after, it burst open. Evelyn flounced out into the hall with Grandpa following, saying, again in a raised voice: "Young lady, you are not *FIT* to tie Alice's shoelaces... You ought to be ashamed of yourself!"

For some time after this event Evelyn was unwelcome in her father's house. But, in reality, the heated exchange happened to be the proverbial straw that broke the camel's back—and this is where the rest of Evelyn's tale may be told.

By the time the family had reached their threshold with Auntie Evelyn's insistence on interfering in my father's romantic life, things were already nearing the boiling point—under circumstances that I was only to learn when it was determined (like oh so many things in my life, it seems) when "old enough" to finally know!

As it turned out, my grandmother James had inadvertently discovered something one day while placing a vase that had been moved in the drawing room. As she picked it up, it made a rattling noise as though something were inside. She shook it and then held it upside down, playing with it for a while to dislodge whatever seemed to be trapped in it until, finally, a rolled up piece of paper fell out on which was written a letter—and not just any letter. It was a letter sent by a lover of Auntie's, arranging for their secret *tryst* in London while she was to be there on business, and containing information that made it clear this was just one correspondence in what was an ongoing, clandestine love affair between Evelyn and another man! Grandmother knew, too, very well, who the man was as well—a prominent Buxton businessman from a very well-known family like their own... She was simply horrified! Never had there been such scandalous behaviour in the family! She took the news immediately to Grandfather James.

Grandpa took over at once. Summoning Evelyn, he demanded the liaison stop immediately. Evelyn who, at that time especially, was, of course, risking nearly everything she had worked for professionally, not to mention the family's reputation and her prized social status in one grand and amorous gesture, agreed to end the affair, thereby saving everyone a public scandal, but, still, now, irrevocably and ultimately the family knew. It was something she could never undo, and it would mean a great rift between them. For certain things would never quite be the same with her parents. Unsurprisingly, at least to those who were in-the-know, shortly thereafter Evelyn and her photographer husband announced their divorce.

Many years later, as I approached young womanhood, it seemed too that for a time I would be next in line to receive Evelyn's attentions where matters and manners of society came to bear. I distinctly remember her coming to our house one day for a visit.

Mother answered the door and there she stood, an elegant and stately lady still, perfectly dressed and carefully made up. She said she'd come to discuss giving me an official "coming out party" and to make a debutante of me in the town where she was now living—which might've meant Stockport, Manchester, or even London, as she was an active member of society circles in each place. To complete my ascent up the social ladder, she also suggested sending me to a finishing school in Switzerland, so I would then have the proper background to move in the right circles throughout my life. Mother, who had rubbed shoulders with enough aristocracy in her life of service, said that she didn't believe in encouraging what she conceived of as a life of snobbery and pretence, and was not at all supportive of either idea. Father agreed. They declined the offer on the spot.

Auntie, who thought nothing good enough unless it was dripping with titled people who could "open doors" to high society was obviously upset, yet, sensing inevitable defeat on these issues, countered by begging my parents to at least let her send me to a private school for the rest of my education; she would pay. Mum and Dad declined this too, firmly stating that the school I was in was perfectly adequate and of a high standard—in fact, it was a scholarship school and I had passed all the examinations to be accepted.

The matter reached an impasse, and the visit concluded just so. Nevertheless, over the years, Evelyn came and went, and we continued to see her fairly regularly. She reluctantly but finally gave up trying to get her way when it came to my path to adulthood. While I agree with my parents' ultimate decisions on all counts, I had and have much gratitude to Evelyn for her concern for me and that she considered me worth bothering with at all. Among her attentions that received no qualms from my parents were her continuing practice of giving me books to read, ones that had also been her girls' favourites when my age; a treasure of schoolgirl stories galore! I absolutely revelled in their every page. A small victory for Evelyn, perhaps, but still oh-so rewarding for me, gifts that were as lasting and important, if not more so, than any invitation to any social affair I can imagine.

~~~
~~~

I never actually knew my grandfather James, but so wish I had. He died four years before I was born and, because he had served our little town from 1902 until 1916 as the Superintendent of Police, it was through his reputation that he lived on so vividly in both Buxton and my imagination that I almost came to feel at times I had known him. The townspeople called him "Super James" (short for Superintendent, of course, but one can't help but love the alternate possibility of its meaning) and by all accounts he was "super"— everything to everyone: a true English gentleman who acted as father-confessor, psychologist, *confidant* to the lovelorn, best friend, children's advisor, and, by so many accounts, all-around hero. I often reflected on the fact that it must have been a lot of pressure being one of his children, not only because one would have to be on one's best behaviour at all times, but because his standards were so very high. An excerpt from his obituary in the the *Buxton Advertiser*, somewhat says it all:

> *"By the death of Mr. Samuel James, ex-Superintendent of Police, Buxton has lost one of its most popular and unassuming residents, a man who was known and respected all over the town by people in all walks of life; who loved to crack a joke and laugh, and who could claim many more good friends than it is the lot of the average man to have."*

Stories about Grandpa's life in law enforcement have often come to mind over the years, especially whenever I watched American television in the 1960s and being struck that he, in essence, seemed the real British forerunner of the fictional

Sheriff Andy Taylor character played by Andy Griffith; the Buxton jailhouse sounding just like a slice of an English "Mayberry."

In particular, just like on its fictional American TV counterpart, every Saturday night the man everyone somewhat recognized as "the town drunk" would stagger into the Buxton Police Station and Grandpa would dutifully lock him up in a cell for the night to sober up. Come Sunday morning, Grandma would cook a full English breakfast complete with all its traditional trimmings—crumpets, bacon, eggs, both fried bread and tomatoes, and, of course, tea—which she would serve to him. Talk about more "guest" than prisoner! After this, Grandpa would see that he had a good hot bath and—part fatherly advice, part lecture—would turn him loose to go home to his wife and family. Of course, the fellow would more often as not be back the following week and, in my humble opinion, milked the whole ritual for all it was worth. One well imagines his wife's opinion of these episodes, while not having to have much imagination at all to divine the answer.

With the living quarters for Chief and family attached to the jail, home could present challenges as well. On one occasion, Dad told me that Grandpa had a dangerous prisoner in custody—an accused murderer and thoroughly bad lot—awaiting transfer to a jail in another city, who, somehow, managed to escape from his cell during the early morning hours. Grandma was in the kitchen cooking breakfast, and, as she was deaf, she never heard a thing when he crept up behind her and placed a knife to her throat. Putting her in front of him, he took her hostage and made his way into the street. Once there, he threw her violently to the ground—an act which added not only to her potential harm but also, as she was six months pregnant with my Auntie Dorothy, to her baby's as well. Fortuitously, no further or permanent damage was done and he was recaptured, but Grandma was understandably traumatized by the whole episode. She was always a brave woman, but it must have been very hard for her around these types of people at times.

In all, Grandpa served on the police force thirty-four years, the very picture of dutiful dedication, efficiency, good nature and fair dealing. During the latter part of his life, he suffered with heart trouble, afflicted nearly constantly with angina. In those days there were no further tests or effective treatments other than rest and as quiet a life as possible. My mother said that the sound of his measured steps as he would walk down the hallway of the James home at night to wind the huge grandfather clock at the foot of the stairs would live in her memory forever.

My father and mother were far away in the wilds of Canada when Grandpa died and never got the chance to say goodbye. The whole town turned out to pay their respects. He lies in Buxton's Fairfield churchyard.

~~~

Grandmother James, as previously noted, was deaf from an early age but we found ways to communicate. Most of her life was spent in silence and, toward its end (as she eventually lost her sight), in darkness as well. I remember our visits when she was unable to see anymore. She would place her hands over my face and say, "Ah, Kathleen, my dear girl," identifying me through touch alone.

She was born in London, within the sound of the storied Bow Bells of St. Mary's Church in Cheapside—a true Cockney—and, as typical of so many residents of the mean
~~~

streets of Dickensian London's notorious East End, into poverty. In my memories of her, she always seems frail and, befitting notions of a true old-world Victorian grandmother, to wear long, high-necked black velvet dresses with white lace peeking over the collars. She had come far from a life of abject poverty, one which saw her put to work as a maid at age eight in the London home of some well-to-do family. She was said to be so tiny at that time that they stood her on an orange box to wash their dishes.

At that point in her life Grandma could still hear, and her employers owned a piano to which she was very much attracted. Pianos during that era always had locks on them; I remember my first piano having one, although it was kept open. The one in this London home, however, was always locked so no one outside the family could play it. One can only guess that this must have made it even more attractive to her, and when the people were out, she said she would creep into the drawing room to sit beneath its keyboard, get her small hands between the top and bottom panels, and pluck the piano strings in attempts to make whatever music she could. When I was growing up she would admonish me, saying: "Kath, if you ever have the chance to learn to play the piano, you must. I never had the opportunity, but you must try! It is a wonderful thing to do."

On the very rare occasions she would come to our house, she would sit in the room while I played piano even though she couldn't hear it. She could see, though, and I knew watching her in turn that she was proud I'd learned to play. Perhaps if she could have heard she might not have been so impressed, but we'll leave that speculation as it is and focus on the happiness it brought to us both instead.

Grandma was fortunate in that she had a lifetime pension

from the police force and was thus well cared for as she aged. The pension allowed her to employ live-in care and, thus, she had a constant companion who cooked, cleaned, and was housed in an apartment in the house. Eventually, though, Grandma needed the services of a nursing home, which was, actually, a beautiful place that overlooked the Pavilion Gardens near where I was born.

One Sunday morning, age twelve, I went with Dad to visit her there, and while we sat holding her hands, she leaned suddenly forward and uttered a sharp sigh. She then lay back again and was gone… just like that, passing away right in front of our eyes.

Dad, numb with an incomprehension that quickly turned to shock, began to tremble, his eyes filling with tears. This was my first encounter with death, and I somehow knew inherently that I had to remain calm and strong for his sake. Taking him gently by the hand, I led him from her room to a sitting room down the hall where we sat quietly holding hands until we were ready to face the world again. Arrangements were made, and Grandma was laid to rest beside Grandpa at Fairfield; she had been ninety-two years old.

This event remained in my mind for a long time after, making me realize how precious and fleeting life really is, and instilling in me the idea that one should spend as much time as possible with those they love in this short life of ours.

Chapter 2

Mother's parents have always remained somewhat of a mystery. Anything I have ever pieced together about her large, fractured, and fractious family is based largely on her recollections up to the point when she left home, and those portrayed a life fraught with hardship, grief, and uncertainty.

To begin with, neither her father, a firm Protestant, nor her mother, a devout Catholic, would budge in their devotion to their chosen faiths. With twelve children to raise, they reached an equitably functional plan (if not necessarily ingenious in its ability to unite them), by deciding that rather than designating one religion for the whole family, they would bring the children up in abeyance to each denomination alternately—the first child, Catholic, the next Protestant, and so on and so on, back and forth, making the family a minor microcosm of a religious conflict not out of step with national discourse at the time. My mother's birth order meant that she was raised Protestant, or, Anglican, an adherent to the teachings of the Church of England.

Beyond the obvious complications raised in implementation

of this plan, more were added when some of the children (the youngest) came to be raised, through both Grandma's departure from the marriage and her eventual death, with different last names. My Grandfather's name on Mother's side was Shaw; my Grandmother's maiden name, Simpson. A household split in faith and with a matriarch and patriarch divided physically would not only fall, but also lent shaky determinations to the children's surnames: my mother, as one of the youngest, would go into adult life as Alice Simpson—*never* Shaw at her mother's behest, and certainly not hyphenated; the very least reason for this being, as she would joke in a rather less ladylike fashion than was her custom, that the assignation (pun intended) of initials in the arrangement made monogramming her luggage absolutely prohibitive: "Those three initials would never have allowed me to travel with *any* dignity."

The brother to whom my mother felt closest was ten years older than she and the eldest, Isaac Shaw. Named for their father, Isaac left home before my mother had achieved an age into double digits. His departure, she would ever-remember, was one of the first and truly bitter sadnesses doled out in an already tumultuous early life. On the whole she knew her brothers and sisters very little by the time things began to change (even more dramatically), the next few years compounding a near assurance that she would never know where in the world to find most of them as she carried on with her life.

When my grandmother Simpson died at age forty-seven, Mother's older siblings, much like Isaac, were mostly grown and gone, too, leaving her and three others behind with a father seemingly unable to cope with life. By all family accounts, Grandfather Shaw was always a difficult man with a quick temper, prone to heavy drinking, and, when doing so, to move quickly from merely difficult to nearly impossible. Subsequent fragmentary narrative histories become nearly untraceable past a point, but whatever the case, it remains clear that there was always a great deal of unhappiness in the home and the children were neither ever a significant priority beyond their rank and file adumbration in the family pecking order, nor particularly, adequately, or affectionately cared either for or about.

Eventually, Grandfather Shaw took another wife who, purportedly of similar disposition, habit, and general attitude toward children on the whole (and most certainly his), helped compound a nearly completely disastrous situation into an irreparable and final one. After Grandma Simpson's death, this drama culminated with an attempt to send the four youngest children—my mother included—to an orphanage. As to how it was foiled, the exact details are also lost, but what is clear is that thanks to the eldest daughter of Grandfather Shaw's new spouse, a schoolteacher and an obviously empathic one, the children were taken in as her own charges. My mother grew into a teenager in her household, along with her three younger "Simpson" siblings. If Mum ever spoke of these things, an act she was hard-pressed to do, she always related it with a sense of shame; one I have always assumed was self-ascribed for the failure of her family (more acutely and accurately her father) to live up to what she justifiably considered the absolute minimum of familial responsibility to its most vulnerable members. But, this is ultimately a superficial sign of a deeper wound about "appearances." On a much deeper level, one cannot (at least I cannot) imagine the agony it must have caused her and her siblings to have their remaining living parent confirm how valueless and unloved they were. The obvious lack of even enough fatherly affection to not allow them to be callously cast aside must have wounded deeply, making it either very difficult or very easy for my mother to move forward with, if not exactly courage, then, at least resolve.

My mother, desperately missing a real home, lacking the only brother with whom she felt safe, and with her remaining siblings dutifully (if perhaps not lovingly) cared for or scattered who knows where, chose the moment to seize her independence and strike out for some possible happiness over further heartbreak—obtaining her first lady's companionship post and removing herself once and for all from her unhappy circumstances at age twenty.

~~~

Mother's subsequent situation in service suited her. She had always been prim and proper, her siblings calling her, even at her young age, "Lady A." How fitting then that she first ended up in the employ of the titled Lady and then the Shirt sisters.

Her first foray—the one that had ended with her ladyship's trip to Monte Carlo—fostered the next. Her ladyship, a very wealthy, middle-aged heiress who lived in a huge mansion in Birmingham waited on by a full staff of servants, had my mother begin her employment by sending her to a school where she was trained to run the household. Her studies of "domestic science" included household management, interior decorating, entertaining, correspondence, and all the other related tasks required of a social secretary. Mum loved learning about, and inevitably handling, all the circumstances surrounding the execution of these matters, and then, putting her education to work supervising the housekeeper, maids,
~~~

cook, gardener and chauffer, as well as arranging household social engagements, dinners, and banquets. She planned menus, supervised table settings and guest lists, as well as coordinated the final seating arrangements of all attendees. She also accompanied her mistress in a carriage on social calls for the sole purpose of presenting her ladyship's calling card on a silver tray at the door of each of her destinations prior to her ladyship alighting from the carriage herself. It was an exciting and challenging job and she enjoyed it immensely. It most assuredly gave her confidence in taking her next position with the Shirt sisters in Buxton seamlessly, a relationship that would add even more dimension to her life than she could ever have imagined. She had yet to know it, but she was about to enter into a position that would establish more than one lifelong relationship—one that would see her taken into a home in which she was loved more like a daughter than an employee, and one that would inevitably introduce her to her own life as a member of a family of her own.

Chapter 3

The eldest of the daughters Shirt, Margaret, was the sedate and serious one. Her younger sister, Emily, was flighty and full of fun. Emily loved social occasions, parties, and lunching with her large circle of friends. Both were very active in the Buxton congregation of the Anglican Church and helped in its many charities, fundraising events, and church-sponsored town activities.

On one of those dreary afternoons of constant English rain not long after Mum entered their employ, one far too miserable to venture outdoors and with the entire household finding itself without much to do, Miss Margaret said to Mother, "Alice, why don't you go up to the attic and find a book? There are cartons of books up there just longing to be read."

A bookworm to begin with, Mum climbed the steep attic stairs and seated herself among the boxes, trunks, discarded bric-a-brac and treasures to search for an interesting tale to while away the gloomy afternoon. There were so many, dusty, heavy, and full of the promise of literary enjoyment. She set aside a few likely candidates before spotting a large trunk she thought would only contain more, but, as she pried it open, found it filled instead with objects shrouded in protective cloth. She unwrapped one and found something metallic and blackened with age. She called downstairs, and the Shirt sisters came up to see what she had found.

Mummy said, "I'm sorry, I wasn't meaning to pry, but looking for the books I came upon these. May I unwrap them?"

"Oh, those," Miss Emily said, "just throw them out. They're no good any more. We've been meaning to get rid of them. They belonged to Mother and Father but they've turned black and ugly."

Mum unwrapped the first one and she knew exactly what they were, having supervised the prior care and cleaning of similar objects in her ladyship's household. Obtaining permission, she hauled them all downstairs to the kitchen.

Using silver polish she began working. For days she cleaned, polished, and buffed each newly unwrapped piece, until what emerged before her were beautiful silver teapots, hot water jugs, a coffee pot, cheese board, and a lovely silver basket with a handle, each embossed with flowers and unique designs. They were simply exquisite.

Miss Margaret and Miss Emily were astounded to find that these things were not in fact ruined at all, they looked as good as new, and so thankful Mother had not followed their instructions to throw them away. The newly discovered treasures were installed in the china cabinet in the drawing room, and throughout my childhood I would help clean them for the holidays every year. Many years later, when both the sisters passed, they left the silver to Mummy to be handed down to me when I grew up and married. They reside in my home in a handsome cabinet worthy of their history, and I still polish them, lovingly recalling Mum and the sisters, and how fortunate I am to have them and the memories they represent.

Soon after their first incidental meeting on the day my father had been at the Shirt household to troubleshoot the electrical problem that ended in afternoon tea, Dad and Mum arranged to go out together on their first date. The Misses Shirt wanted, of course, to know where she was going, and she told them she was going for a walk with the young gentleman who had been sent to fix the electricity in their home. They were there when he arrived and wanted to know just who he was. He told them his name was Cecil Roberry James.

Miss Margaret asked, "Are you any relation to Superintendent James?"

"Yes, I'm his youngest son," he replied.

"Oh, well then, that's all right," she said. "But you will have to have Alice home for nine o'clock."

With that approval, Mum and Dad started to keep regular company. Their courtship lasted for about two years, during which time they discussed, as couples throughout time always have, planning their future together. My father, although settled on my mother, was still unsettled in knowing just where he wanted to be and how he wanted to live. He had been building quite a career for himself as a very respected member of staff at the Electricity Department, but he still hankered to explore the possibilities of unknown places and faraway climes. Grandpa James wanted him to go into banking, as his talent for mathematics was so impressive, but Dad had no interest in pursuing it. Over the years, I have often wondered if Grandpa was ever disappointed that none of his sons were interested in law enforcement. I know my Great Grandfather, like him, was on the police force, but whatever might have been the basis of any form of family tradition certainly halted with my father and his brothers.

After much discussion over these two years they kept company prior to marrying, my parents finally agreed that Daddy should fulfil his ongoing curiosity to find out just where they might begin their lives together. He would begin first by going to Australia. He had relatives who had settled in Melbourne and had always toyed with the idea of going to visit to explore opportunities there. Soon after they became engaged, he set sail for "down under" to find work, and to prepare things so that Mother could inevitably follow.

Upon his arrival, he stayed with Grandpa's relatives, his career training in Buxton serving him well. He fairly quickly obtained a position supervising the installation of electrical lighting plants in the Australian Outback, an adventure that saw him deciding to stay on "in the bush" on a sheep station in New South Wales. The job lasted only until the romance wore off and he realized it certainly wasn't what he truly wanted to do for the rest of his life. But Dad liked Australia and was anxious to get settled in Melbourne again so that he could send for Mother.

After returning to the city and once again acquiring employment in his field, he booked her passage on a ship for the long journey while both, with assistance from his various aunts and uncles, planned their wedding.

Chapter 4

The voyage from England to Australia in those days was a rough excursion for anyone, much less a young lady alone—a tremendous eight-week undertaking. Mother, scared (who wouldn't be), her feelings undoubtedly compounded by the Misses Shirt, who by this time looked upon her as a daughter and had all but become her guardians, really didn't want to see her to go at all. They wanted her close to them in England, not knowing what might lie ahead of her on such a distant and unknown continent. But, as intimidated as she might've been by the idea of possibly overwhelming circumstances, Mother was armed with an indomitable spirit, determination, and the courage of the convictions that had seen her make a successful new life for herself beyond her family, and would not be deterred. She simply *had* to go, love would accomplish the rest.

Facing the ever-turbulent seas of the notorious Cape of Good Hope, with storms so severe that the ship that carried her bobbed around like a toy on the ocean, Mother was convinced that all aboard would perish. For days no one was allowed to venture out of their cabins. She was, of course, horribly seasick too, so much so that she spent most of her time in the ship's infirmary, causing the ship's doctor to venture the grave concern they would have to bury her at sea. She lost a full two stones (twenty-eight pounds) in all. In the end, it was the doctor who saved her life through the most unlikely restorative powers of Guinness Stout. She hated every sip, but apparently, its highly caloric, iron-rich composition built up her strength, sustaining her when she couldn't keep anything else down.

Despite, or perhaps due in part to her near abject condition during the ordeal, the ship's doctor also seemed to somehow fall in love with his patient. He didn't want the voyage to end. Young, handsome, and charming, by Mum's account, he was apparently completely bowled over, requiring her to explain gently her reason for making the voyage in the first place. With regrets expressed, each stepped back onto their separate paths.

When the ship docked, Mum, thin and weak, found that the bridal trousseau she'd had packed in her trunk in the ship's hold did not fit her. Extensive alterations would have to be made. Nevertheless, within weeks all was in place, and Mum and Dad were married at the home of a relative in Melbourne called "Tanderra"—a native aboriginal word meaning, "a pleasant place to stay." It was evidently a lovely setting: a beautiful house surrounded with wide verandas, its grounds and gardens lush with flowering fruit trees. Mum's mid-calf length dress of cream coloured heavy lace over *peau-de-soie* was embellished with fresh orange blossoms from the trees on the property, woven into her headdress and bouquet as well. Daddy wore a dark double-breasted suit. They made a handsome couple, as evinced by the wedding photograph that sits on the desk where I write.

During this period of time, homes in Australia and England

were given names, chosen by their owners. Names that were of special importance in the lives of those who resided therein. Unfortunately, this does not seem to be the practice any more, which is regrettable, as it lent a certain atmosphere and charm to the property. It seems now that only the stately homes or mansions are named. The homes in this memoir you will notice all had a name. The Post Offices throughout the country recognized these names and I am sure it helped the postman a great deal as they came to know those names on their route, especially in the small towns and villages.

Adjusting to life in Australia was difficult for Mum. Coming from England, where it was cool and damp, to the often relentlessly hot climate south of the equator was a tremendous adjustment. Temperatures could often rise to well over 100 degrees in the sun and just slightly less in the shade. At one time she told me that they didn't experience any rain for six months. When it finally did, she ran out into the middle of the road to stand in the drenching downpour until she was soaked through to the skin.

In order to expand their social circle my father became a Freemason. This opened many doors both socially and professionally. The Masonic Lodge also gave them the chance to return to the dance floor and, as they had once danced the nights away in the Pavilion Gardens in Buxton, they danced at the many balls and formal affairs thrown there (The Gold Ball! The Tennis Ball! It went on...), allowing Mum to get dressed up in a series of beautiful ball gowns. She often spoke of how they loved to attend these soirees and the many lovely people they met with whom they became friends.

Toward the end of their second year in Australia, Mother became pregnant. They were so excited—their first baby! But Mum also couldn't help but think how she wanted to share the experience with her loved ones in England. By this point she was not only really suffering with the climate and thoroughly disenchanted with the heat, but was also sick of another bane of life down under: mosquitoes—which were both huge and seemingly drawn to her in particular. She had even taken to packing newspapers inside her stockings just to keep her legs from being bitten, and causing she and Dad to have to sleep constantly beneath netting to protect themselves at night.

One day, while out shopping in an Italian market near their home, an old woman approached Mum and said in her best English, "Little lady, you going to have trouble...," to which, understandably perplexed, Mother replied, "What do you mean?"

The lady continued, "You have trouble with that baby you carrying. You call the doctor. Go see him! Tell him it not turn."

The interaction unnerved her. She was close to her delivery date and she took the lady's warning to heart. She went to see her doctor as soon as she could, but, as it turned out he had gone to England for three months for further medical training, and she was left instead with a new, younger, and less experienced colleague; one who quickly and adamantly dismissed the woman's concerns as "nonsense."

When her delivery day came, it became abundantly clear that, in fact, it wasn't nonsense—the baby in fact had not turned. It was to be a breach birth, and Mother, small and narrow-hipped, was in for a terrible labour. With neither the depth of knowledge, adequate staffing, nor the most sophisticated of facilities at their disposal, and the contemporary practices of obstetrics not being what it is now, they first, as she described it, used rollers on her abdomen in what sounded like an early attempt at a still-used technique in applying gentle abdominal pressure to attempt to get the baby to turn downward, head first, for delivery. It was a long and torturous procedure. And, in the end, the pain of it would only be compounded. It was a girl. She lived only enough time to be given a name, "Gloria."

My mother never really got over the loss. Its immediate consequence was that it stoked Mum's desire to go home—England—which, with Father's complete understanding, they returned to just as soon as she was able to travel.

Their families in England, by blood and adoption, were saddened by the circumstances, but happy to have them back. My father, received with open arms at the Electricity Works, resumed building the two of them a steady life once more. It seemed to work, at least for a short time. But their loss had unsettled them profoundly, and in ways that even the comfort of familiar surroundings and family could not fully restore or resolve. Father, especially, wasn't quite ready to call their days of searching for something else over just yet, and, after what amounted to only months, another continent beckoned. They planned once again to seek a fresh start. This time it would be Mum who had at least part of their possible answer.

Chapter 5

Mum's older sister, Grace, left England when Mother was still a young child, just as Isaac had. But, unlike Isaac, Mum knew where Grace had gone. She and her husband, Tom, lived in Sault Ste. Marie in southern Ontario, Canada, very near the U.S./Canadian border. While the sisters hadn't seen each other for years, the connection was evidently strong enough to spark a new if distant dream and the promise of reconnection. And so, off they went, setting sail with only the certainty of the uncertain ahead of them.

Once in Sault Ste. Marie, they found an apartment and Dad, once again, looked for work. Shortly thereafter, Mother once again became pregnant and, this time, they sought and found a truly brilliant obstetrician committed to monitoring the pregnancy full term and well prepared for any eventualities for the coming birth.

On August 9, 1931, Mother delivered a healthy baby boy they named after his grandfather—Samuel Raymond James. Sam was a golden-haired, blue-eyed darling, and they were ecstatic, but, as is so often the case, as one aspect of good fortune comes into our lives, its opposite marks another.

At this crucial moment, with a new baby to care for and

Father searching for work, the Great Depression hit Canada, and the few jobs that were available were going to Canadian nationals first. As immigrants who had spent nearly all their money getting settled and having the baby, Mum and Dad found themselves with a seemingly overwhelming conundrum.

As it turned out, Grace and Tom owned acreage about forty miles east of the city in the wilds of southern Ontario—a place called Dunn's Valley. With no means of transportation to get there, and no real knowledge of it beyond its whereabouts and an acquaintance with a few of only its very few inhabitants, they made Mum and Dad an offer: if they could get there, Grace and Tom would give them a couple of acres of the parcel to homestead, introduce them to the farmers thereabouts, and give them a chance to start a life at least until the worst of the Depression was over; another gamble, but, on the whole, a feasible idea.

Although my Dad had never built a house and really knew nothing about what it entailed, he set out alone to Dunn's Valley with some flour sacks and other provisions on his back to do just that. Upon arrival and after taking in the proverbial lay of the land, it was arranged that, with the help of a farmer from the area returning from the city, Mum and baby Sam would come to the spot to join him. All they had to shelter them was a large tent they could live in until the house was built.

Their first night, tent fully set up and Sam fed and put to bed, Mum cooked their dinner over an open campfire. As the evening wore on, its flames began to die out, leaving only glowing embers. Suddenly, out in the darkness just beyond the perimeter of their camp there came a single eerie howl. Then another. Then more, as other creatures joined in. Mum looking at Dad, said she could see even in the dim light of the waning fire that the hair on his arms and the back of his neck was standing straight up.

"What's that?" she asked.

"Oh, it's nothing," he lied.

It was wolves, and they were, by the sound of things, surrounding the campsite. With no weapon beyond the axe he used to chop their firewood, Dad, thought fast. Having read as many adventure stories throughout his youth as he could absorb, he knew that, at least in the world of theoretical and literary wolves, they were said to never come near an open fire. He went to work immediately, coaxing their own fire's embers until it roared back to a blaze. He sat, stoking it throughout the night until the first signs of dawn appeared on the horizon. It worked! They had made it through the very first long and, for a time, harrowing night in their distant new home, safe and sound.

As the days in Dunn's Valley unfolded, neighbouring farmers helped and advised them on any number of practical concerns. Dad successfully built a small (and, upon visiting it many years later I can vouch, it was indeed very small) cabin, cultivating a vegetable garden alongside to sustain his burgeoning family. He also worked for some of the farmers in return for milk and other much needed food and supplies. With the cabin built, the family getting on its feet, and things settling down into a more normal daily routine, it wouldn't be long though before they were reminded that while their location might be remote, life, and even death, beyond the valley went on, and, in truth, could even reach them with chilling ease. One day, a telegram was delivered care of Aunt Grace. It revealed that my baby brother's namesake, Samuel James, was gone; dead of a heart attack at age sixty-nine.

It was a blow. It had been nearly three challenging yet liberating and eventful years during which they had, through often herculean effort, established a new life. The grim news was further compounded by the anxiety of wanting to go back to England for the funeral, but times still not being good enough to have the financial means to do so, much less with any requisite speed. Even if they had the money they simply would not be able to get there in time. The realization lent a sudden perspective. After some discussion, there was no question in their minds—it was time to go home to Buxton.

In the end, it would be Miss Emily Shirt who, close to the centre of their former lives in Buxton, reached out to rescue them by sending tickets to board a ship back to England. They jumped at the opportunity, leaving their tiny home behind nearly as quickly as they had seemingly come to it.

Upon their return, Dad went back to work again at the Electricity Works as a supervisor in charge of metering, and, within just months of re-establishing themselves in familiar surroundings, Mum was pregnant again, this time with a girl. I, Kathleen Audrey James, was about to make my entrance into this world.

Chapter 6

With Grandfather's passing and their return to England, the wanderlust that had sparked my parents' adventures seemed finally to wane. They would now settle for the next seventeen years, Buxton's admixture of rural and rugged geography, tended urban village surroundings, and cultivated residents seeming finally to strike them as having the correct balance in suiting their personalities and needs.

Perched at the edge of the moors along the river Wye, its town centre anchored by ornamental buildings, winding streets, and sheltering gardens, Buxton has always seemed to me the best of all worlds. In my young mind, especially, it was a fairy-tale place full of wonder, and yet, never any wonder that my parents finally welcomed it as a calm and tranquil home after such woolly adventures.

Situated at the crossroads of several Roman-era roads, my little hometown was dubbed *Aquae Arnemetiae* by the Romans drawn to its ancient spa; the name meaning, "Waters of the Goddess of the Grove." The locale actually dates much farther back than Roman occupation to the Bronze and Iron Ages, remaining popular with Christian pilgrims who would "take the waters" and pay their respects at the town's Chapel of St.

Anne, the patron saint to whom I am told, "mothers, women in labour, single or unattached women, miners, and those seeking shelter from storms" all offer prayers. I've always felt those miners must have felt in rather odd company, but such are the mysteries of faith.

Key to its more modern history, the Dukes of Devonshire were largely responsible for Buxton's development from the eighteenth century on, each descendant adding to the legacy to this day. In 1780 William Cavendish, Fifth Duke of Devonshire, sponsored construction of Buxton's Crescent, a central architectural town feature modelled on Bath's Georgian-era precursor. At its centre, carved out of stone, is the Cavendish crest. In addition to its noteworthy architectural details and history, the Devonshire Royal Hospital boasted the largest unsupported dome in the world for quite some time. Made of slate, it was designed by architect Robert Rippon Duke in 1881, becoming at once both a marvel of engineering, and an important health treatment centre for patients from all over the world.

During the latter half of the nineteenth century, the town truly grew into the fashionable spa for which it holds it most renown, its beautiful hotels and rooming houses popular among resort-goers and a bustling cultural destination for the well-to-do throughout history. In 1894, the Eighth Duke of Devonshire opened The Pump Room, a location where one could go to the mineral well to take a glass of the now-famous Buxton waters and to sit, drink, and in turn take in the locale's beautiful surroundings. Daddy would take Sam and I there on Saturday morning outings and we would take a glass—which is now bottled commercially and sold all over England. On our 1997 visit, a bottle of Buxton Water awaited us in our rooms at the Old Hall Hotel, and we seemed to notice its presence in each supermarket and shop everywhere we went from there to London.

For all of its reputation as a resort for others, Buxton was also solidly steeped in Derbyshire county tradition. Each year, beginning in May and continuing through September, the town holds its traditional Wells Dressing Festival, a custom celebrated throughout the county. The festival's origins can be traced back to the 1500s— by some estimations, even as far back as Celtic and Roman times—when the wells of Tissington purportedly kept the village free from the plague. At least since then, villages throughout Derbyshire decorate their wells each year with religious scenes made from flower buds, petals and leaves, somewhat recalling the efforts for the annual Rose Bowl Parade in Pasadena, California, but on what is certainly a smaller scale. Thousands of buds and petals of all colours go into making up the decorations of the wells, after which they are then blessed in a religious ceremony. In Buxton, St. Anne's Well, located adjacent the Crescent, was decorated, and from my earliest recollections, also inspired a beauty contest to determine both a Wells Dressing Queen and her Ladies in Waiting—it was a distinction every Buxton girl in my day dreamt of owning at least once. My schoolmate Brenda was Queen the year I left England. St. Anne's Well is still decorated each year, people from near and far still flock to see it.

Behind and to the north of what became our home on Anncroft Road, stretched miles of wild moorland that bloomed every spring with purple heather that lasted well on throughout summer. The heart of town had shops in Spring Gardens, and The Slopes behind town hall had winding, graded paths and tree-lined lanes and were all located near my favourite place of all—the Pavilion Gardens.

Occupying twelve acres of land donated by the Seventh

Duke of Devonshire, the Pavilion Gardens was Buxton's cultural hub, replete with its delicate glass-walled, high-domed concert hall. It remains one of the town's most recognizable structures. Outside the glass hall the surrounding gardens featured tennis courts where a miniature version of Wimbledon took place at the end of each season, as well as putting and bowling greens, a lake with beautiful white swans and paddle boats, and acres of walking paths that meandered through its parkland. In my memories of these places I loved so, I also remember fondly the Saturday mornings Sam and I spent at Collins Café, drinking coffee or tea as we looked down on the busy shoppers in Spring Gardens, and the countless times we strolled under the weeping willows along the Wye on the paths in the Serpentine as we made our way downtown with Mum to do our shopping.

Famously, or infamously, (depending on your interpretations of royal history, its ties to Catholicism and the rise of the Church of England), Mary, Queen of Scots, under the watchful eye of her jailer the Earl of Shrewsbury, came to Buxton fairly regularly. Imprisoned by Queen Elizabeth I, Mary was considered to have a rightful claim as heir to the British throne. Elizabeth, after years of intrigue, finally had settled any claims that the crown would be anyone's but her own rather decisively. After keeping Mary under a kind of "house arrest" for years, Elizabeth signed a writ that saw Mary beheaded at London's dreaded "Bloody Tower"—undoubtedly solving a few of Elizabeth's problems and, frankly, Mary's as well. Mary remained in Buxton under house arrest in the Old Hall Hotel for two-and-a-half years or so, scratching several messages in Latin into the glass of its windows with her diamond ring, including her final farewell to the town. I guess some people really do lose their heads after seeing Buxton (a terrible joke, and apologies to those who think, as I do, that Mary was probably set up to look more guilty of intrigue or treason than she actually was).

Today, The Old Hall Hotel, recognized among the oldest if not *the* oldest hotel in England, is also still well-recognized as the best in town. When I was a young girl, I passed by it on my way to school or into town several times a week, envying the people at the white clad tables I spied through the dining room windows where they sat, elegant and serene: "Ah, how I would like to stay there," I would say quietly to myself going by, a fantasy I never dreamt I would realize until fifty years later when Sam and I and our spouses travelled to England for a reunion with our childhood.

When we returned on that trip, our room was just doors down from Mary's old room on the second floor, the Bridal Suite, "Mary's Bower." Some say Mary still walks the hallways, and, one night, downstairs in the dining room I longed to sit in all those years before, I realized I had forgotten something in our room. Not thinking for even a moment of the legend, I ran upstairs and passed through the glass doors that lead past Mary's Bower when, suddenly, I became very aware that the hallway had become noticeably and almost bitterly cold. I remember that I shuddered just as the thought passed through my mind that they ought to turn the heat up in the place, and then it hit me—no, it wasn't *that* kind of cold. It wasn't just chilly or like a draft coming in from somewhere. It was swift, piercing, bone-chilling... Remembering the legend, I retrieved the forgotten item and rushed back downstairs. When I settled back at our table, I must have looked a bit pale, as Sam asked, "What's the matter, did you see a ghost?"

"Almost," I replied, adding nothing more and secretly wondering if I very nearly had!

Father, World War I,
Circa 1916

Mum's engagement photograph

Dad engagement photograph at his parent's home in Buxton

Mom and Dad's Wedding photograph, Melbourne, Australia September 1, 1929

Grandpa James, Superintendent of Police, Buxton

Taking dolly for a walk

Childhood home in Buxton "Tanderra" on left

Helping Daddy mow the lawn at "Tanderra"

My favourite photo of Mom, Sam and I

Taking a nap

Kathleen four years old

Hamming it up with banjo

Sam and I at Tanderra

Chapter 7

Shortly before my birth in 1935, Miss Margaret Shirt had passed away after a short illness. It was really then that Miss Emily, who'd brought my parents back from Canada, became an almost immediate and important part of my life. She was, first, my godmother, but also a surrogate grandmother to my brother and I, loving and spoiling us throughout our young lives. When they returned from Canada, Mother and Father began living with her in her large home which, they all agreed, they should now name "Tanderra" after the home where my parents married in Australia. This new Tanderra was a beautiful half-timbered structure on a corner in a well-established Buxton neighbourhood with tree-lined streets and well-kept gardens.

When Sam was little, he could not say "Auntie Emily," and, for whatever reason, began calling her "Cubby." Cubby she would be from that moment on. We had wonderful times with her as we grew. Every holiday she and Mum would cook family dinners. At Christmas we would have a real feast, the silver pieces the Shirt sisters had given Mum playing an elegant role in the table setting. At these occasions there were always "crackers" on each plate (typically English party favours that make a "pop" when you pull them from the ends). We loved the noise they made just before we looked eagerly inside them for the little treasures and paper hats or crowns each contained; the latter in which we all paraded around for the rest of the evening.

After dinner, the table cleared, we would play the old English card games of Happy Family and Auction. Both are games of memory. In Happy Family one matches cards of various suits named after fictional families with a humorous rendering of one of its four members illustrating each card (father, mother, son and daughter) per suit. The object, naturally, is to complete as many suits as possible and the winner determined by the most families one collects. Auction also requires guessing who possesses certain cards needed to complete its two-card sets, with the additional activity of bidding (using small sea shells as currency) on sight-unseen "lots" you suspect might complete your own collection. The real challenge is not only to collect as many sets as possible, but, doing so while trying not to overbid or bid on the wrong lots or run out of "money."

It was loads of silly fun, and Sam, who had more than a mischievous sense of humour, would always try to win by cheating or somehow pulling the wool over Cubby's eyes, and which usually ended with her chasing him around with a soda siphon and threatening to "squirt it down his neck." They teased each other unmercifully, those two, but she would always win, and it was wonderful to see her throw aside her dignified persona to become a complete child in pursuing him with so much glee and laughter.

Stepping back into her more dignified role, Cubby also proudly took us to church with her on Sunday mornings. I was very young when this first began and Sam about seven.

Until about age twelve, little boys wore short pants and knee socks in those days. Cubby would always give Sam sixpence to put in the collection-plate, which, he would immediately put down his sock. Then, when the collection plate came around, lo-and-behold, Sam just couldn't seem to fish the coin out (surprise!) leaving Cubby with nearly no choice but to give him another one. Sunday after Sunday Sam pulled this little scheme (talk about having things worked out to a science!). To top it off, by the time Sunday service was over, Cubby had always somehow "forgotten" she'd doubled up on the sixpence and Sammy was off and running sixpence to the good... Oh, my big brother!

But Sam was never a real source of discomfort, at least for me. I was, however, most embarrassed in church because Cubby would simply not let me use the kneeling pads that pulled down from the pew in front of us when it was time to pray. Cubby would let Sam kneel, but told me I was too young—I could kneel "when I reached the age of five." So, there I sat in our pew while everyone else knelt. I was simply mortified. As far as I was concerned, I was already a big girl and I would always go home after to complain to Mother. It was a grievance I never did resolve and an early sign I was ready to jolly well do as I wished.

Issues of "church & state" were quickly forgotten though when, back at Tanderra, Cubby would let me play dress-up in her beautiful silk dresses. I would put my hair up and wear her lovely necklaces, pins and other jewellery, all the while traipsing around pretending to be "a great lady" with Cubby playing along to the hilt. Whenever I ran out of steam and outfits, the two of us would then sit at the little table in the alcove by her bay window overlooking the garden, have some tea, and eat the little "Maids of Honour" and "Fairy Cakes" she made. It was our special time and we had lots of fun. On Saturday mornings after the war when both Cubby and I were getting a bit older, I would ride my bike the three miles or so from our house to her flat on Bath Road to visit and do some light housework and dusting. My task, specifically, involved a set of chairs among her collection of amazing Victorian-era furniture that had curlicues all around their legs and she was simply unable to bend down to dust. I would arrive, let myself in the front door and then call out to her: "Cubby, it's Kath! I've come to dust your legs!" After I was done, she would always treat me to a full English breakfast with all the trimmings and we would chat about our week's activities, swapping tales of our adventures... Such lovely, cherished memories.

Cubby shopping in Buxton

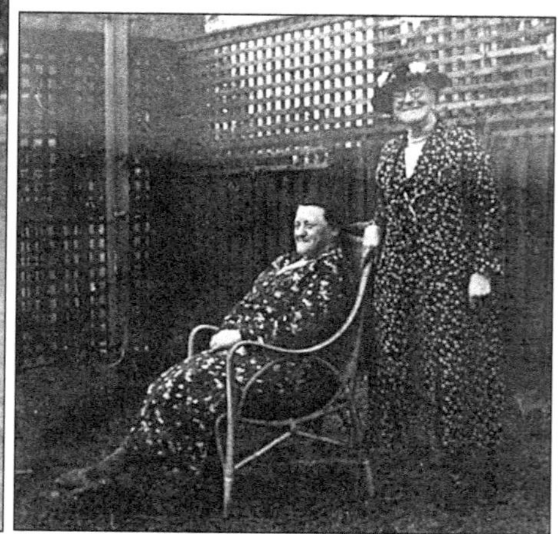

My two Godmother's, Cubby (standing & Mrs. Taylor, her friend, sitting)

Chapter 8

From the moment I was born, Sam was usually (and, at first, even unusually) very protective of me. When people approached my perambulator when Mum had us out walking, he would stand between them and it and say, "Go away! You can't have her!" leading Mum to have to explain that they were not going to take me away and only wanted to see and admire the new baby. Of course as I grew older things changed, and Sam became the very picture of what one perhaps envisions as a precocious older brother.

On one occasion when I was about two, as we pretended to paint the tool shed in our back garden with paintbrushes dipped into cans of water, he put up a stepladder to "help" me climb up onto the shed's flat roof with him. After doing so, he went down again, removed it, and left me stranded up there. Luckily, Mum came out to see what we were doing. "Where's Kath?" she inquired. Sam pointed upward and giggled. Mother, horrified, kept my attention while she put the stepladder back up so that she could coax me down.

Despite these usual brotherly pranks, on the whole, Sam looked out for me to make sure I wasn't left out or bullied by anyone (anyone but him, of course), and it was nice to have a big brother. I adored him at that age and followed him everywhere. I'm sure as he got older I often made quite a nuisance of myself, but, truthfully, he never really complained.

When I was three years old I ended up with a rather serious illness involving my kidneys. Again, in a time with no quick solutions like penicillin or antibiotics, there was little treatment for these things aside from rest and time. After enough of the former and a bit too much of the latter with no sign of improvement, Mum decided to call the doctor, who, it turned out, was away. Instead, the service sent a young doctor to Tanderra instead, fresh off the boat from Poland. After examining me he said the fever I was running was beginning to become dangerously high, noticing that my skin even seemed transparent and waxen, otherworldly, as though a light was shining behind it. It was a pallor that denoted to him that if something wasn't done pretty quickly I might not make it!

He instructed her to make fresh barley water and feed it to me regularly throughout the night. So there Mum sat, spooning me the cloudy and unpleasant liquid, during which time I remember Sam bringing a lacy cream-coloured shawl with a square cut-out pattern into the room, placing it across my crib as he peeked through in an attempt to try to make me laugh. I remember vividly Mum saying, "Don't excite her, Sammy." I also remember I asked her to sing to me. I wanted to hear her to sing, "Now the Day is Over," a Church of England hymn I loved. She did, crying all the while as I fell into a deep sleep. When I woke up the next morning my fever had broken and I was much better. The episode is one of my earliest and strongest memories and, to this day, if I close my eyes I can still hear Mum singing and crying.

Our family years at Tanderra with Cubby were happy

ones. She would very often lunch and shop with her friends and they were always on-the-go doing something or going somewhere. One of my favourite memories was the day she said she had a surprise for Sam and I and, sure enough, soon a moving van arrived to unload the biggest rocking horse we had ever seen—two tiers of seats on each end of the rocker to sit on, and so big that about eight children could climb on and there would still be room! It took up the entire drawing room and one needed a stepladder just to get up into the saddle. It was made of wood and painted red, blue, green, and gold and had reins of dark brown leather... It was just spectacular! We named it "Dobbin."

The only trouble was that nothing else but Dobbin could fit in the drawing room and it was the only room in which Dobbin could fit. With no other activity possible in the space he took up entirely, it was soon clear that Dobbin would have to go. We begged Cubby not to take him back and she was as disappointed at the idea of having to do so... So, as ever resourceful as she was kind, Cubby decided instead to give our amazing horse to the local orphanage for their playroom and then, going back to the furniture store where she got him, ordered us a smaller, more modest version that would fit in our home and it was all accomplished before we even knew what we'd missed. The children at the orphanage continually sent messages telling her how much they loved their enormous horse, and new Dobbin fit in our playroom perfectly.

Cubby—such a philanthropic, generous, loving, and lovely lady, always wanting to make someone, or, more accurately, *everyone* happy.

As lovely as living with Cubby was, after a while Mum and Dad decided they wanted a house of their own and began planning to build one. It was time. Cubby actually wanted to go back to "Belgrave," the brownstone she also owned on Buxton's Bath Road—Tanderra, large as it was, took quite a bit of upkeep, and Belgrave was much better-suited to her lifestyle now that she was alone. Located on the edge of the Pavilion Gardens, Belgrave also afforded her easiest access to all the activities she so enjoyed.

In the meanwhile, Dad began working in consultation with a building contractor on a site he and Mum selected in the quiet little village of Burbage, about two miles northwest of Buxton proper. Located just below the rim of Axe Edge, Burbage had bus service to the other villages 'round about the area and into Buxton itself for convenience of shopping and errands. They made a down payment and, just as the builder began work on our new home, a stop-order was issued by the government to all construction companies that they were to "cease building new homes." This moratorium, issued all over England, meant something *very big* was afoot, and it was the first occurrence that brought the reality of the impending war into sharp focus.

To add to the sheer inconvenience of the situation, Dad had a further talk with the builder and, as it turned out, in addition to the moratorium on actual construction, all down payments paid on new construction were now frozen as well. My parents it seemed, like so many others to be sure, could not now (and, in fact, would never) get the money back that they'd already invested—it was, inevitably, "lost" in the wartime shuffle along with so many other things big and small. Adding insult to injury, it was also getting increasingly difficult to find a house, flat or, in fact, any space at all to buy or even rent. Daddy, reluctantly but with little choice, accepted a rental on a semi-detached house a few streets south of the recently thwarted building site where we could at least live. It was certainly not ideal, but ideal wasn't an option; it was take it or leave it. Where and when the next opportunity, if any, might come along was anybody's guess. They took it, and we all said hello to our new home at Burbage's 4 Anncroft Road.

Located on the last lot in a *cul-de-sac* just before one reached a couple of open lots and fields that spread out for miles to meet the moors, 4 Anncroft Road was two stories tall, but, obviously, still much smaller than our spacious digs with Cubby at Tanderra. My parents named the new house "Bayswater," this time after the place in Australia where they spent their honeymoon.

Chapter 9

Sam and I actually really loved our new neighbourhood. It was far more open and free than in town, and we could roam and explore the surrounding fields to our hearts' content. Making friends with other children living in the area rather quickly, we spent hours playing around the little brook that meandered through the fields across the road from us—jumping across it and catching tadpoles to raise to "froghood," and just doing the sorts of wonderful things one does as children around a rambling little brook. In places, and particularly at its base, the stream contained yellow ochre that caused us both to name it "Ochre Brook" (which we pronounced okkerbrook) and so many times to get into trouble as our socks ended up its orange-yellow hue. Pleasant, with green countryside stretching out across the roadway beyond the small garden in front of the house, Anncroft Road also looked out on a small farm in an adjacent field, owned by a man who raised hay, cattle and horses, and who had a donkey I befriended and called, "Jinny Donkey." I would save him a treat from my lunch every day, and, after I started school, he would come to the rear fence at 4:15 sharp, braying loudly until I raced to meet him.

There was also a long stretch of garden at the side of the house and a larger one in back. I began having tea parties with my dolls on the back lawn, inviting my new friends to join in. On days when I didn't have companions to play with, I would set up my toy tea set on a little table and have a good old gossip with my two largest dolls, Sally and Mary, who were about the size of eighteen-month-old children. They were good if somewhat silent company and we seldom disagreed.

The other side of the house bordered our neighbour's back garden, a charming old retired couple who were very fond of children. In their multi-level back garden with its greenhouses and chicken coop, they raised the most glorious tomatoes you've ever seen. They *smelled* like tomatoes, unlike the ones so often found in today's supermarkets that smell and taste like nothing at all. When they were ripe, the old man would invite Sam and I into the smaller of the greenhouses and tell us to help ourselves to as many of the tiny red cherry ones as we could eat, and to take home any we could not. They were delicious and as sweet as candy.

The old man had been a manager in the cotton mills of Delph, Lancashire at one time, but we affectionately dubbed him "Gepetto" after the creator of the storybook character *Pinocchio* because, underneath his garage at the street level, he had a woodworking shop where he spent most of his time making toys. He crafted beautiful scooters, sleds, wagons, trains, trucks, doll houses and miniature furniture, figurines, and countless other items made from wood and all professionally finished in bright colours, which he gave to the children in the neighbourhood. Needless to say, everyone loved him. He gave of himself to make others happy, and knowing how hard things would soon become during those scary times, he often filled a gap in what would seem an often cruel world. Sam and I learned a lot from his selfless example—primarily that one doesn't always need to be compensated by money or material things, sometimes the smile on a child's face provides the greatest joy of all.

Gepetto's granddaughter, Mavis, was also from Delph. Her parents lived and worked there in the cotton mills. She came to stay every year on summer holidays and had this marvellously "broad" Lancashire accent that I loved to try to imitate, so thick with its regional pronunciations and colloquial annunciations it could barely, at times, be understood by anyone beyond the region. As we grew older I looked forward to seeing Mavis with great excitement. She was, as they used to say in the day, a bit of a "lusty lass," and even though we were the same age, was far more worldly and wise in ways that made me begin to take notice of things in life besides my dolls and the staid ways of the local children. Much farther ahead in life and coming from a different environment in a mill town, Mavis seemed to be growing up faster—she even had lipstick hidden in her purse that she would apply standing in front of the mirror along with all kinds of other compacts and tubes of stuff, encouraging me to do the same. I'd follow her lead and put it on, then try to wipe it all off before going home. It seemed nearly indelible and didn't come off all that easily. I knew I'd be in real trouble coming home all made-up like a starry-eyed showgirl with a head full of nonsense relayed in a completely different accent... Mum would have a fit. She thought Mavis was leading me astray anyway, but I loved being with her and felt quite grown up when she was around.

In due course, Mavis also managed to develop a huge crush on Sam, and, before you could say "Bob's Your Uncle," was following him around until I finally got the impression she only wanted to be *around me* to be *near* him. From that point on, whenever he and his friends went tramping around up on the moors, she would ask me if we could go along. She simply adored him. I thought it very silly. Sam was, of course, flattered to have a pretty, red apple-cheeked young girl chasing him everywhere, but, truthfully, just wasn't that interested in girls yet, and, once again in his ever-protective way, also warned me not to get into things with her that might lead to trouble. Frankly, I didn't know what he was talking about and then got to the point where I thought the whole thing all quite strange and disorienting.

It was almost immediately after we moved to Bayswater I was enrolled in kindergarten at the local council school. Just a short walk from the house, the school building itself was old and somewhat rundown, and I wasn't much impressed with my first encounters with school life at all. We drew, we learned letters and numbers, we played with coloured blocks and soft, mouldable plasticine. It all bored me to tears. I marked my time until I could make the move up to Standard I.

Chapter 10

My birthday, 1940... Five years old! I remember the day well—*the* big turning point in my life! Or, so I believed. Age five meant I was a grown-up. No longer a baby. A real person! Time to take charge of my life! I still don't know where I got this idea, but things were different, and I felt I just had to shoulder my own responsibilities—be more aggressive! Take charge!

As I walked in front of Burbage Church in the village on that day I felt older, taller; I felt free. Looking back now, one wonders if this all stemmed from Cubby's comment that when I was finally "a big girl" I could kneel to pray in church with the rest of the congregation. Undoubtedly, it had some effect, but, whatever the factors that had awakened these sensibilities they had captured my mind as I began Standard I. I was changing, and things around me would too, in a big way! Little did I know...

Settled in at Bayswater, through with kindergarten and prepared for all the new experiences being "grown up" would bring, I was ready for the challenge. Yet, despite my newly acquired status at the ripe old age of five, I began to sense there were certain things even I still could not quite understand, and, definitely, picking up on anxieties in Mum and Dad. Knowing deep down that whatever these might be, the two of them would undoubtedly make sure they were well taken care of in due course, I needn't worry overly about it.

Instead, I simply looked forward to being in the same grown-up school as Sam, which, alone gave me a feeling of confidence, accomplishment, and the comfort of knowing I had a big brother in the same building to call on. Sam, four years ahead of me, was on the cusp of going on to higher education at The Buxton College, and I tagged along with him and his friends as much as I could, playing "football" (soccer) and cricket when they would let me. I was actually a pretty good soccer player, and enjoyed cricket too, even though they were both definitely considered boy's games.

I recognize now that these days, in many ways, were truly among my last experiencing that feeling one has as a child that the world and its wonders are at one's fingertips, easy to count out and count on. On the whole things looked quite rosy, and I really hadn't a care in the world I could name. The realities of war were obviously things I could never have conceived of in any way at that point, my little life, understandably, very full of childhood concerns however grown-up I imagined or was determined to be. Playmates, family life, school… only later did I realize how hard my parents had worked to shield us at from what was not only a plausible threat, but, as it turned out to be, an absolute inevitability.

~~~

Friday, September 1, 1939, Adolf Hitler, on the heels of an already growing list of atrocities seen and unseen, had given orders for German troops to invade Poland—an outrage (among so many even at that historical moment) that would
~~~

finally force a shift from wan political posturing to decisive military response. The first but largely unsubstantiated news reports suggested the Poles were having some success in resisting the Nazi invasion, but Britain had vowed to protect Poland should it be attacked, and, duty-bound made it clear they would: if German troops were not withdrawn immediately, an official declaration of war would follow.

Britons went on about their weekends with wirelesses (radios) on. In perfectly ironic contrast to the beautiful Sunday morning that was September 3, British Prime Minister Neville Chamberlain gloomily addressed the nation, replacing any guesswork about if Britain would go to war with the certainty of when: *"I am speaking to you from the Cabinet Room at No. 10 Downing Street,"* his dour announcement began: *"This morning the British Ambassador in Berlin handed the German Government a final note stating that, unless we heard from them by 11 o'clock that they were prepared at once to withdraw their troops from Poland, a state of war would exist between us... no such undertaking has been received... this country is at war with Germany."*

It seemed then as though everything went quiet—as if a great conversation had been interrupted by the gravest news. The kind of silence one imagines in the experience of air suddenly being sucked from a room; laden with dread and the anticipation of what the next sound would be and when it would be heard. It was a silence inevitably broken by the most unimaginable and absurdly violent onslaught one might conceive—one that would hold us all in its sway for five years and altering everything and everyone it touched.

Chapter 11

As my preoccupations with adulthood kept me busy, Britain had indeed been preparing for war. By 1938, any member of the adult public paying even the slightest bit of attention could scarcely miss the signs of increased governmental activity and the nation's build-up to it. Money was actively being poured into building the Royal Air Force as it recruited enlistees to fly its new airplanes. Pamphlets and booklets with such titles as, *The Protection of Your Home Against Air Raids,* were being circulated to the nation's populace to educate us all about the ominous possibilities of such things as poison gas attacks, bombing, and evacuation plans. Seemingly overnight, thirty-eight million gas masks were ready to distribute.

In January 1939, the government had published *The National Service Handbook*—forty-eight pages of fitness qualifications and age requirements with regard to all variety of wartime service from regular and reserve forces to the Women's Land Army and the office of Civil Defence. The greatest call for assistance was for air raid wardens—men, age thirty or above, women above age twenty-five—who would be responsible for duties ranging from panic control to first aid. Air raid wardens were the jacks-of-all-trades of civil defence, seeing to it that people used their gas masks properly, went to the appropriate shelters during raids, and that homeowners and shopkeepers blacked out windows and followed general rules that would help maintain as much order as possible in moments of extreme terror and chaos.

The administration of the national Air Raid Precautions unit (A.R.P.), formed committees in every town to train people on the home front how to survive air attacks, and thousands of people answered the call, my father included. Three nights a week during the war he would be responsible for fire-watching at the town Electricity Works, setting out with a tin helmet and a bucket full of sand to put out flash fires from incendiary bombs (a bomb which contains an incendiary agent designed to start a fire when it explodes), to peer into the darkness of blackened-out Buxton for any signs of light or enemy fire. In urban centres, the A.R.P. was also tasked with an energetic plan to evacuate women and children to more rural and out-of-the-way locales. It was a process that saw a half-million volunteer evacuees leave London and other prime target cities to take up residence in the homes of relatives and strangers alike, as far away from the building storm-front as possible.

Registration for evacuation remained voluntary (although it was strongly encouraged), but the billeting of evacuees was mandatory. Rural families adjusted to housing new children, some of who had never left the cities of their birth before. Evacuees old enough to be aware of what was happening faced the traumas of separation and isolation from parents who, in sending them away from potential harm, now suffered the potential grief of perhaps never seeing them again to add to mounting fears of bombs and bullets. Later on, during the

"London Blitz," I remember going to the pictures with Mum and watching the *Movietone News* reports on the evacuations. There on the big screen, Gracie Fields, the most popular singer of the day stood on a London train platform surrounded by hundreds of children packed up and ready to leave. She sang a song we all knew well:

"Wish me luck as you wave me good-bye,
Cheerio, on my way, here I go...
'til we meet once again, you and I,
Wish me luck as you wave me good-bye!"

Around her, mothers wept as stunned children of every age boarded trains headed for the north of England and Scotland. It was this scene that suddenly defined what the war really meant—loss of family, loss of home. From that moment on and a time after, my greatest fear was that someday, perhaps soon, the war would separate us and that I too might have to leave Mum, Dad, and Sam behind. Like the children on the screen, I blinked away tears but I did not cry. "Keep a stiff upper lip," was our constant refrain, and I succeeded in doing so, most of the time.

Soon after the declaration of war, we were all issued national identity cards that we used throughout. These individual numbers were not only for identification should something happen and they needed to figure out who you were, but also to allot ration cards and other official government documentation. My number was RBFK-1444. Looking at it in retrospect—and I know I'm not alone in this observation among those members of my generation—the whole thing at times was like living in the middle of an episode of the British TV comedy show "Dad's Army" (which still airs on Public

Broadcasting Service in America every now and then), only it was *real*, and not always easy to see the humour in it.

Chapter 12

Accepting the sobering idea that in order to survive each would have to compromise and alter our lifestyle was a bitter pill. Poor, wealthy, old, young, no one escaped hardships. Speaking in nearby Manchester on January 27, 1940, less than six months prior to becoming Prime Minister, the then First Lord of the Admiralty, Winston Churchill, set the tone as he rallied the nation he would soon lead in earnest: "*Come then, let us to the task, to the battle, to the toil—each to our part each to our station... Let us go forward together in all parts of the Empire, in all parts of the island. There is not a week, nor a day, nor an hour to lose.*"

Indeed, it seemed not. Those manufacturers who had not already been silently retooling for the war effort, quickly began turning their plants and production facilities to make weapons and supplies—bombs, bullets, tanks, planes, helmets... As men were called up to military service the nation's workforce began to suffer for labour, and British women stepped in to "man" the factories as members of the Women's Land Army, as well as working the nation's fields and farms producing food in case of potential siege. As islanders, dependent on goods and supplies no longer obtainable due to surrounding seas already rumoured to be teeming with enemy ships and U-Boats full of torpedoes, we all began to prepare to go it on our own and become as completely self-sufficient as possible.

Everyone was expected to "do their bit," no matter how large or small, and conserving resources would be the first rule in this new way of life. This meant rationing, first of food and "petrol"—gasoline, and as these began to be regulated the blackouts began. We had nothing left to do but get our houses in order and wait for signs of the enemy. And indeed we would wait, as it turned out, for some time.

~~~

After years of speculation, intense efforts in initial national preparedness, and then the official declaration of war, the reality was that, at its beginning, the war turned out to be tremendously anti-climatic; "hurry up and wait," as the old saying goes. As a result, the first eight months of British wartime has become known as "The Phoney War," as threats of German attack began to sound more like grand overstatement. While many men and women had already begun to assume extra duties in civil defence organizations, enforced blackouts plunged us all into darkness every night, bomb shelters sprang up and bunkers dug down, and the food items we not only loved but needed became scarce, there were still no squadrons of German bombers overhead or marked signs of planned invasion, nor any noticeable troop movement by our own soldiers either. Some of the children who had been evacuated in those early days in September 1939 were even returning home. Despite all this, we had to carry on as though the threat was imminent, and then, suddenly, in April 1940, it did and with frightening immediacy. Whatever appeared "phoney" finally gave way to reality and the news began to pour in.
~~~

A coordinated effort led by British and French troops had landed in Norway to confront Hitler's army, but the Nazi's had beaten them to the punch. Within two weeks, these allied troops were forced to abandon the endeavour, dashing any early hopes of stemming or turning back German progress.

Nazi forces then quickly overtook not just Norway, but also Denmark, Luxembourg and Belgium. On May 10th, The Netherlands fell and German tanks swiftly entered France too, which was brought to surrender and an official armistice that, if nothing else, assured Paris would avoid being reduced to a smouldering heap prior to occupation. That same day too, Britain's Parliament called for the now rapidly ailing Neville Chamberlain to submit his resignation as Prime Minister for failing in adequately prosecuting Britain's role in the growing conflict. This would be a significant turn that would almost assure a full head-on collision between Britain and Germany. With Chamberlain out, the kettle was about to be put on full boil.

While Chamberlain, publicly, had indeed sounded as if he meant business in dealing with Hitler, privately he had much less commitment to the enterprise. In examining the eight months since that fateful Sunday when the gauntlet was thrown down more in frustration than anger, what is clear now is that Chamberlain all but considered Britain's ultimate fate as one of inevitable capitulation under the most favourable terms that could be negotiated. His every effort—however couched in the rhetoric of preserving British lives and maintaining enough good will to assure Britons "peace for our time"—had only provided Hitler more time to achieve his aspirations. Chamberlain's grand plan had become fairly evident within the meager protests and half-hearted diplomatic gestures offered up as early as March 1938, when Germany annexed Austria. A year-and-a-half later it had opened the door further for the Nazi's enslavement of Czechoslovakia, and their move on Poland.

During the summit that culminated in the signing of the Munich Agreement (September 1939), he actually implored his political counterpart, the Fuhrer, to at least try to abstain from bombing Prague too heavily, or killing too many citizens should they decide to resist Nazi efforts too strenuously. I'm sure any Czech representatives attending the summit would have expressed their gratitude for this hollow gesture toward their countrymen with a distinctly different one had they been invited to participate in the summit (they hadn't). And so, for those nations whose moments had yet to come in facing Hitler's aggression—including Britain's—Chamberlain's "*grin and bear* it" approach was the official plan.

Returning from Munich that September, Chamberlain carried the paper with his and Hitler's signatures—proof of his good deeds on behalf of his own beloved England. He reportedly held it aloft while entreating his gob-smacked supporters outside 10 Downing Street to, "*Go home and get a nice, quiet sleep*," as the Nazi *blitzkrieg* ramped up in preparations to turn Western Europe, day by day, country by country, into a very different continent with a rapidly developing and decidedly fascist future.

When Chamberlain was finally urged with little remaining politesse to step down as PM, he did, and Winston Churchill was thrust wholly into the unholy mess Neville had helped create. Churchill became our new PM one week before my fifth birthday.

Chapter 13

Of course, I knew absolutely nothing of all these political or military machinations. For my part, these months were merely a precursor to my own four-year tour of duty in the little space between our living room curtains and windows at Bayswater, face glued to the panes as I looked out for lights in the sky coming from between the houses across Anncroft Road. Whatever suspicions I had at the time about things changing were affirmed, just as my innocence was abruptly and, perhaps, finally shattered when Dad arrived home from work one night with four boxes that I thought were presents. And, in a way, they were—though certainly not the kind Sam or I were used to.

Dad opened one of the boxes. Inside was a funny-looking, khaki-coloured thing with goggles attached that connected to a tube like an elephant trunk, and a thing that looked like a can at the bottom! Dad removed it from the box and fastened it over his head, immediately transformed into a monster. He had to take it off because, frankly, it was horrific and scared me to death. I started to cry. He explained, putting his arm around my shoulder: "Look, Kath, it's all right. We need these to be safe... There's even one here for you too."

"Oh boy, what a treat," I thought. A British Government Issue gas mask we were to carry at all times wherever we went, ready to wear at a moment's notice, and, no doubt, suitable for any and all occasions. Dad opened the other three boxes. Our masks were, at least, not as ugly as his. Adult men's masks were the funny-looking "elephant" gas masks. As air raid wardens or even potential combatants, they were specially designed for "dangerous situations" (as if a possible gas attack was somehow less so to others in the community). He would wear it several times a week when he fire-watched for the A.R.P. Each mask came in its own satchel with a button-snap to keep them closed. When unsnapped, you pulled the mask out by its straps. Ours were more of a tan colour and made of rubber-like material with one clear oval window over the eyes made of a thick material called Perspex. At the bottom there was a bright green cover, which, I learned later, was a filter, but seemed to me at the time nothing more than a can with holes punched in it.

Dad took mine by the straps and, soothing me as he did, placed it gently over my head, adjusting it to fit over my curls. The contraption felt so strange and smelled horribly of rubber and chemicals. It was, to say the least, quite unpleasant, and I, understandably, didn't like it at all. Mum and Sam's were like mine. They remained fairly taciturn as they looked them over.

At school, our teachers told us what to do with the masks and we were simply to obey. We were to keep our masks on our desks where we could reach them, pick them up immediately when the sirens went, place them, again, immediately, over our heads, and then, breathe normally. Immediacy for those of you who missed it, was the key we were told, because some of the bombs might just be gas bombs, and the fumes from these could kill very quickly (Oh, how very nice thank you, what a cheery thought!). When not in use, the masks were to be kept in their cases and, using the strap, worn either over our heads crosswise or hung down our backs like backpacks. Being children, we would find all sorts of creative ways to carry them as time went on—around our necks and straight down the front of our clothes, twisted round our belts... Safety first! Fashionable always.

The mounting evidence was making it suddenly very clear to me that this "Hitler person" was trying to destroy us! I certainly hoped I would never have to put that awful, smelly thing on, but, of course, no sooner did that thought pop into in my head when the sirens sounded and away we went, teachers prodding us along as we donned them, to proceed to the air-raid shelters. From that point on we had drills every day to rehearse our speed in affixing these weird-looking wardrobe items to our heads and proceeding in a speedy but orderly fashion to our shelters. After a while it became second nature, just another part of life. We would be required to return them to the government after the war. Gladly.

Chapter 14

June 1940 brought news of British forces in action that made the previous April's fiasco in Norway pale in comparison. Our *full*, active-duty combat ground forces had been deployed to stave off Hitler's advances on the Continent and they made the headlines with nearly all-encompassing disaster. Pinned down on the beach at Dunkirk in northern France without enough Royal Navy support to facilitate their evacuation, they had been all but driven into the English Channel by the Germans. The had only narrowly escaped total annihilation through the thoroughly herculean efforts of hundreds of British non-combatants in small watercraft, who had imperilled themselves to perform the evacuations in what certainly must still stand as one of the most miraculous feats in military civil defence history—thousands of retreating soldiers rescued against all odds from a hopeless situation. This miracle (code name, "Operation Dynamo") had been set in motion by Churchill, who was spending his first weeks at 10 Downing Street trying to figure out how to lead a country whose situation had spiralled so far out of control, and so quickly, that describing it as desperate would have seemed to those in the know as optimistic.

With chilling efficacy, German forces were very suddenly and uncomfortably situated across the English Channel, their presence able to be seen from Britain's southern shores, not to mention felt by those living at the perimeter of British rule: the Nazis had taken control of the Channel Islands—Jersey, Guernsey, Alderney, Sark, and Herm—and established airbases along both France's northern and Belgium's western coasts; bases from which they would be able to stage a full onslaught on the British mainland. Britain was now the last holdout in Hitler's complete sweep of Europe. His forces prepared to snatch the last jewel in the crown, and with it his total domination.

Churchill, faced with the choice of trading words or blows, chose the latter, while never losing his considerable skill in the former in steeling us for the struggle: "*We shall fight them on the beaches. We shall fight them in the streets. We shall never surrender.*"

In towns, particularly those along England's southern coast, citizens trained for potential hand-to-hand combat with invading troops. Inland, residents were encouraged to strew out-of-use cars, farming equipment, old tires, and any other miscellaneous junk they could accumulate in the surrounding fields to hamper the landing of German planes or troops.

On July 10th, the "Battle of Britain" began. Hermann Goering's Luftwaffe was the first tool to achieve the air superiority that would make invasion of the mainland possible. Success would mean a devastated infrastructure, a demoralized populace, and a crippled military. Goering assured his Fuhrer that it should only be about a fortnight before it was a *fait accompli*. The battle would, in fact, last well-over 110 days, and from August through October the Germans would suffer not only the losses of 1,800 aircraft and 2,500 fliers, but also the favourable time and weather conditions needed to move forward with their plan. Despite their seeming invincibility and much-touted superiority, the Nazis had somehow seriously miscalculated where our little island was concerned.

Their first blunder was almost undoubtedly allowing the allied forces at Dunkirk to retreat. Perhaps in his desire for Britain and Germany to remain on quasi-friendly terms after the "inevitable" surrender, Hitler failed—one assumes more through arrogance than magnanimity—to order the final, crushing blow: "He who fights and runs away, lives to fight another day," as the saying goes.

The next critical mistake was of a more technological nature. The Nazis lacked a full understanding of the Royal Air Force's crucial incorporation of Radar-based systems to accurately pinpoint movements of German squadrons. This allowed R.A.F. pilots to meet the threats posed by the Luftwaffe with increased success, which, coupled with British industry's ability to out-produce German aircraft (especially with regard to fighter planes, and the new Supermarine Spitfire in particular), and the well-coordinated efforts of both Royal Air Force leadership and its legion of young pilots intent on either protecting their home or avenging defeats suffered elsewhere, meant the Germans had finally run into unprecedented and formidable resistance. They had underestimated their opponent and overplayed their hand. The first defeat on his path to global acquiescence, Hitler was left with little choice but to abandon invasion plans for England in order to turn his forces eastward in the daunting task of gaining dominance on the Russian Front.

Reflecting both on this and a moment very soon thereafter within his national radio broadcast on May 10, 1942—two years to-the-day from his appointment as Prime Minister—Churchill, with his inimitable brand of rhetorical flourish, elevated his countrymen just as he scolded those who had given England little more than a veritable wish of, "good luck, you're going to need it:"

> *"All the world, even our best friends, thought that our end had come. Accordingly, we prepared ourselves to conquer or to perish. We were united in that solemn, majestic hour; we were all equally resolved at least to go down fighting. We cast calculation to the winds; no wavering voice was heard; we hurled defiance at our foes; we faced our duty and, by the mercy of God, we were preserved. It fell to me in those days to express the sentiments and resolves of the British nation in that supreme crisis of its life. That was to be an honour far beyond any dreams or ambitions I had ever nursed, and it is one that cannot be taken away."*

Nevertheless, the cost of the endeavor should never be underestimated. In the end, while England lost less aircraft (around 1,600) and airmen (around 1,500) than the enemy during the Battle of Britain, it was still war, and it was still on. While the option of invasion had at least momentarily been swept from the table, it would still be a long and brutal time before we would be allowed to forget that the Nazis meant to exact a heavy toll for the trouble Britain caused them.

~~~

The Battle of Britain gave way to the worst days of what is referred to as "The Blitz," and while each populous city of strategic or industrial importance would suffer recurrences of German attacks throughout the war, the individual and
~~~

collective Blitzes they suffered during the nine months of the first and most debilitating phase of German air bombardment were the deadliest. London, Liverpool, Birmingham, Manchester, and Sheffield each suffered heavily from September 1940 until May 1941, with London—easiest to reach and the most populace of all—the hardest hit. Beginning Saturday, September 7, 1940 (Black Saturday), our capital was bombed for fifty-seven straight days. Buildings that had stood for hundreds of years disintegrated in the flames. Terrorized and sleep-deprived, its citizens spent the first of many nights in air raid shelters and on Underground subway platforms, emerging in the morning hours to inventory the mounting damage, and to try to carry on with some semblance of a routine that looked like normal life.

On May 10, 1941, the largest German air raid directed against London during this first wave of attacks killed over 1,400 and maimed many more. In the nine months of The Blitz, Britain's national death toll would reach over 43,000.

Chapter 15

Recognizing that this was all really happening whether we liked it or not, there was no choice but for us to try to maintain our own daily routine too. Interrupted by the occasional air-raid siren followed by "all-clear" in due course, we went on with a resolve not to let it interfere with the pursuit of education, family life, and the development of our interests and talents whatever they may be. Each day presented a challenge to approach life as normally as we could, just as we accepted the idea that life could change dramatically at any moment.

At the tender age of five, I had certainly already formulated a rather strong opinion that this whole war thing, whatever the case, was incredibly stupid, and I was pretty put out on some days that things had been allowed to get this point by so-called adults. Nevertheless, they had, and, speaking as an adult now myself, I was determined to move along with life despite the fact that the world was wholly intent on mucking it all up and destroying itself.

For the most part school went on as usual. Between drills and actual air raids it seemed we were spending a fair share of time in the shelters in the corners of the school playground.

Camouflaged with sandbags, each class was assigned a different shelter, which we would go to along with our teachers to proceed with daily lessons. As most are aware, it tends to rain a lot in England, so, all in all the shelters were rather a damp experience, turning very cold especially during winter, as they were, understandably, unheated. Sometimes when it rained or snowed, a foot or more of water would collect, but we were undeterred; we sat with our feet tucked under us clad in our raingear and Wellington boots (Wellie-Bobs). We didn't mind and we felt safe there, and there was a lot to be said for that. Most of the boys thought the whole thing nothing but a barrel of fun, a great adventure. Those who couldn't find room in the often-overcrowded shelters were more than game to crouch under the tables in the library for protection against the possibility of flying glass until the "all-clear" sounded. I remember thinking they were *very* silly indeed—but then boys that age usually are!

Every once in a while, I would see the front page of the newspaper we received on our doorstep in the morning. One day in particular there was a full-length photograph of Hitler in uniform. He looked very frightening with his swastika armband, riding boots and crop, a grim-looking scowl affixed on his pinched face, his ridiculous little moustache stuck in the centre. It was "a face..." as my father would sometimes joke when referring to those whose demeanours lacked a certain elemental attraction, "...only a mother could love." I wasn't sure I could be convinced he even had one, just as I could also never be convinced either that even if he did that she could rise to the occasion in appraising his with any warmth.

In the photograph, his arm was raised in the typical salute to, well... himself, I guessed. I looked at it and stuck my tongue straight out—a thing I was *never* permitted to do. I looked around. I wasn't caught, but I'll bet even if Mum had seen me, she wouldn't have punished me. Knowing her, she might have joined me. Having got away with it that time only encouraged me, and, from then on, every time I saw his picture I stuck out my tongue and made all the nasty faces I could think of, and all the while thinking that if I ever did see him in the flesh that I would kick him straight in the shins! Somebody had to stop him, and I fancied that with a little of my mother's indomitable spirit running through my veins and a good, swift right foot aimed just so, it might just be me. Imagine the headlines: "Buxton Girl Kicks Fuhrer! Peace In Our Time at Last!" So much for Neville Chamberlain...

~~~

Thinking back it seems to me that my life as a child was not only regulated, but was defined by loud sounds. In school it was bells—to begin the school day, change classes, end the day, summon us for Sunday services... bells, bells, bells. But, at this particular point it was definitely sirens. The siren that indicated air raid was characterized by a loud whine that began at a low frequency and then grew louder as it climbed in pitch, higher and higher to a crescendo, then dropped again to repeat itself all over, rising and falling at fever pitch to urge us to action. After the raid was over, the long, single, unwavering high-pitched note of the "all-clear" would sound for several seconds to signal that it was safe to come out of hiding. There was no mistaking one siren for the other, we knew each immediately.

Sometimes at night, when well and truly pitch dark with everyone barricaded indoors behind blackout curtains and not a sliver of light showing, we would go out to sit on the front steps at Bayswater to watch the sky. It certainly was
~~~

a busy sky. At first, everything was black, and then, before you knew it, it began, the sky lighting up to the northeast in the direction of shipbuilding port of Liverpool, or, closer, Manchester, known well as a centre for the manufacture of munitions and other industrial support in Britain's war effort. Between the two cities, as well as the industrial centres of Birmingham and Derby to the south, it seemed as if we would see bombing taking place practically every night during those first two years of the war, each one a source of flashing explosions and loud booms.

I remember vividly one day at the start of my second year in Standard I, hearing the sirens at mid-afternoon just as we were readying ourselves to leave our last class of the day. Gathering our schoolbooks for the trek home we were heading for the cloakroom to don outside gear when the relentless wail began.

I picked up my pace and located the peg where my coat hung, my wellie-bobs sitting on the floor just beneath. Pulling both on quickly, I turned to look around. Our class shared the cloakroom with the infants, kindergarteners, and four-year-olds, and the little ones were hurrying as fast as they could to put their coats and hats on, some crying and clearly panicked by the urgency and anxiety the sirens always stirred in us. Some seemed frozen in the moment and called out for their mums.

Across the cloakroom I saw their teacher, Miss Nivens—a sturdy, older woman standing in a brown dress wringing her hands and silently but very noticeably crying too. As an adult reflecting back on that moment I can now better imagine what an incredible responsibility it must've been to have charge of all of those children with the great possibility that enemy planes would soon be overhead... They couldn't just be let out into the streets. She called out for all to get their gas masks on to proceed with her to the shelters.

As some of the little ones were having such trouble putting on their gear, I, ready to go, started around the room helping, reassuring them as I went: just say a little prayer, it'll all be behind us in a minute or two and we can go home. "Let's help Miss Nivens get to the shelter. Be quick! No time to lose," I chirped with as much cheer as I could muster through my own mounting anxiety.

And then, just as, at that very moment, I became suddenly aware that Mum was there. She had hurried to school when she'd heard the sirens. Evidently, rushing to come get me, doors opened all along our street and other mothers called out: "Are you going to get Kathleen and Sammy, Mrs. James? Will you bring my (Sally, David, or whomever they asked for) back?"

"Yes, whoever I can, I will!" she vowed.

She looked at me and addressed Miss Nivens: "Let me take all the children going my direction, Miss Nivens!"

Surprised, but undoubtedly grateful for another adult to assist her, Miss Nivens quickly replied, "Oh, thank you, Mrs. James, please, I would be ever so grateful if you would," and then began to cry again, a bit more visibly. Mum turned, drew her close and spoke to her softly, telling me later she had simply encouraged her to put on a brave face so the children didn't see she was scared. She then looked over to see me busily buttoning up the little ones, murmuring my little encouragements, and told me later too how proud she was of what a "little missionary" I had been in the moment.

Calling out the names of children requested, Mum assembled us all into a small group and we left for our neighbourhood. Miss Nivens and the other children headed to the shelters. It wasn't just a drill, and the planes were getting closer. Once our little troop had left the school grounds, Mum instructed us to move single file with our backs against the stone walls that lined the streets on our way toward Anncroft Road.

We sidestepped our way home, stopping at garden gates along the way to dispense the appropriate children, all the while neither stepping into the street nor even the middle of the sidewalk to avoid making ourselves into targets; we were warned constantly that any sign of movement an enemy pilot detected could cause them to swoop down to, at the very least terrorize, if not devastate, whatever presented itself as a target.

Such were the rules of war as we understood them, and well before any of the guidelines set forth in the 1949 Geneva Convention sought to end violence perpetrated against non-combatants—well, at least in theory. Historical evidence has suggested otherwise, and I'm forever cynical regarding these matters, as the sole aim of waging war is to visit enough destruction, terror, suffering and, ultimately, death, to bend another to one's will. Ideally, emerging as victor means breaking your quarry entirely. Nothing more ever need be done after assuring total subjugation. The ways and means of victory may be negotiable, but rules or reasonable measures under such circumstances only present in the end, an obvious affront to human intelligence, and let's not even speak of morality. In war, these are delusions. Nothing more. The line from Robert Burns's *Man Was Made to Mourn*, perhaps says it best in summation of power's constant war on fellow-feeling, and while he was not addressing war itself, it applies— "man's inhumanity to man." Indeed.

Finally, after making sure everyone else had got to their

homes safe and sound, our mission accomplished, we arrived back home.

By the time Father came home from work, Mum's heroism was a thing of the past. But, as she told him the story, he wasn't quite so, shall we say, *blasé*. In fact, he grew *very* angry. Evidently, as he explained from the A.R.P., and in turn his own perspective in its diligent service, what Mum had done was very much, "against all the rules" to put it mildly. She should never have gone out on the streets or to the school in the first place! In doing so she had not only made a target of herself, but had endangered the lives of the children she'd collected and her own daughter, as well—putting us all in grave, even mortal, danger!

"Oh dear," Mum said, absolutely stricken with horror as the thought sunk in. She'd only done what she thought needed to be done in an emergency. She was mortified to think she had put us further in harm's way, promising Dad never to do anything like that again. Dad, assured that he had relayed things in no uncertain terms and we now fully understood, finally calmed himself, dropping the subject and retreating into a vindicated if somewhat sullen silence in the other room.

Of course, all said and done, I saw both perspectives. I just felt badly for Mum that in her attempt to do the right thing she had ended up in such trouble. She was the only one brave enough to venture out, and the other mothers certainly happy to see her go to collect us. They were, of course, very grateful, and asked her if, or when, it happened again, if she would do the same. Mum explained that it had been brought to her attention rather energetically that while it appeared the proper course of action in theory, in practice it just wasn't the smartest thing to do, adding that we all just had to trust in the school to protect us until any raid was well over. Then she would be happy to go and collect everyone again.

If this particular incident did anything, it helped shed additional perspective on the fact that, up until this time at least, we had still been taking our lives for granted. As creatures of habit, a little deviation from expected routine or one's schedule might present an annoying inconvenience at most. Under the new state of "normality"—war—not following proscribed protocols could be deadly. Now that every aspect of life could change instantly, one needed to develop a sudden adaptability at the sound of the siren and then readjust again after the danger had passed. These are not easy adjustments to make without a bit of practice. Some people never got the chance; it was just over.

It certainly made me sensitive to the plight of the thousands of men and women who were sleeping night after night in London underground stations, and the tens-of-thousands of people abroad who had already suffered losses of homes and loved ones as they were plunged further into days filled with horror as their new state of "normal." If I hadn't known it before, I most assuredly knew now—at the centre of the flashes we witnessed on the horizon, watching in fear, awe, and yet at a still relatively safe remove in the dark on the front steps at Bayswater, meant there were those who would not be as fortunate as we were on that night, or any other in the future—ever. Some would never have a second chance to learn to cope, they would simply be gone for good. No wonder Father was angry.

Chapter 16

Besides food and petrol, clothing, paper, building supplies, heating fuel (coal and coke), and even electricity was also meted out in rations. Every day our electricity was on for a few short peak hours and then turned off again to conserve it. Mother would schedule cooking, baking, washing and anything else for which she used electricity to take advantage of these periods. It was a huge task and she was superb at making it work, on many occasions forsaking the range top entirely to cook over a coal fire in our living room hearth. When they finally got around to rationing coal, she would often bake lovely cakes, scones, or cook tasty meals under the fire grate. Coal was really the only source of heat in our home as central heating was unavailable. When we retired at night, the fire would eventually die out and the house would chill off. I would hear Mum setting the fire downstairs anew just before dawn. There was many a time during the winter months when we awakened upstairs to find frost had developed on our coverlets overnight. It certainly taught us to be hardy.

The darkening day-to-day world around us was met in kind with the darkened world of blackouts in our homes.

Thick, black material was allotted to everyone, and Mum, like nearly every British housewife, sewed floor-to-ceiling blackout curtains, which were then threaded onto rods and placed over every window. As dusk fell and lights turned on, the curtains were drawn tight to make sure that not even a chink of light could show through. In our living room, the blackout curtains still left a half-moon-shaped space between them and the very top of the window. I began spending a great deal of time looking out into the pitch black sky, relieved by the occasional searchlight joining my efforts in scanning it for signs of danger.

On the *cul-de-sac* at Bayswater traffic was always sparse. Most of the cars in our neighbourhood were put up on blocks for the duration of the war due to petrol rationing. Those few cars one saw out at night had the top half of their headlights either covered with black paper, cardboard and tape, or dimmed with paint. On main roads between towns—and even some places in town—"cat's eyes" were installed; devices about six inches square made of rubber and light-reflective material that formed a double line of glowing yellow lights down the middle of the road to navigate by. Their covers were bright yellow and spring-loaded so they would not break when cars ran over them.

A.R.P. patrols were out every night in town looking for lights and hammering on doors: "Put that light out!" They kept careful track, and if your non-compliance was habitual, you were fined. I often thought of Dad out there policing around the Electricity Works neighbourhood—being "Super James's" son must have rubbed off at least a little bit, and he could certainly be firm and authoritarian when the need arose.

With all that darkness in those young years, It's no wonder that years later I stood transfixed at the centre of New York's

Times Square, so in love with the lights and the freedom and peace they represented.

~~~

Dad, of course, wasn't the only one capable of being the authoritarian in our household. For as gentle and soft-hearted as Mum could be, Sam called her "The Sarge" for a reason, and she rounded us up with nearly military rigour and attention to detail. In emergencies—real or perceived—our lovely, gentle, and otherwise seemingly fragile English Rose-of-a-mother turned into an intractable force with an iron will; one best to obey. To me she was, as so many mothers were to their families, among the unsung heroes of wartime. Women who kept homes together, hearts close, clothes mended, meals cooked and hearths burning... I truly believe if Hitler himself had come up our front walk, Mum would have dealt with him single-handedly and unequivocally, put him in the dustbin, and then turned on a heel to put the kettle on and finish her day's household duties.

One morning the sirens sounded just after Daddy had left for work on his bicycle, and Mum stood at the foot of the stairs to marshal us into action: "Come on children! Air raid! Bring your toothbrushes and toothpaste and dress warmly! Kath—put on your liberty-bodice! Hurry, we must go before the planes come!"

Our house had neither a basement nor an air raid shelter, so, whenever we were there and the sirens went, we had to evacuate. This was different from the night-time routine, as darkness meant at least a certain amount of safety provided blackout curtains were drawn.

Sam and I looked at one another. Where on earth were we going? And *why, in the name of all that was holy* did we need
~~~

toothbrushes, toothpaste, and, me, my—*Liberty Bodice*!? This was "The Sarge" all over. So very English and concerned with the details of "keeping up appearances."

For those unfamiliar with the so-called "liberty bodice" (and who, at this stage in history, is?), it was a sleeveless undergarment for girls that slipped over the head and pulled down to the waistline where a set of four suspenders were attached—two front, two back—to hold one's stockings up. Truth be told, and this must've had something to do with Mum's directive, it did a fairly good job of keeping one warm... Nevertheless, this was simply the very last thing I would have thought to have taken along when evacuating. It was always of such importance to Mum that I be properly attired—even in cases of extreme emergency—she felt my "uniform" incomplete and not up to civilized standards without it. Apparently, if one were to be captured or killed by the enemy, it wouldn't do *at all* not to be dressed properly for the occasion. With raised eyebrows I shrugged at Sam, sighed, and obeyed.

After heading downstairs, Mum led Sam and I to the end of the *cul-de-sac* where we climbed over a stile that separated us from the field beyond. Once we reached that, a little way further along we headed up a hillock where she instructed us to lay face down and stay very still. We lay side-by-side listening and waiting for the throb of the German aircraft, which even at that age we quickly became able to discern from British and (later in the war) their American counterparts. They all had completely different notes—the allied planes were usually smoother and higher-pitched—and recognizing the difference quickly became essential as enemy planes would once in a while sneak through British defences undetected and unaccompanied by the sirens' warnings. One learned to live with an ear cocked heavenward for the dreaded note of the German planes.

Finally, after laying in wait for what seemed like a very long time, the planes passed over and the long all-clear siren sounded in the distance. We breathed a collective sigh of relief. Mum's instincts were seemingly spot-on this time—we were safest in the field because the enemy would aim for the more built-up areas (of course, little did we know at that point, what some of those seemingly open spaces actually helped conceal, but more on that aside in a bit).

When we got up, I looked across the fields and into the distance. The surrounding countryside looked untouched, the amazing English landscape seemed transplanted in reverse from a nineteenth-century landscape painting with the addition of the distinctly fresh smell of moor and heather lending the scene's momentary, if only illusory, sense that, perhaps, everything remained unspoiled after all. Yet, realizing that we were also hiding in a field at all meant that somewhere out there beyond the gaze, someone was intent on making it and us their conquest, and our home *their* domain. I wondered how that could be. How could these so-called "grown-ups," with all their years of knowledge and experience, be so surely and cruelly misguided? How did *any of this* make sense? These sorts of crazy things only happened in stories, didn't they? I couldn't grasp it, even with the morning's happenings making the reality abundantly clear. I wanted to go up onto a rooftop and shout at the top of my voice, "*STOP IT!* Just *stop*! Think about what you're doing!" But, clearly, it was a bit late for all that, and on it, and we, would go.

Not long after this episode—in fact, on Sunday, December 22, 1940—we journeyed to Manchester for a church-sponsored convention at the Free Trade Hall, a large public facility used by a host of groups from surrounding communities for such gatherings. On this outwardly peaceful afternoon, as we listened quietly to the day's sermon, the air raid sirens went again. Over the loudspeaker, the minister announced that we were to evacuate the building immediately—not to talk or linger with any goodbyes, just gather our families and belongings together as quickly as possible and proceed calmly to the doors.

Mum and Dad gathered us together and rushed us out of the building to the charabanc (chartered bus) on which we'd arrived. Once it was fully loaded with people, our driver wasted no time in getting us all on the road back to Buxton. As we got further away we could hear the sound of muffled explosions as the bombs began to rain down on the already much-damaged city behind us.

Opening the *Buxton Advertiser* a day or so later, we came upon an incredible photograph of the very building we had so hastily evacuated—it was nearly completely demolished, with only a couple walls left still standing and the others no more than a few feet tall; rubble, a literal shell of its former self. What an escape. From then on, I never asked again why I had to do something when told to do it. My "bit" in this war effort was clearly and simply to cooperate and obey instructions so as not give my parents anything else to worry about. They, and we, had enough already.

Chapter 17

While getting used to the idea of rationing seems fairly straightforward, I can tell you that in daily practice it is extremely difficult. As it went, every person, paperwork filled out and ID numbers and cards accounted for, was issued a ration book containing a set of different coloured coupons to cover one month's supply of each different food group: butter, sugar, milk, eggs, bread, potatoes... everything. Under rationing, anything you can think of that seems common in one's daily diet can, and often did, become rare luxuries. Fruit, for instance, was almost impossible to obtain. I did not even see a banana until I was eleven years old—they were completely exotic commodities! It was always a great treat to find an orange or an apple in the toe of a Christmas stocking or, if especially lucky, one of each! Treasures to be savoured.

Toffees (candies) had their own coupons, and these, understandably, were the ones with which Sam and I were most concerned. We were allowed to have our own to spend as "allowance money" on whatever sweets we could get, but, unfortunately, due to a rather underdeveloped sense of self-restraint, they just never lasted past about the second week of the month, meaning a rather long stretch without treats.

It was a good thing Mum didn't share this trait or we would have starved to death pretty early on. I've always felt I learned a lot from her example in nearly every aspect of my life, but as to any lessons regarding my sweet tooth, they just really never took.

We were allocated meat protein (beef or pork) once a week equal in weight to that of about the size of a hamburger. Again our ever-resourceful mother found all sorts of things to substitute for it. One day a week she could also obtain fresh fish from the fish market—that filled the bill for a day's meal. I remember toward the end of the war we had access to whale meat, its dark reddish-blue colour stands out in my mind. One certainly doesn't see a lot of that about these days, and for a number of very good reasons; not the least of which is its taste. For Christmas dinner, if you put your name down early enough, one might get a chicken—a tremendous treat for all—or, occasionally, Mum might even obtain a rabbit to cook, which I would never eat, as all I could see in my mind's eye were their sweet little noses and cotton tails. I just couldn't bring myself to indulge.

Eggs too were scarce. We were allowed one per week per person. Mummy and Daddy would give up their ration so that Sam and I could have the extra nutrition. Mum learned to bake eggless cakes as well as learning how best to apportion the little margarine we would get for scones. With dairy products in general a concern, milk at school was allotted us at a pint a day during mid-morning break to ensure strong bones and teeth. It was served lukewarm as we didn't have refrigeration.

Mum also obtained a wartime cookbook with all sorts of wonderful, unheard of recipes that kept us fed and healthy. The end of the month was always lean as one waited for a new month's batch of coupons, and, again, I have to praise her for her tremendous planning, but we never went hungry. Somehow she worked her magic and we enjoyed nearly everything we were fed. While she was always the menu planner and scheduler, once in a while, one of the local farmers would call dad to fix something electrical and he would go by to help and then come home with *four* or even *six* fresh eggs to add to the mix. Those were banner days, and we enjoyed those eggs as though they had been laid by the proverbial golden goose itself!

To really give you an idea of what the deprivations of such basic foodstuffs have on a young mind and the habits one develops in dealing with the reality of there only being so much to go around, I share a brief tale of one of my experiences on our family's later American holiday in New Jersey.

On this particular day, the lady of the house was baking and, after giving me money, distinctly foreign to me for a couple of reasons (currency? No coupons?), I was sent off to the corner grocery store for a dozen eggs and five pounds of sugar... I managed, somehow, not to react to what initially sounded like a very "tall order" to begin with!

Walking down the street and around the corner to a little Mom & Pop grocery store, I reluctantly went inside to find two or three customers already standing at a counter waiting to be served, and then a few more that walked in just behind me. With all these people present, all I could think was that I just didn't know *how* I was going to accomplish this. How in the world was I going to ask for *ONE DOZEN* eggs, and *FIVE POUNDS* of sugar? I had never even *seen* that many eggs or that much sugar before, much less been able to *buy* them!

Too shy and ashamed yet to ask, I looked around and

then sidled around to the back of the store to make myself inconspicuous. All around me were big glass bottles full of candies, stacks of chocolate bars, canned goods and fruit of *all* kinds just stacked up; everything we either couldn't get or were still rationed back home even with the war well over. I simply couldn't believe my eyes. These people didn't know they were born, I thought! They had *everything* and *a LOT* of it! They must not have had a war here...

I watched and listened as the people around me completed their purchases and as others entered the shop, and I just kept moving back behind them so they would go ahead of me. I hoped against hope that I be allowed to be the very last and only customer left to be waited on—only then did I feel I could ask my unspeakable questions without everyone staring at me in horror.

Then, the motherly owner, spying me at the back of the crowd called out: "Honey, you've been here a long time and you keep letting everyone go ahead of you... You're next! Come up here and tell me how I can help you!"

No longer invisible and unable to shrink away or hold back any longer, I moved as close to the counter as I could, leaned over (so no one around me could hear how greedy I obviously was), and whispered haltingly: "May I... please... have... um... a *dozen* eggs?" She looked at me, and repeated my order in a loud voice, "A *DOZEN EGGS*!?" In my mind I was screaming, "Shhhhhhhh!" I cringed, wanting to crawl into a hole. "*SURE!*" she said, whirling around to reach into the cooler case to produce a carton of eggs, flipping it open, and then, holding it out so *everybody* could see them!

My mind was swimming. So that's how they packed them, I thought first—a dozen in a box. I looked around me and was stunned that no one seemed to be paying even the slightest bit of attention to me. Thank goodness! "What else can I get you?" asked the storeowner. Again, I whispered, "May I please have... *five* pounds of... *sugar*?"

"Five pounds of sugar, honey... *Sure!*"

I so wished she wouldn't *shout* like that—now *everybody* was surely staring at me! She reached back again to casually produce a five-pound bag of sugar and placed it on the counter in front of me with a thud. "Will that be all?" she asked. Would that be all? Wasn't that enough? Truth be told, I wanted desperately to buy some candy for myself too... no ration coupons to worry about and "anything I wanted?!" I daren't. This was *enough* extravagance for one day. Sheepishly, I slunk out of the store, still feeling guilty, greedy, and decidedly embarrassed. Quickly retracing my steps, I returned to our hostess with the contraband, and entreated her, saying, "Oh please, don't ever ask me to do that again."

"Do what?" she asked, genuinely perplexed. I explained to her how awful I'd felt for asking for so much, to which she laughed and told me not to be silly. "That was nothing! People ask for much more than that every day."

Amazing, I thought, this really was a wonderful country... I really couldn't believe it.

Chapter 18

There was a separate ration book for clothing and shoes, with just enough coupons for each person to acquire one new outfit per year. This presented challenges if one had growing children. A new dress or coat was always a rare treat, but Mum devised all sorts of ways to lengthen dresses and skirts, as well as Sam's pant legs. In the case of my dresses, she would put on false hems by inserting a strip of another material close in colour just a few inches from the hemline. In school, my girl classmates and I eventually occupied ourselves, too, in our spare time, contributing our knitting skills to making scarves for British troops in khaki or Royal Air Force blue. Princess Elizabeth (Queen Elizabeth II) was sixteen years old at the time, and it was widely reported that she and her sister, Princess Margaret, knitted constantly. As we all admired the Princesses very much, we tried to knit in every moment we could find. We subsequently received more than a few letters of gratitude from soldiers at the front for our warm and woolly handiwork.

Daddy got into the act too, in a different way, buying kits of rubber soles and heels to mend our shoes in his little workshop attached to the house. He became quite a cobbler as the war stretched on; a thing he had certainly never done before. Like him, everyone seemed to rise to whatever occasion was necessary, and instead of complaining about the shortages we faced, we tried to find creative ways around them. It was a great lesson in problem-solving to learn to work around those things we couldn't change.

Then there was paper—it's amazing what one takes for granted until it's needed. Whenever we went shopping there were no paper bags given out at the market. Mum would take along a cloth or string bag to carry her purchases home. Every scrap of paper we could recycle, we did. Books and magazines were printed on the cheapest rough paper available, and I still have the wartime copy of *Jane Eyre* and *Wuthering Heights* that I purchased with saved-up pocket money. I've carried it with me as a favourite all these years. On the frontispiece it states that the book is printed "in complete conformity with authorized means and measures," and stamped, "Book Production War Economy Standard." The pages are a dirty-white colour, not at all like the sleek white pages of today's books.

I loved books and still do. The books that I managed to retain are still among my most treasured possessions, read and reread over and over again. My book collection at the time, needless to say, was very small, and there were many times when Aunty Evelyn made contributions to my small library. I relished the fact they belonged to me then and still do.

Beyond the many things we had to conserve, there were also many things confiscated by the British government for the good of the war effort. All manner of metal objects, aluminium pots and pans, iron railings, anything that could be melted down for their raw materials were fair game, and there were often drives for donations of these kinds of articles.

One day on my way home from school I was visiting Cubby at Bath Road.

We were sitting in front of the second-floor bay window of her flat looking out over the street when an army lorry pulled up. Two uniformed soldiers jumped out and, after going to the back of the truck, were joined there by two more. They jumped up from where they sat to help the driver and his comrade lower some pretty serious-looking equipment down onto the street. Cubby, straining to see out, said, "What are they doing here?" Then, almost as soon as she'd asked the question, she realized and gasped with alarm: "Oh, Kath, they're going to cut off my ornamental iron fence! They just can't! They haven't even asked me!"

Sure enough, I looked down and saw that the equipment they had was a welding tool with a flame coming out the end, and they were starting to cut off the beautiful wrought iron railings that sat atop the stone wall that surrounded Cubby's little garden in front of her brownstone. We both charged downstairs and Cubby flung open the front door.

"You have no right to remove those railings! They belong to me!" Cubby said forcefully. "Oh yes, we do," one of the soldiers answered back, continuing: "Instructions from headquarters... to be melted down. Don't you know there's a war on? All the railings in town are going—your turn to donate."

"Indeed I do," Cubby spluttered indignantly. "But, it would be nice if you had *asked*. You might have come to the door and informed me what you were doing. This is *my* house, it doesn't belong to the government."

Sorry, Madam," said the soldier. "We haven't the time for formalities."

All during the conversation, the other soldiers had been busy expediently chopping off the railings and, as soon as they had finished, they loaded them on the truck and drove away before we could even process what had happened. Needless to say, they were never replaced, nor was any compensation received for them. Cubby, like it or not, had donated and "done her bit" for the cause.

In addition to the knitting of scarves and "donating" (willingly or not) household metal and iron goods, there was also a big national campaign called "Dig for Victory," for which everyone was advised to dig up sections of their lawn and flower beds to grow vegetables. Daddy, for whom gardening was not only something he loved, but was very good at, was only too eager to comply—digging up the entire side lawn of our place to begin raising just about every vegetable you can think of. With him very much preoccupied as head of the household and with his work and A.R.P duties, mother hemming, sewing, shopping, cooking, and providing the comforts around our home, it was Sam and I who were assigned to keep up with things in The Victory Garden. It gave us something productive to do with any extra time we had; not that there seemed much of it with everything else there was to do.

The Victory Garden was yet another of those common English experiences key to understanding how we survived such lean times. Living off the land best we knew how, we weeded and watered, and Sam and I earned a penny for every caterpillar we picked off the cabbages. Sam hated gardening with a passion and would do anything to get out of it, but he liked his vegetables and ate heartily whenever our little crops were ready. Like my father, I loved gardening but, unlike Sam or the rest of the family, I hated vegetables, so my sole focus in doing more than my fair share of weeding was earning the extra money paid for picking those pesky caterpillars from the cabbages.

Mum, it should be said, was actually quite upset about my aversion to vegetables, even crying on occasion over my "saucy plate." She, as she often stated firmly, was convinced I would never actually reach adulthood because of this failure. Truthfully, I was about the age of forty before I finally acquired a taste for them at all. Now I enjoy them, at least in balanced and sparing amounts. If I enjoyed the riches of the experience the Victory Garden provided, it was more the process of planting, tending, and watering that appealed to me. I loved watering the plants, which reminds me of a small story about my vegetable-loving gardening partner, Sam...

At the top of our Victory Garden stood a little tool shed, in front of which was a robust and flourishing stand of rhubarb. When it would get red and ripe, Mum would pick it and make the most delicious rhubarb pie and stewed rhubarb and custard. These were incomparable. I loved them and I have never tasted anything their like since. Sam, too, in particular, loved these rhubarb dishes until, suddenly and out of the blue one day, he declared he didn't like rhubarb anymore, and refused to eat anything she prepared using it. Mum couldn't understand at all. Rhubarb dishes were always so clearly among his favourite things and he so often pleaded with her to make them.

It would take many years—well into our adult lives—before this mystery was solved, and that only with Sam's confession. It seems that instead of taking time away from outdoor playtime to go inside to use the bathroom, the little rascal would instead "wee-wee" into the rhubarb bushes. He said he loved the loud sound peeing onto the huge firm leaves made—it "fascinated" him...

As adults, Sam had a stand of rhubarb planted in clear view

of the road on the side of his house. Its prominent location made it impossible for the repeat of any such shenanigans, and that was the only reason any of us agreed to eat the homemade rhubarb treats created in his family kitchen. Even still, he would look at all our faces around the table at family gatherings with a wry and knowing look whenever they were served. Boys will indeed always be boys!

In the end, our Victory Garden alleviated a serious problem in feeding our family, as those like it did for so many on our island. Between our home-grown supply and Mummy's ingenuity in stretching rations, we remained fed and healthy... One simply had to be careful of the rhubarb, evidently, but then again, I didn't like to eat vegetables anyway.

Chapter 19

Our main means of transportation during the war years was either by bus, train, bicycle or "Shanks's pony," a slang term everyone used for one's legs—walking. The local bus service was quite adequate, and we used it constantly. Buses ran regularly into the outlying rural communities, and we took advantage of them for outings, picnics, and little sightseeing excursions, especially in the spring and summer. Trains left Buxton on a regular basis for the larger cities such as Stockport, Manchester, and the little villages and hamlets in between, but, all in all, we stayed pretty close to home with so much uncertainty and never knowing if bombing or some other development might actually prevent us from returning home. We missed our car tremendously. With the distances we would have to have travelled and no access to petrol, we didn't get to see our relatives very often, and they, of course, were in exactly the same position.

Dad had adjusted to the challenges in transportation by riding his bicycle pretty much everywhere, which not only provided him his to-and-fro from work and other duties expediently, but also offered some recreation and a feeling of normalcy as well. He and Sam rode all over the Derbyshire

Dales at weekends and holidays for fun, but I was still too little, and, even if I had mastered riding, would've tired well before those two. My taking part was not yet an option.

Cubby had bought Sam a beautiful bicycle when he was old enough, and the boys' rides made me look forward to the day when it would be my turn to have a bike too. As it turned out, that day came about midway through the war when she asked Mum to bring me to the bicycle shop in Buxton to pick out my birthday present... I was so excited! A real bicycle of my own, and a new one! Sam came along to lend advice.

I remember how the bicycle shop smelled; that rubbery smell of all those new tires. I sat on all the girl's bikes to find just the right one, so it took me a long time. I wanted to be sure! Finally, we selected a shiny, black Hercules with gold pin striping. It had a leather satchel attached to back of the seat containing a flat tire kit, a tin of bike polish, and a cloth. A tire pump was attached to the frame above the crankshaft, and, on the handlebars, there was a shiny silver bell that I could ring with my thumb to warn people of my approach. It was simply beautiful, and I didn't sleep for several nights after I got it home with anticipation of seeing it again the next morning. I loved the way it looked. Now all I had to do was learn to ride it!

Fortunately, the flat, even pavement of the *cul-de-sac* at Bayswater was perfect for learning to ride. The task of teaching me naturally fell to Daddy and Sam, who were very patient with the process. As there was no such thing as training wheels in those days, the two of them spent a fair number of hours running along by my side and holding onto the seat of the Hercules to steady me. I thought I'd never learn and spent a lot of time falling off and scraping my knees. I was just about ready to concede it as hopeless, that I would never be a bicyclist when, one day, Sam and Dad set off with me starting way at the end of the street, and, with words of encouragement like, "Keep going, Kath, you're doing fine!" and "Pedal, pedal, that's the way!" I really began to feel good... after all, I couldn't fall off with them holding me up so safely.

Just past the halfway point down the road, I looked back over my shoulder to say something and no one was there. Looking farther back, I glimpsed, however briefly, the two of them standing at the far end, huge grins on their faces... I was *ALONE*. I had ridden that entire way all by myself! I panicked immediately and promptly fell off the bike.

"Why did you let go of me?" I asked when they caught up to me. I was a bit put out with them for the lack of warning. "Because, if we didn't, you'd never learn," they said. The next few times were better, and, I finally gained enough confidence to ride on my own. I finally knew the feeling of independence Sam and Dad had when they were off riding. Here was something I could go out and do in the world all by myself if I wanted... Another turning point in life and one that definitely beat Shanks's Pony!

When I finally mastered the skill, they couldn't get me off the Hercules. I loved and treasured that bike, and we spent many happy miles together, and whenever I wasn't riding it, I was polishing it to a high shine.

Chapter 20

It's probably very fair to say that our collective sense of well-being during the war was inextricably linked to how London and its citizens were fairing. London was as a kind of 'magnetic north' to one's location no matter what direction it may have actually been in one's relation to it. It was from London that we got our news and, if that news was coming over the wireless, we knew we were still afloat; it gave us a better sense of what we might expect closer at hand.

Every night at nine o'clock we gathered in the living room to listen to the news introduced by the majestic chime of Big Ben—the event of the day and our chance to hear what was happening in London and around the world. When London's Westminster took several direct bomb hits during the May '41 Blitz (May 10th! Something seemed always to happen *that day* every year!), the huge bell, which, had in fact been cracked for years, seemed to me to then chime in a decidedly odd, off-key note that was almost funny. But despite the pasting the capital was taking or how the big bell sounded, the BBC knew it was a symbol for the whole Empire and, as long as it could be heard, we could, and indeed *must*, go on... As the old Timex commercials used to say, we may have been taking a licking, but we kept on ticking!

Another symbol of our survival, the Royal Family, also played their role as well, turning their attention and duties to touring bombed-out London neighbourhoods to visit those who had lost homes and loved ones. Queen Elizabeth went everywhere with King George, the duo photographed navigating the rubble, smiling as best they could as they urged the people to endure, to hope, to never give up. They always dressed impeccably, too, reminding all to maintain their dignity at all costs and in spite of the circumstances. Of course, their presence and ever-tony demeanour sparked its fair share of backlash, too. Some of the populace in London's East End reportedly booed the couple, whose sudden appearance signalled nothing more than the hollow gesture of out-of-touch bluebloods with no real possibility of ever being threatened. It was a viewpoint not unsurprisingly fuelled by a number of increasing class and political disenfranchisements, for some, perhaps, furthered by the reality that King George's ties to the enemy were both too clear and too close for comfort.

It should be recalled that the Royal Family were the Saxe-Coburg-Gothas until George changed their surname to "Windsor" to create distance between them and their German ancestry. Perceptions changed, at least for some, after Buckingham Palace was bombed in September 1940, causing the "Queen Mum" to declare: "I'm glad we've been bombed. It makes me feel I can look the East End in the face." It was not an insignificant statement from a number of perspectives.

Many Americans, I know, too, are ever quick to sneer at the Royal family as a collection of uppity snobs whose actions belong to a world of pantomimes and costume dramas served up for public relations or marketing purposes and (certainly in more recent times), sheer tourism. But from my perspective, an acknowledgment of their function at that time should never be conflated solely with the more frivolous or trivial aspects of commerce.

Public relations during wartime (*aka* propaganda) was, just as it remains today, an all-important tool in achieving victory. The Nazis were indeed the most virulent and successful example of the phenomenon, one that, up until the Battle of Britain, had all but allowed them victory after victory through the advantage of fearful perceptions that were (as discovered later) in some cases, less reality than the numerous myths they relayed to the world.

There were many British people during the war years who viewed news of Royal excursions as sincere expressions of resoluteness, tenacity, courage and leadership, ones reinforcing Churchill's messages of positive national dignity and camaraderie in almost retaliatory measure for the fearful, diabolical, and murderous scourge projected by Hitler's power-hungry killing machine, the Third Reich. For those who only equate the Monarchy with its clothes, jewellery and spectacle, it should be noted that they also did, in fact, ultimately refuse evacuation; choosing instead to tough it out in London with "the people," and, as Queen Elizabeth explained the decision: "The children will not leave unless I do. I shall not leave unless their father does, and the King will not leave the country in any circumstances whatsoever."

Chapter 21

Imagining Germany in my very young years and, truthfully, at other times, I've often asked: How could a whole nation allow such a ruthless, twisted, and hateful person like Hitler to rise to power? How and why could a nation be held in thrall by a person so thoroughly committed to championing the absolute worst in humanity's lexicon of behaviours, stunted in the very least in upholding even basic values of empathy, compassion, and fellow-feeling? How could they have followed someone like that as their leader? Historical purviews providing answers yet years ahead of me, I was incredulous in comprehending the phenomenon then. Armed with a more complete familiarity of particular historical accounts and with the bloody details now all quantified, qualified, and (theoretically) accounted for, it is still blindingly difficult now. Add to these cold hard facts the further complexities introduced through tenets of faith and Christian teachings to "love" one's enemies and to forgive "those that trespass against us," can too often be of little help, and I still find myself asking more questions than I can answer, and, while I neither hate anyone and truly believe that exacting judgment over others also exacts a price on the judge, I still have wondered how could anyone affiliated with the Nazis be forgiven, much less be loved.

There remain those for whom it is beyond *my* personal capacity to muster compassion, understanding, or even the pretence of forgiveness. My fear—and it is, with recognition that fear itself is the heart's blood of each anger and hatred—is that human beings will never truly shed a certain predisposition toward believing in and acting upon delusional ideologies that drive their pursuits of power to the ends taken however absurd (be they political, religious, societal or cultural). It is sad to think that the subtle mechanisms of human reasoning seem always to give way to the darkest aspects of the Darwinian model—"survival of the fittest" with "fittest" reductively defined by "most able to inflict cruel and deadly force." It is a law that ignores the uniquely human potential of empathy and is adjudicated through the celebration of might over right. It is more often accompanied by the loss of humanity and even life.

At this stage in human history, it is abundantly clear that no Western powers escape justifiable accusations of oppression, subjugation, and destruction of innocent lives in their quests for power. England's centuries-old list of conquests and colonisations certainly rank among those in need of reckoning squarely, and in so doing one must acknowledge one's birthright as the beneficiary of truly ill-gotten gains somewhere down the line. Let us also not forget, too, that Allied forces were ultimately joined, aided, and did abet a like-minded sociopath to Germany's Hitler in the figure of Joseph Stalin, whose genocidal record over a lifetime in power offers a grim bookend to the Fuhrer's own. If peacetime politics make "strange bedfellows," wartime politics, it seems, make positively deplorable and often shameful ones.

What history will ever provide a requisite narrative of a bridge too far in human estimations of achieving aims at the expense of others? When I look around me even now, I see spectres of what drove that hateful little man forward in other world leaders and am reminded that it can happen again. The greatest catastrophes, they say, are the result of the accumulation of smaller, even seemingly minor incidents, decisions, or events, and there is a whole world full of those who would still bend others to their will at any and every cost.

Chapter 22

It is a natural phenomenon for children to play games that mimic and reflect the world around them. We observed carefully and, even in the course of playing, tried making sense of the world and its problems through the things we acted out on the playground. Boys especially seemed to always be playing war games and pretending to be soldiers. Everywhere one looked, pint-sized officers and junior combatants fascinated with the mechanisms, machinery, and technologies of war led their own little armies to enact their fascinations with action and bravery. Very often, within these games, the world, for better and worse, comes briefly and tellingly into focus.

Diagonally across from where our house stood, just down in a little hollow, was an old, small grey farmhouse in which lived a family of four. The mother stayed at home, the father worked in the limestone quarries nearby. They had two sons, the eldest about sixteen and a quiet and agreeable enough chap, the younger by two or so years, Donald, was a different matter entirely.

Challenged by a physiological condition that manifested itself in a pronounced curvature of his spine, resulted in Donald walking with both a pronounced stoop and a somewhat sideways gait. It does not take much imagination to surmise that the severity of this condition caused him not only a degree of physical discomfort, even pain, but also what must have been an unquantifiable but acute amount of psychological distress as well.

Donald was an unfriendly boy who seemed never able to look into your eyes when the chance to converse arose. He seemed to internalize the war in a very serious way indeed, and one that seemed to turn his physically wracked state and his almost undoubted feelings of difference into a miniaturized though extremely volatile manifestation of the very enemy himself: Donald very obviously and honestly fancied himself the embodiment of Hitler; we even, and yes cruelly though quite accurately so, called him, "Little Hitler," and he took great pains to look the part. He wore his hair swept severely left over his forehead just like the real Fuhrer, and, had he been old enough to grow a moustache, one can also fairly assume its probable style.

True to this adopted persona, Donald had also taken to "recruiting" boys in the neighbourhood (at least those of whom seemed either impressionable or "naïve" enough, to follow along) whom he conscripted and drilled into his own little army using his very own brand of martial brutality to achieve its quasi-military precision. Eventually, the army grew to about fifteen or so young boys whom he "trained" daily after school, lining them up on the street in front of our house for inspection, noting any infractions of whatever rules he had developed for their appearance or conduct, and then, punishing them. Severely. This most often involved turning them around, about-face away from him, and then kicking them repeatedly as hard as he could in the backs of the legs, buttocks, and the base of their spines in order to knock them down, after which, he would continue his ministrations of either kicking or beating them with the riding crop that he wielded. This would go on until the "recruit" begged for mercy.

He was an absolutely diabolical little tyrant! His followers—as absolutely daft as I imagined them to be for allowing themselves to be subjected to this kind of sadistic treatment—were clearly and visibly terrified of him and, as they subjected themselves to being ritualistically abused, obediently offered up Nazi salutes as they went goose-stepping up and down Anncroft Road. It. Was. Absurd. Simply, mad. A dark mirror held up to a world that seemed rife for chilling enactments of depraved sadomasochistic cruelty and victimization.

Not content with the marching and drilling, beatings and otherwise humiliation of these boys, Donald also taught them how to make little bombs in bottles and pipes—working them up, all said and done, into a potentially crack neighbourhood junior terror squad. At one point in the war whenever we heard explosions, we were never quite sure whether Manchester was going up in smoke again, or if it was simply Little Hitler with yet another explosive device. Looking back, I think it was actually Mum who named him, "Little Hitler," and, after any loud report, would often call out: "What was that, Manchester or Little Hitler?"

"Little Hitler, Mum!"

To which she would respond, "Oh, well, that's all right then."

This bizarre if, honestly, quite unsettling little neighbourhood drama went on for quite some time. Sam and I watched with initial amusement, then, befuddled incredulity, and, finally, horror, as his unmerciful mistreatment of the boys reached a point of the psychopathic.

At some point along the line, Mum saw Donald's mother on the bus to downtown Buxton and decided to have a word with her about whether *she* had concerns about her son's behaviour. It was a query met, as Mum relayed, with a mouthful of "bad words," an admonishment to "mind her own business," and, the penultimate phrase in the vast universe of maternally available verbal trump cards in parental culpability: "My boy would never do anything of the sort! He's a good boy!" Upon hearing this, I asked Sam if he thought she might be blind or deaf, and to which, if I remember correctly, he responded, "No. Just stupid."

Where Donald was concerned, it was nearly inevitable things would probably not resolve fully until something very bad happened, and, as it turned out, it did in the form of a real feud with a neighbourhood boy named Peter, who, ironically, was the brother of a local police officer. The denouement was reached when Donald threw one of his homemade bombs at Peter—filled with pepper. It exploded near Peter's head and blinded him for what turned out to be quite some time. For a while the doctors had grave doubts as to his regaining his sight at all, but after some time in the Manchester Eye Hospital, most of it did return, although there was evidently some irreversible damage that he was told he'd have to live with (isn't there always?).

The positive result of what was nearly a *very* tragic set of events was that our neighbourhood terror squad was no more... I'm not sure exactly what happened to Donald or where he went, but we never saw him again. His reign of terror on Anncroft Road was over. We were heartily glad to see our local chapter of the "Hitler Youth Organization" disbanded. Peace in our time restored, at least on our street, to make way again for the larger war. Enough of "Boy's inhumanity to boys," there was enough of the grown-up kind to be had.

Chapter 23

Between Derbyshire's county seat, Derby, thirty miles to the southeast; Sheffield twenty miles due east; Leeds (forty miles) to the northeast; Birmingham (fifty miles) nearly due south; and Stockport, Manchester and Liverpool, (located respectively thirteen, twenty, and forty-five miles to the north/northwest) there were a real host of prime targets surrounding Buxton on which the Germans focused their bombing. If one looks at a map, one realizes fairly quickly that Buxton was at the epicentre of these targets, which was certainly enough, but, there were also a couple closer at hand that kept things more than a bit interesting for the average Buxtonian on some days.

For miles surrounding our bucolic Peak District home, there were two clandestine RAF storage hubs that were vital to Britain's overall war efforts. The hills were indeed alive with the most volatile and incendiary materials—including RAF munitions and airplane fuel, and lethal and undetonated German ordinance. Unexploded gas bombs were trundled in and out via railroad lines running north of town below the edge of the moors that stretched seemingly endlessly on west to the outskirts of Manchester. Bombs destined for various airfields and squadrons were also ferried to and fro along these lines throughout the English Midlands. All these functions were hidden away at an installation we called "McAlpine's," which, as it began to accrue more use after 1940 and as its presence known to German intelligence, then became a sought-after target.

The name "McAlpine's" was attributable to a large civil and defence industry construction company founded by Sir Robert McAlpine & Sons, which, in our area, was overseen and run by son Alfred McAlpine. The McAlpine family was (and continues to be) among the largest civic building contractors in Britain, responsible for everything from the construction of aqueducts, railway tunnels and fuel bunkers for the British government, well-before the war, and continuing on through London's 2012 Olympic stadium project and to the present day. The location's historically accurate name was actually Harpur Hill, named after the neighbouring hamlet near Axe Edge. Harpur Hill was comprised of no less than 500 acres of underground weapons storage built around an old quarry, and, as such, was the largest munitions depot in the whole of England.

We may not (mercifully) have known that at the time, but we obviously knew about its location, as it was almost quite literally in our backyard. If we had known the full story, I'm not sure we would have been able to even sleep at night. Add to that that it was also a fairly commonly held notion among some locals that, as the war wore on, German spies knew of its location and contents, *as well as* the nearby limestone quarries at Whaley Bridge/Furness Vale—about six miles to the north/northwest between Buxton and Stockport—which also concealed a very large underground RAF fuel depot. Whatever monikers ascribed to each, it helped explain why, whenever we would begin to get used to periods of quiet, the Luftwaffe would decide to return—each time (it seemed at least to me) getting closer than the last.

When the Nazis developed the V-1 in 1944, and their raids suddenly seemed to shift with renewed and desperate intensity to the area, Mum would often get upset because I became transfixed with the pilotless rocket planes. “Buzz-bombs” or “doodlebugs” as we called them, came complete with a stream of flame streaking out behind, as they buzzed, rattled, and roared with a distinct and only slightly more diabolical sound than the silence that signalled their drop straight down from the sky when the engines stopped.

If you became suddenly aware of it going very quiet after you had registered one’s approach, it probably meant you were already in trouble. Launched by the thousands from German bases in France, these vicious objects were nothing more than the sum total the “V” in their name suggested—“vengeance” weapons that blindly plagued England with increasing frequency as the Germans became aware that they were losing the war.

Mum and Dad once told the story of a friend who, riding his bicycle along a country lane in the south of England one night, heard the approach of a doodlebug behind him. Glancing back over his shoulder, he saw that it was traveling in the same direction and catching up fast. He pedalled as hard as he could in the pitch dark as the thing spewed fire and issued its horrendous noise until he finally spotted a lane off to his right. Taking it, he watched, with at least some sense of relief, as it then went silently straight on and exploded.

In the cities, monstrous barrage balloons hovered like silver-grey elephants scattered in the skies; beasts tethered from ground wires floating above to interfere with these menaces. In Manchester and Stockport we saw them afloat whenever we travelled through, their awkward, cumbersome presence the constant reminder of dangers somehow never far from mind. Unknown to many at the time, besides its explosive warhead, the V-1 was also armed with sharp metal blades along the front edges of its wings; cable cutters to deal with barrage balloon ground wires. I'm glad I didn't know that, either... The balloons always seemed of little value to me and, at least from my vantage point, the bombs appeared chillingly on target. The Germans may well have been losing the war, but they were still winning a few too many battles for my liking.

Looking at a map of Europe now always reminds me how very close those weapons were. Two hundred miles or so across the Channel to Buxton would've seemed a long way to a little girl, but certainly not to an advancing army. London was barely half that distance from their source and had real problems with V-1s as the summer of '44 went on. I really didn't understand, which again was undoubtedly just as well, but the horrors haunted me constantly enough, and I always had one ear cocked listening for that terrible hoarse-throated sound. I knew too the direction they came from—straight up-country from the south through the gap between the houses across the road from the front of our house where I'd stationed myself at the window to watch for them.

Insecure and terrified out of my wits almost constantly, I would often run home as fast as I could at the end of my school days, holding my breath for what seemed the whole time down the long road. When I reached the corner at Anncroft Road, I'd peek up it to see if our house was still standing. Assured that it was, only then would I exhale and, with a long sigh of relief, begin to breathe again. It was OK, Mum was safe... Another day of reprieve. So often in my mind I envisioned a plane or doodlebug bombing our street and Mum being unable to escape; or imagined that moment of realization that Daddy was not coming home from work because the Electricity Works were demolished; or Sam, Cubby, or Grandma caught in an air raid... On and on. Fear never far, if it ever did leave my mind at all.

Such is the horrific effect war has on children. Of course, in those days nobody ever really asked how children felt about anything, but war, I'm telling you, can force one to live in holy terror. "You can't spend your life looking for doodlebugs!" Mother would scold. Undeterred, I just knew that if I ever really did see one coming, I would be the one to save us all!

Air raids and flying bombs were not the only things we were taught to fear. Warnings issued at school, in the newspapers, and over the wireless carried daily admonitions that had tremendous effect. We were cautioned not to talk to strangers or volunteer information to anyone we did not know, as it was "known" there were German spies around; possibly even in town. It was a lonely feeling sometimes not to feel able to talk to someone who addressed you, but we took it very seriously. If spies were indeed all over the island looking for information, we knew enough not to speak too openly about our surroundings and invite the reprisals that seemed, inevitably, to come from the air.

There were objects too that were always to be viewed with suspicion, as they might be bombs or explosive devices. Who knew what the enemy might be capable of? "DON'T PICK ANYTHING UP!" was a mantra drummed into our dear little heads on a daily basis, as some of the devices and munitions dropped or jettisoned by enemy planes on the way back from their raids on the cities (land mines were often deployed on small parachutes) were often brightly coloured and, thus, attractive to children. In no uncertain terms we were to go near things we didn't recognize.

Of course, Sam and his pals' inquisitiveness always trumped whatever warnings were to be observed, they were interested in anything unusual for its potential to thrill. Truth be told, I was just as eager, at least some of the time.

Sam's friend Arthur, the thoroughly likeable son of our next-door neighbour, was just a bit older than Sam and seemed always to be in on the game. Typical boys with inquiring minds, he and Sam spent a lot of time together roaming the moors "looking for stuff," despite any and every warning otherwise. Shell casings, pieces of detonated bombs, debris from crashed airplanes... any items they could carry along they would often bring home. Some things were harmless—Sam got into his own little business of making rings, jewellery and other trinkets out of Perspex and glass from downed airplanes—but, on one occasion, the boys claimed to have actually come across an unexploded bomb. They said that it was OK, as they had taken the detonator off to render it harmless! How they would've known what to do is beyond me, and, frankly, I'm still somewhat unsure of the veracity of the story, but, knowing them, it could very well have been true; it was one of those occasions I really didn't *want* to know.

Scared but sworn to secrecy, I could never tell our parents when they were out scouting around, and I always carried the secret fear that someday they wouldn't come back. Those agonizing hours I waited for them... If my parents *had* known even *half* of what those two got up to, they would never have let Sam out of the house again. For the most part they were fearless and nothing deterred them. I was much less so, and so often theirs were excursions I was disinterested in joining. But there were others...

Chapter 24

At some point in 1944, Sam and I noticed something odd as we watched from our living room window. Easily spotted in their black and white habits, a small group of nuns had taken to daily walks up to the moors via the road that ran perpendicular to the end of Anncroft Road. Their behaviour, plainly stated, seems as innocuous as it sounds, save for some specifics. To explain: the convent from which the nuns walked was in the centre of town, and a fair way off from our house; far enough that even at our age we could not fathom just what was to be gained by walking so far in order to go even *further*. Why—with all the truly pretty, picturesque, or peaceful strolls one might take in any direction—and, one could add, far less strenuous ones—did these nuns (in full habits) choose this one?

Day after day for a few weeks the procession of six went by our house at the same hour (always one in the afternoon, *always six* nuns) to walk the rather steep hill to the moors. And every day we waited to see them go and then return again after about two hours. It was like clockwork. They would go up, and then in two hours' time come back down the hill to head for town. There was really no other route back from the moor.

For those unfamiliar with moors and moorlands, it's worth a moment to elaborate: First, they are, on the whole, windswept, austere, and rough surroundings. There is good reason they have long been represented by writers like the Brontes as such lonely, wild and untrammelled places. They are often the site of howling winds and dense fog, squalling rain, and, in winter, damp and bitter cold. Manchester's surrounding moors fan out due northeast/east and south to meet Buxton's, extending to their topmost reaches all the way to the Dark Peaks of England's South Pennine Mountains (about twenty-five miles north from the centre of Buxton as the crow flies).

These distant yet shared grounds were then, as they remain now, sparsely populated spots where secrets may lie undisturbed for years, even decades. Saddleworth Moor, infamous for the horrific "Moors Murders" perpetrated by Ian Brady and Myra Hindley in the mid-1960s reveal a telling example, with evidence of the duo's final victim thought only to have been discovered in 2017. The investigation was first opened in 1965. Second, while Buxton and its environs are touted for nature walks and recreational hiking, it should be remembered these were times well before current daily practices associated with health consciousness became the norm. There was no running, bicycling, fitness groups training for marathons or races or the like. While we did camp on the moors edges and tramp around a bit along some of the long-abandoned Roman roads that cut across them, the moors were certainly neither frequented recreationally, nor were they park-like. They were where civilization largely ceased, save for the occasional farm and its wandering flocks of sheep.

Dotted with out-of-use quarries and pierced with unmarked mineshafts and wells, they were left largely to the grouse and the occasional hunting or shooting party. Choked in bramble, heather, and nettle there were only concealed cloughs, ravines and caves into, if one weren't cautious, one might vanish. The moors north of Level Lane where the nuns set off were the site of old coal mines, disused and flooded. When I was still quite young, a neighbour of ours, evidently despondent over her husband's infidelity, intentionally sought one out. It took a while to figure out where she'd gone. Mum shielded us from the sordid details of the episode's sad conclusion.

And so, to continue the tale with another rhetorical question—just what *exactly* was this gaggle of fusty nuns doing going up there day after day? It was strange. Each day, we watched and counted, until, one day, after a noticeably much shorter period of time than the usual two hours, the nuns came down the hill and we counted again. *Seven*... How could six go up and seven come down? Did they just happen along a lost nun wandering around and decide to bring her home? It made no sense. It was clearly an investigative job for my brother and his pal Ronnie Dixon; one on which the duo was only too eager to set out... without me! They wouldn't let me go. I was, it turned out, "only a girl!"

"Nonsense!" I protested. I implored them, as unhappy at being slighted as unhappy gets. In fact—indignant! I note now these as the first stirrings of my fury as a woman denied equality or rights. I was about to really launch into it all when Sam explained: First, they really didn't know what they would find and he didn't want to endanger me, and, "Besides...," he added, "... if we don't come back in a reasonable time, it's got to be you that sounds the alarm and tells Dad to come and look for us."

I still didn't like it, but, begrudgingly, had to admit that it actually made sense. Terrific. My usual role—the lookout.

Watch and wait. Well, OK, but neither happily nor patiently, I'm afraid.

With it settled for the moment, the boys set off. At the time, I actually suspected they might've even followed the nuns before, at least part of the way—how else would they know how far to go, or the path they chose? They evidently kept going until they joined the old Roman road and, following that for quite a way, came to the well-known ruins of a long-uninhabited farmhouse we called "the halfway house," due to its location on the long trek from the far edge of the moor to town.

Searching around there, the boys saw nothing much out of the ordinary until, a little farther along, they came upon a large, mangled object which, as they approached it, became the clearly recognisable remains of an airplane—Sam claimed it was a German one! By the looks of things, he said, it had been there for some time, and there appeared to be no signs of life around either it or the scrub-covered moor between them and the farmhouse. Weighing their apprehension against overwhelming curiosity, the boys backtracked to take another look there, where, poking around the farmhouse's exterior walls, they found footprints that appeared quite fresh.

They entered the broken down house, climbing over piles of rubble and junk, and, as they did, began to encounter tell-tale signs of things seemingly having recently been disturbed. Foremost, there were some stones that looked as if they'd been arranged in a heap, under which, they found upon dragging a few aside and sweeping some dirt and loose gravel away, was the outline of the original access trapdoor to the farmhouse cellar. With little debate, pounding hearts, and collective breath held, they lifted the latch and pulled back the door to reveal a set of rough, uneven stairs leading down into the dark hole beneath the house. With no clue as to what awaited and no means of lighting the way, they quickly agreed to cover it up again and return the next day with flashlights to investigate further.

They were very excited when they returned home to tell me about the whole thing. I already wanted to tell Daddy, but they said that I'd better not—invoking the veiled threat that must now echo throughout the entire history of juvenile relationships in every culture across the planet: "Nothing good ever happens to little nippers who tattle to Mum and Dad." I resented that too. I wouldn't tell if they didn't want me to, as I knew they'd never trust me again. I swore again that I wouldn't.

None of us slept much that night in anticipation of what they might find the next day, and when daylight came the boys were ready to go back to the moors. I was still very upset. Then, I thought about it: What if something truly awful is there like bombs or explosives, hidden weapons, or... perhaps worse—a *body*! The possibilities of these realizations certainly didn't make me feel any better, and now the whole thing had turned really quite sinister. I was beginning to feel really frightened for them. Nevertheless, I went ahead and agreed to cover for their absence but told them not to be too long or I would have to sound the alarm. I then proceeded to await their return as I had the day prior, but with an increased sense of anxiety. I just knew something was afoot, and I waited with bated breath for what seemed an eternity.

Equipped now with flashlights and cricket bats for protection, the boys returned to the scene. Cautiously retracing their actions, they opened the hatch and, this time, shinnied down into the darkness beneath the floor. They were either very brave or very foolhardy, or, as are most who place themselves in potential peril, an admixture of both.

In the corner of the dank cellar they quickly discovered a pile of freshly emptied food tins, as well as some food wrappers that indicated the recent presence of someone who had hidden there for a time and had provisions—*all* British-made with the clearly recognizable black wartime labels affixed; ration goods.

We had a meeting when they'd returned that left us pretty clear conclusions—a little voice in my head said: "Deduction, my dear Watson... *It was the nuns!*" They'd been taking the food to the downed German pilot from that plane (or a spy!), one who by now had either already infiltrated the area or would very soon, and, in either case, had used the farmhouse to lay low until the timing was right to move along or (in the case of a downed or injured airman), was well enough to travel. It was obvious! The nuns had supplied him, and when it was time they smuggled him out in one of their habits to assure that he could be guided to safe harbour. Who would notice, much less suspect them? Who would be on the lookout for a bunch of nuns on a quiet stroll, or keep track of where they went? We would—we did!

Could it be true? We certainly didn't imagine either the nuns "habits" (pun intended) or the shift in their number, but, as we all know, circumstantial evidence never stands up in court. The intrigue could never be solved. As we were trained by Dad and Mum to "keep our own counsel," it was finally by this edict that our lips were sealed. Neither of them ever knew of the adventure until we told them years later. We didn't want to worry them and, besides, if anyone asked them, they could honestly say they did not know—as far as Sam and I were concerned it was for their protection too.

Chalk it all up to just one among many secret stories never revealed, I suppose, and with so many now gone having never told anything of what they knew, another "mystery" never unearthed. And, speaking of...

One day, Daddy came home with a cardboard box about eight inches high, ten inches long, and about six inches wide—another present for my brother and I, but a much better one than that grotty old gas mask! We opened the box and there, curled up in a tight ball, was a little creature—a hedgehog!

Riding his bicycle home from the office, Dad was passing through a country lane when he spotted him. He was rather a large hedgehog as hedgehogs go, and his quills were very sharp—it was difficult to pick him up at first because he was so spiky, but, we soon got used to it. We named him "Snuffles," as he, indeed, made a sort of snuffling sound making his way across the floor.

I took him to school one day to the equivalent of "show and tell," but he was very reclusive and curled up in a tight ball and wouldn't come out. The children in my class poked at him to try to make him move and were disappointed because he didn't do any tricks. Personally, I didn't think he needed to impress anybody with tricks: hedgehogs are hedgehogs and are quite independent. He just didn't like attention. I took him home. But Snuffles still would not uncurl and not even to eat. He just stayed rolled up. After several days, and without being able to detect a heartbeat under all those sharp quills, we came to the sad conclusion that he was dead.

On a fittingly rainy day for a funeral, my brother, borrowing one of Dad's removable white collars fitted backwards and with his raincoat back to front to look more reverential, armed us both with prayer books to recite the Church of England burial service over Snuffles in the side garden. We stood there in the rain, serious and sombre, to give him a proper and fitting send-off. We mourned, sang a hymn for the dead, and lowered him into a small grave we had dug. We threw in a flower and a shovelful of dirt, and said our sad and tearful good-byes. After filling in the hole, we erected a little wooden cross with an epitaph that read: "R.I.P. Dear Snuffles. An Uncommon Hedgehog who will be greatly missed."

As one imagines, it only took three days for my ever-inquisitive brother to say, "I want to go dig Snuffles up to see if he's still there."

"Of course, he's still *there*," I replied. "Where else *would* he be?"

"Well... It's the third day and he might have 'risen,'" he responded.

"Hedgehogs don't rise from the dead!" I said, with a resigned practicality.

"How do *you* know? Bet he's not there," said Sam.

"He's *there*," I replied firmly, adding, "Don't be so silly."

"I'm digging him up!" he said.

Not to be left out, off we set to exhume the body of the dear departed Snuffles, and— lo and behold—when the last shovelful of dirt was removed we looked down into the grave to find the box was pried OPEN and Snuffles nowhere to be found!

"I *TOLD* you!" said my brother. "He has risen!"

"Piffle!" I shot back... "He wasn't dead then in the first place, and, anyway, now he's gone, and so he must be alive *somewhere*."

We went inside and got out the Church of England Hymnal again, this time to sing with great joy and vigour an appropriate hymn: "Snuffles the Hedgehog has risen today... Hallelujah!" We obviously never saw him again. He got going while the getting was good, and who could blame him? He was either out there somewhere living a happy hedgehog life, or had been received into hedgehog-heaven, leaving us yet another miracle to ponder... First, six nuns turn to seven, and now, a hedgehog was resurrected in the English Midlands. Someone should write a book, but who'd believe it?

King George VI and Queen Elizabeth (present Queen Elizabeth's mother) visiting rubble in London Blitz

Little boy crying and looking at the bombed-out ruins of his home. Note the dog looking down on him.

Chapter 25

On Christmas Eve 1944, Hitler sent us a present and not a welcome one. I was asleep in my little bed cosy and warm, but strangely dreaming of being in the middle of an air raid and the house being bombed. I awoke abruptly and, outside, I heard it— *that* horrible, loud noise! Jumping out of bed, not quite yet awake and in full panic mode, I turned and immediately ran head-on into the side of the wardrobe. "Hmm," I thought, groggily, "it must be the wreckage!" Thoroughly dazed and awakening from dream to reality I made my way cautiously along to lift the heavy blackout curtain in my room and looked into the skies... there, coming straight toward the house, was an object in the sky with a ball of fire shooting out the back! A doodlebug! They had caught me sleeping on the job!

The vibration and noise seemed to shake the house to its foundation. This was it—it was going to destroy us all! Awakened from one nightmare into a very real one, I spun around again and ran out into the hallway, this time managing to avoid hitting anything and calling for Mum and Dad. Sam was already out there, bewildered still half asleep. Dad, quickly confirmed I wasn't dreaming, saying firmly but reassuringly: "Stay calm... we'll be all right as long as the engine keeps going. Everyone get downstairs."

We hurried down to the living room. Sam and Dad quickly pushed the biggest furniture against the front windows so that, if they shattered, we wouldn't be hurt by the flying glass. Mum once again quickly offered the one comfort that placated us during every crisis, saying, "Never mind, I'll put the kettle on and we'll have a cup of tea." Tea. *The* answer for all ills, pains, air raids, trials, tribulations (real or imagined), and any-and-all of the other devastations that took place throughout my childhood and well beyond! Tea, I am happy to say, always works!

We sat huddled together, kettle on the boil, listening intently for the noise overhead to stop, and, all the while, praying it wouldn't. In the end it went over, exploding on the moors north of the house. We looked at each other with relief and, joining hands, Daddy said a prayer of thanks.

In a farmhouse not far away, lived a school chum of my brother's, John. He too was fast asleep that Christmas Eve until that same noise awakened him. When the doodlebug hit, John said his bed careened across the room, hit the wall, and he ended up on the floor. He called it, "a real rude awakening." I'll say, but at least he'd lived to tell the tale!

Just before the war ended, our family took yet another short trip to Manchester, and truly, and for the first time I really understood what a bomb could do and just what those lights in the sky at night really meant. Street after street levelled. Only deep holes and piles of rubble left. The exterior walls of the tallest apartment buildings were still partially standing, the rest of the buildings' structures were completely blown away. The interior walls, along with the contents of each apartment, lay in heaps at the bottom of a huge crater at the centre. I remember vividly, standing on the edge of it all and looking up to see what colour the walls were in each flat on every floor. It looked so strange. No floors, hallways, or rooms, no partitions; just a vertical floor-by-floor display of walls decorated differently top to bottom.

What made an additionally indelible impression on my mind was when I then looked down deep into the crater and saw a doll amongst the debris. Crushed and mangled, it sat there with a toy lorry and pram (baby carriage); toys that had belonged to living, breathing children... Where were they? What happened to them? Were they alive? I could only wonder... Something was drastically wrong in our world for anyone to feel the need to resort to this kind of violence to settle differences. It was insane.

Chapter 26

Whenever I am asked about my childhood, I have to answer that on the whole, even in the midst of a war, we managed to live a life filled with undeniably and genuinely happy moments. Among the most important thing one learns during wartime, too, is that courage is cultivated, and my Mum and Dad were nothing short of incredible in that regard. They were rare and unselfish parents who made sure Sam and I were both physically and emotionally taken care of, dedicated to putting us first. There were many times, I am well sure, that they put aside their desires to their own detriment—true parents in every sense of the word—and I will never be able to express my thanks for all they did. If they were ever truly afraid (and I'm sure they were), they very rarely let it show, and they set a fine example that taught us how to cope, largely by keeping busy. Continuing to do everyday things, setting goals and reaching them, and not being frightened into inactivity all became our salvation.

There were no hysterics or "poor us" sentiments expressed, and if we were not exactly fearless or without heartache, at the very least we were together. A sense of value and what was important in life were instilled that transcended ambitions, social status, wealth or the attainment of material things. They were secondary concerns; it was being together and having our family and loved ones around us that mattered most. I discovered that helping wherever and whomever I could helped me too, and this led to some perspective whenever feeling, as I did at times, that I was living on the edge of an unknown I could not possibly grasp.

It was also always a good thing finding those with a sense of humour still intact too. At least some of the "indomitable British spirit" may be found in things to laugh at. The comedians on the wireless seemed to poke fun at everyone in nearly every situation, teaching us to laugh at ourselves. When one couldn't seem to find solace or the laughter would not come, praying kept fear in some abeyance as well. We often read the Bible to learn to strive to be good people when nearly every other message suggested the rest of humanity had abandoned the notion forever.

To further ensure a sense of normalcy in our lives, Mum and Dad would often entertain friends on the weekend and include Sam and I in the fun. Almost never were we banished to our rooms to let the grown-ups have fun "without the children." Mum would prepare light refreshments or cakes to have with tea, and we would play parlour games and have no end of laughs. We played Charades, Blind Man's Bluff, Musical Chairs, and a couple others that were as improvisational as they were unnamed.

If the company stayed for the weekend, Sam would always use the circumstance as his chance to do the thing he liked best—play tricks on them by short-sheeting the bed, or, another favourite, putting a sewing bobbin on a long string attached to a can under it and hiding to wait until it was quiet. Then, of course, string in hand, he would slowly pull it along as the unsuspecting guests searched for the source of the noise. They were always good sports and had a good laugh at our silly pranks.

My parents also felt it was important to enjoy the great outdoors and to learn to be close to nature. Dad said it was good for us to learn to "rough-it," because one never knew if circumstances might arise in which we would have to live off the land. Every summer, at least once, we would go for our equivalent of a camping trip.

I suppose I really don't have an adventurous bone in my body when all is said and done, and I silently but certainly hoped that "living off the land" would never be something I truly had to experience—usually as I pondered the mysteries of just why in the world my mother ever agreed to their foray into the wilds of Canada. Give me home, a warm bed, and a book...

Nevertheless, I didn't complain and went along with the rest on these excursions, helping pack what most would undoubtedly picture as the quintessential English picnic basket replete with cutlery, china plates and cups, tablecloth and linen napkins and real drinking glasses (roughing it should only be so much so!) We packed sandwiches, salads, and fruit from the ration larder, and we carried a metal pot to boil water for tea, because, after all, what expedition would be complete without it when four o'clock came around?

Mum and I had a "girls" pup tent all to ourselves. Sam and Dad shared a bigger, "man-size" tent. We didn't have sleeping bags, we just simply packed our blankets and pillows for the cool nights in "the woods." Everyone thought it great fun, and it was clear that Mum, as prim and proper as she could be, had certainly spent her fair share of time in a tent; she was always quite resourceful and quite easily caught up in the spirit of things. What an adventure! Off we'd go to hike up to the edge of the moor to pitch our tents, and then to pick bilberries off the low bushes amongst the heather, the grouse flying out from beneath as we went. They had a funny cry that sounded both plaintive and also mimicked a harsh warning—it sounded for all the world like, "G'back, G'back"—which made us feel as though we were invading their territory, which, of course, we were.

One summer, as we planned our annual excursion, Dad invited a friend who had been "bombed-out" in London to come along. He'd lost his business as well as his flat and everything in it in an air raid one terrible night, landing in Buxton with only the clothes he stood up in and a few small personal belongings scavenged from the wreckage. A lifetime city dweller, he was nevertheless full of enthusiasm and agreed readily to the adventure. I doubted he had ever even seen farm animals before, much less having an occasion to rough-it in the woods!

We huffed and puffed our way along with tents and gear, picnic basket, and a collection of small twigs to start a campfire. Finding a spot of colour, we set up camp and settled down for the evening. It was so peaceful. Not a sound outside of nature to be heard, no sirens, no planes. We enjoyed dinner and sat around until dusk, extinguishing our campfire so as not to create any light that could be seen from the air. We told stories, and Sam and I listened as the grown-ups related their experiences in different parts of the world. Of course, we also told ghost stories and had a proper sing-song of English folk tunes too. Mummy and Daddy loved to sing, and we all joined in until we were sleepy, turning in tired but content.

In the wee hours of the morning I awakened to a strange noise. There was something outside—snorting and pushing against the bottom of the tent right by my head! Adrenaline pumping, I nudged Mum while trying not to make a sound. She awoke and immediately called out for Dad: "Robey, Robey! There's some kind of animal trying to get in our tent!"

Dad, Sam, and our London guest came on the run to rescue us from the wild beast, which, in fact, turned out to be a cow along with a small herd of friends. I still didn't like it— the cows I knew had long, sharp curved horns and would toss you if they didn't like you. I'd been chased by one near Bayswater and was still convinced they were vicious. The men chased the cattle, and we watched them go, trampling the supplies and gear stacked outside our tents as they did. That was enough roughing it for me. I was very happy to be going back to the house.

Chapter 27

As things settled down in the skies above, and I became somewhat less preoccupied with either scouring them for doodlebugs, or convinced that every time I left the house it would be bombed into oblivion, I began to look forward to coming home from school in the afternoons to spend time with Mum, who would be doing afternoon chores with the wireless on. We listened to so many popular BBC programs. After the war, our favourite was a popular daytime radio "soap opera" called "Mrs. Dale's Diary", which she listened to religiously. In the winter when it got dark early, I would hurry home to a roaring fireplace in the living room where Mummy would have the kettle on the boil and some scrumptious scones or cakes to enjoy while we sat in our easy chairs listening to the thoughts and adventures of Mrs. Dale and husband Jim, the physician. I loved it. We so enjoyed those brief times of cosy camaraderie in a busy day— just carefree girls.

Mum and Dad both loved the radio, and while I wouldn't say ours was an overly musical household, Sam loved trad-jazz—New Orleans and Dixieland—as well as the Big Band music that had become the rage. He had, somehow (though I'm not quite sure how or when), even learned to play the drums with some real skill. My tastes turned toward both classical music and the popular songs of the day. I loved the performers on the radio and very much related to the spirit of some of those songs. They reinforced my sense of collective camaraderie, and the lyrics still echo in my head even now. I remember most vividly Vera Lynn's *The White Cliffs of Dover*: "*There'll be peace and laughter forever after, tomorrow, when the world is free...*", and Gracie Fields's, *When the Lights Go On Again All Over the World*.

As my musical interests grew, I kept telling Mummy that I really wanted to take piano lessons. She explained that, while it would be fine with her, the obvious problem was that we didn't have a piano, and, at the moment, could ill-afford to get one. It was a problem. I knew such luxuries were definitely not a first priority and decided after a short while that it was pretty thoughtless of me to keep going on about it. I resigned myself to forget about learning, although I spoke to Cubby about it one day while visiting, relaying the story of my grandmother's frustrated childhood experiences with the locked piano.

To my surprise, she told me she played! I had no idea! Sure enough, the next time we were together at a house where they had a piano, she played for me, very sweetly and with a full command of a whole repertoire of old time songs of her era. She was eighty-four, and while it was clear that her fingers weren't what they once were—plagued as she was by arthritis and a right index finger that didn't work quite as well due to the loss of a tendon in an accident—her memory was as sharp as a teenager's, and she still managed to "tickle the ivories" with real verve. I loved to listen to her, and I wanted to play like that. I thought about it constantly.

Not long after that, Mum and I were home one day, me

looking out of the bow window in the living room and whiling away the time to see what kind of a day it was, when I heard a vehicle approaching. There was a huge van coming up the street. It slowed and then stopped just outside our house. I yelled to Mum in the other room. "Mummy, Mummy, there's a moving van outside."

"Oh?" she answered, "It must be for one of the neighbours."

"No, it stopped here in front," I persisted.

"It must be a mistake, Kath," she replied.

Typical nosy neighbours, every time a moving or furniture van came down our street, there Mum and I were, glued to the window. We wanted to see whatever new piece of furniture or appliance the neighbours might be getting.

"Mum, they're opening the back doors right by our gate—come quick!"

She finally came to the window and said matter-of-factly, "Oh, I know what that is."

"What? Is it for us? What are we getting!?" My anticipation and excitement grew with each query until I was nearly jumping up and down. From my eight-year old point of view, *anything* new meant a red-letter day.

"Well, let's go out on the step and take a look," Mum finally said.

When the men opened the van doors, I saw it. My eyes opened wider than I ever thought they could, my mouth dropped open, and my heart skipped and almost stopped. It was a piano! A beautiful, *beautiful*, piano, and they were pulling it forward in the truck! I just couldn't believe it!

"Mummy, is it… a mistake!?" I asked, still incredulous.

"No, Kath. It's not a mistake. It's for you… Cubby bought it. Isn't it wonderful?"

Cubby, frequenting the sales rooms in Buxton, was

evidently browsing around one day and found this unusual instrument listed for auction in an estate sale. Made by John Brinsmead & Sons, an old and respected name in British-made pianos, it was constructed of rosewood, a wooden frame and highly polished keys of real ivory, and had all these incredible markings and, I would soon find out, a beautifully warm tone too. For *me*... a piano. Overwhelmed, I sat down on the front step and cried... so happy, so grateful. Now, I could and would really learn to play!

Sure enough, right on the heels of its delivery, along came Cubby. She had walked a mile-and-a half from her home in hopes of reaching our house before her gift did. While she didn't quite make it, she was very happy it had arrived on schedule. I simply smothered her with hugs and kisses as I told her that she had just made me the happiest little girl in the whole wide world.

When the movers had gone, she sat down with me and played some of her old tunes as we waited for the piano tuner she had also ordered to come along, to make sure it was in fine shape for me to begin (it had to be tuned every three months). When he arrived, he took off its front panel to get at the tuning pegs, and there, written on the frame, were the names and dates of every piano tuner that had ever worked on it, dating back through its already eighty-eight-year history! It was simply a treasure, and I couldn't wait to start my lessons. Oh, Cubby, as warm and funny as she was dignified and proper, a true English lady... so good to us. She loved us as though we were her very own, and, as far as I was concerned, we were. I loved her with all my heart.

Chapter 28

"Quick, a convoy!" The cry went up as my schoolmates and I hurried out of the school grounds to watch a parade of American soldiers and all their equipment travel through town. In 1942, America got involved in the war, and we began to get used to troops on the move through the village quite regularly. We actually did call them "Yanks," and they were very often on the way north over the moors to a U.S. base about twelve miles away.

We loved them immediately, and whenever news spread that they were coming through and it coincided with our break or lunchtime, we would rush outside to vie for front row positions on the sidewalk to cheer them on. What we loved most were the brightly wrapped sticks of gum, candies, chocolate bars and pennies they threw! To an eager throng of sweets-deprived kids with wartime piggybanks, it was as close as it got to Christmastime. Such excitement in our sleepy little village, we watched them carefully to absorb every detail while we scooped up all the candy we could.

It was on one of these occasions that I saw the first black person I would ever see; an American soldier. For my part—and I write this with the realization as to how shocking it may seem—as a seven-year-old raised in the English Midlands with a sum total of travels no more than about fifty miles or so in any direction, I simply had no reference point for the experience. I don't think any of the children I knew had seen anyone of any ethnic or racial diversity prior. It certainly made us realise how tiny, homogenous, and sheltered our little corner of the world was.

Years later, after settling in the U.S. in the 1950s, I took a trip with my husband and some friends to the southern United States, where I was horrified to nearly physical illness by the institutionalized and "normalized" racial bigotry I witnessed there. Remembering that very soldier, an American, one of "the good guys, I was suddenly acquainted with a very visceral definition for hypocrisy. That "the land of the free and the home of the brave" would ever allow any of its citizens to be treated so unjustly made me question yet again just what was wrong with our planet. I wondered, after what Nazism had accomplished in nearly destroying the globe, what possible excuse there could be for this, for there certainly was to my mind not a single one.

The Americans we encountered for this first time, were well-liked and trusted nearly without reservation in town. We understood, they were allies and there to help. We were simply grateful, with the older girls seemingly especially keen on them. So many would invite them home to meet their Mums and Dads. With our boys scattered around the globe fighting, dates for young women were few and far between. I know many of our boys probably had a bit of a different perspective, but for us, these handsome and charming lads in their beautifully tailored uniforms of expensive, smooth cloth, so impeccably groomed and polite, seemed wholly delightful. They in turn seemed just as delighted to meet our

English girls and their families—well, our English girls at any rate; families just came in the bargain. They would seem always to have access to everything and arrive with gifts of the "exotic" things we couldn't get: sugar, eggs, butter... fruit and chocolate! Naturally, not too many objected when daughters brought home an American boyfriend bearing extra rations to go along with their charming American personalities.

Wartime romances led to more than a few English girls becoming GI brides and sailing off to America. Who could predict what their presence forecast? It would take a while to find out ... but their confident support somehow signalled things were shifting, that we were on the offensive now. They smiled at us as they marched through as if they knew something we weren't quite sure in believing just yet, and the candies and winks they threw our way were only the signs of sweeter and more hopeful times farther down the road. But they were ahead. Maybe we would get there yet.

Chapter 29

On May 7, 1945, ten days before my tenth birthday, Germany and the European Axis powers officially surrendered to the Allies in Reims, France. Victory in Europe (V-E Day) would be celebrated around the world the next day, May 8. I remember that morning vividly, but not for this reason, but rather two others, and it reminds me how funny it often is in how one remembers auspicious days due to their more trivial aspects. First, there was an earthquake: a rather strong tremor that raised the pavement in the road outside of the Duke of York pub in Buxton by at least three inches. Second, a bird flew down our chimney—ending up in a sooty, flustered and fluttering heap on our hearth.

The war was actually over... could it be true? No more air raids, sirens, blackout curtains or living in a constant state of unrest and fear... We'd even heard Hitler was dead. Everyone took the day off and seemed suddenly to be running to the nearest town square or local pub to celebrate. Suddenly, everything that had determined our lives for over five years—more than half my life—seemed to evaporate overnight.

As far as our neighbourhood, our home, I remember us

as simply dazed by the news—restless, almost as if we were in a state of shock. We wandered around not knowing quite what to do, with ourselves, or next. It was as if a strange torpor had taken hold when one really only really wanted to feel overwhelming and ecstatic joy. In fact, I remember vividly not truly feeling any sense of joy at all—certainly relief that no more killing and bombing would take place, but, no desire to go out to the Buxton town square or outside to hoot and holler. Too much had happened. Too much pain, too much loss to instantly give way to any feelings that, "Well, all over and done with and everything is all right now."

Even at that young age, I had the distinct feeling that it could not just suddenly be OK. Not for me. Time needed to pass. There was so much to be done and so much healing that needed to take place—rebuilding, reconnection to a day-to day life without the shadows of destruction looming. Our life on hold had still been the life we had got used to, despite how beyond one's control or reach it could seem at times. I was soon going on a decade on this earth, but I'm certain now that if I felt this way it was a more common reaction than openly expressed. I've heard that some soldiers feel this way when there is no longer anyone to fight. I'm sure it is a reaction that would now be seen as symptomatic of a kind of Post Traumatic Stress Disorder (PTSD). In that time, it would have probably been put down as a case of civilian "shell-shock."

In fact, so many things didn't return to "normal" quickly. While we no longer had blackout curtains and the mere act of opening windows and leaving the curtains open to enjoy the sights, sounds, and smells of the outdoors coming in the house was like a small slice of heaven, food and clothing were still heavily rationed, along with many common goods and services that would take years to return to pre-war standards. Some British industries and businesses never really did bounce back.

Nevertheless, among the things that were wonderful to have back again was our car! To be able to go into the countryside for rides without worrying where we might end up, much less if it was safe to do so, was amazing. After the last "all-clear" sounded, Daddy made sure he took us for an outing just about every weekend. We would roam around all the places we hadn't or couldn't go before and, for the very first time, I truly realized what a beautiful part of England the Peak District and its surrounding counties were.

I never tired of seeing the different towns, villages and countryside around us—going on tours through the stately homes that began once more be open to the public for us to have a look at. Those were things, for many I'm sure, that had been almost forgotten as we entrenched ourselves in just getting through each day. Only gradually did the previous years begin to subside, and could we begin to give ourselves permission to breathe more deeply and feel at ease again.

Buxton itself seemed to have emerged quite another kind of international community, with an influx of American soldiers, displaced Polish refugees and even German POWs. Our quiet, genteel, polished and posh little town had a new veneer, and with its recent past and a rapidly developing future pushing and pulling us, we moved slowly forward, reminded less and less of the legacy of war through physical manifestations of battles and bombs, but more through the vague suspicions of those around us we did not yet recognize. To be sure there were battle scars. For those who had suffered in Prisoner of War or concentration camps, had lost loved ones and or homes, the wounds were, naturally, very deep. For the rest of us, we'd seen much and been very lucky on the whole, but it still meant that chunks of our childhoods were either lost, or at least, coloured by fearful expectations and experience.

Even as people in the streets embraced and celebrated, churches rang bells in revelry, and wireless reporters positively bubbled and burbled their enthusiasms for recent victories and the newfound optimism peace brought, I remember thinking quite firmly that it was about time everyone came to their senses and stopped the reckless behaviours that had led to the worst of our long-lost years in the first place. I seemed to return to the stubborn resolve I'd latched onto when I became "an adult" at age five, reckoning that it was time to get on with our lives with purpose, as I was very sure our choices would now be extraordinarily important and we better make the right ones and right away!

In seeming lockstep with my general scepticism, it was again the *Movietone* newsreels at the picture shows that confirmed my purview of the state of the world beyond our idyllic, green valleys and wild climes.

Film footage shot by Allied liberation forces of Nazi death camps began to surface, revealing still-living victims unable to walk on their own and people who looked more skeletons than fully formed human beings. People of all ages, ravaged by torture, starvation, chronic abuse and illness, wracked with sickness and despair... the images told the real tale. I simply could not bear to look very long and, even now, can't watch movies that either document or represent those atrocities, as they awaken such a hopeless anxiety and depression that it takes weeks to shake the effects. I can't believe there are even a handful who would ever dare deny that it happened... It did.

And so many of these poor people, it turned out, were Germans themselves—imprisoned and tortured to death by their own countrymen for religious, ethnic, cultural or other personal reasons, and subjected to every vile abomination imaginable (or un). Hideous medical experiments on living breathing people, their skin used for lampshades, families ripped apart... all I knew was that these images and the evidence they revealed just added to every other confusion my young mind was attempting to absorb, and I simply could not.

As I noted before, as my generation recedes into history and first-hand accounts become fewer, I worry we will become inured to the lessons this history teaches. In Germany, those who resisted Nazism and hadn't escaped well before the war wound up living in terror, hiding to survive or, more often than not, dying in the attempt. Even for those who survived such treatment; my heart breaks with you. For those who have ever worn the swastika as an emblem of their affiliation to the ideologies of its maker, my heart remains ever-hardened.

Chapter 30

One balmy, sleepy Sunday afternoon in late summer, 1946, my family and I set off into Buxton to go to church. The local buses didn't run as often on Sundays as during the week, so we walked, leaving home with enough time in hand to arrive in the churchyard thirty minutes before the service was to begin at three o'clock. Dad was presiding minister, so he had to be there early to open the doors and get things ready, but we lingered outside as long as we could to enjoy the fresh air and sunshine.

As we rounded the corner with full expectation of being the first ones there, we saw a tall figure studying the board that provided the schedule of weekly services on the church's front wall. Moving closer, we could see it was a man, dressed in the all-too-familiar clothing of a German Prisoner of War. Made of coarse, rough material in an ugly purplish-brown colour, the upper part of the POW uniform consisted of a waist length "Eisenhower" type jacket emblazoned with a khaki-coloured, diamond shaped patch sewn on the back. The man was tall, six or six-one, clean-shaven and well-groomed with light brown hair that fell in a slight wave across his forehead. His slender figure made him look much more a boy than a man, a characteristic reinforced by an almost sheepish lowering of his head and the shy half-smile on his face. In his hand he clutched a book; a tiny German/English dictionary. He appeared harmless, but I felt a shiver run through me, nonetheless.

Dad stepped forward, extended his hand, and in the halting German he'd picked up during the First World War, welcomed the conspicuously dressed stranger. I couldn't help wonder what people would think of him standing there chatting with a German POW, and I looked around to see who might be watching. No one else had arrived. I wondered, were we supposed to welcome him, too? I hung back to await Mum and Sam's reactions and, just as Dad had they did—I quickly found my hand held out to clasp his firmly. He said hello, his smile widening and his face lighting up warmly. I never expected the enemy to look like this.

His name was Bob, and he appeared both quite surprised and pleased to be greeted in his native tongue. At first, he was reluctant to speak English; embarrassed by his lack of fluency. After reassuring him that if we continued to try to speak German it would be a lot worse, he smiled again and began to tell us how he came to be in town. He explained that he was encamped along with a large number of German POWs about twelve miles north. He seemed too young to me to be a POW, not even out of his teens. In German, Dad asked if he could help and, in English, Bob explained that our church was the same kind to which his family had belonged in Germany. He had grown up in it. Daddy, a minister, welcomed him and invited him in for the service.

Bob was eighteen-and-a-half and had been away from his home near Stuttgart for well over three years. He had just turned fifteen when he last saw his father, who at that time was well into his seventies and in poor health. His mother, he explained, was much younger and it was his guess that she'd had perhaps a much better chance of surviving the war. He had two older siblings, a sister and brother. The family had never ascribed to Nazi beliefs, his brother, refusing outright to either enlist in any Nazi-sponsored groups, much less the army.

Coming home from school one day, he turned the corner to see Nazi SS soldiers in front of his house pushing his brother into a van, his father standing by. He ran to the back door of their home, where his mother met him and breathlessly told him to run—into the forest to hide. She knew they would all be taken and that if he stayed, they would immediately take him too, fearing that, at the very least, he would be forced into the Hitler Youth—a group they hated and feared along with everything else they stood for.

Bob said that as it got later in the war the Nazis became ever-more desperate in their need for soldiers and were "recruiting" younger and younger boys to throw at the advancing Allied forces. She knew too that unless he declared his loyalty to The Third Reich, he would be detained, imprisoned, and very likely tortured or killed. He knew that when the SS came for people, it was the end. They confiscated everything and searched the homes for any evidence of subversive behaviour to prove guilt in at undermining Nazi beliefs, and they always found some justification for taking people to camps without either any further review of specifics, or any hope of vindication.

Before any further information could be obtained and the SS began searching for him as a missing puzzle piece, Bob did what he was told; heading for the outskirts of town and then on into the surrounding woods just as fast and as far as he could. Once there, he dug a shallow hole just big enough to lie down in and where he hid for some time. While he did not know what would happen to his family, he knew enough to guess what fate would hold for them.

One night, asleep in this hideaway, Bob became aware of growing activity around him and that it had to be soldiers approaching. He heard engines he knew were tanks, and that they sounded like they were stopping. Too scared to move, he stayed still, and, before becoming aware of anything else, something suddenly overran him, passing right over his hiding place. He lost consciousness.

When he came to, it was in the back of an American field ambulance. He told us he had awakened staring straight up into the face of an American GI who had one hand firmly planted in the middle of his chest, while in his other he brandished a gleaming dagger, held aloft to make it very clear that if Bob moved, he would use it. In the darkness, frightened out of his mind, he said that his most vivid memory was that of the flashing blade, the whites of the soldier's eyes, and a set of gleaming, clenched teeth.

Upon reaching a place where they could interrogate him, the Americans came fairly quickly to the realization that the scared and starving youngster they'd captured was not a German combatant, but, with no other options in their push to secure the area had to turn him over to their military authorities for processing as a Prisoner of War.

From Germany, Bob was transferred, along with other German POWs, to an American prison camp somewhere in the Southern United States. He was the youngest of a group that were "employed" for a pittance of wages held in credit for their efforts picking cotton. Bob remained there for well over a year. Despite somewhat better treatment than they would almost undoubtedly have received under the French occupation of Stuttgart, or in any of the Soviet camps in the area, Bob relayed that they were still, nevertheless, whipped and beaten if they stopped working for even a moment to wipe the sweat from their eyes.

During this time he managed to establish written contact with some friends of his family in Stuttgart, from whom he learned at least some heartening news: his father, mother, and sister were all still alive, although interred in a German concentration camp. His worst fear was realized when he learned that his older brother, remaining steadfast in his refusal to join Hitler's cause in any way, had been shot in front of them in the camp yard one morning.

After VE day, Bob and his fellow prisoners were eventually informed that they would be going home. Assembled and given new suits of civilian clothing and the little money they'd earned for essentials, they were transported and put aboard a ship bound for Europe. Undoubtedly, as hopeful and excited to be going home as they were apprehensive as to what they would find there, their immediate fate then took another turn that betrayed them seeing it again at all. Halfway across the Atlantic, our British government "bought" them from the Americans so that they could be put to work in the quarries of England as part of the national war reparations effort! (So much for being on the *right* side of history!)

Landing in the South of England, the POWs were assembled again and instructed to place all their belongings in a pile—shoes, new suits, wallets, photographs and personal effects, even their new American issue blankets. After doing so, my beloved countrymen set fire to the lot and issued them POW uniforms like Bob wore. It would be more than another year working in a quarry before Bob would be transferred "upcountry" to the POW camp located just over the moors from Buxton.

Hearing this, Mum and Dad felt nothing but overwhelming compassion. They realized how young he still truly was and how very alone, too. Undoubtedly, they saw in him a lost child that made them wonder just what would have happened to our Sam if he had been in a similar position. The only way they knew how to help Bob was to take him into our family circle to at least try to soften the harshness of his life in a strange country. Explaining to Sam and I how they felt, and their intentions in doing so, they also began teaching us one of the greatest lessons we would ever learn in displaying empathy, love and compassion for those less fortunate than ourselves.

From that point on, Bob, who was allowed on weekends to circulate somewhat freely in and around town (prisoners were given passes), was welcome in our home; Mum simply spread the rations thinner and we all extended a helping hand. Mum and Dad also encouraged him to continue to write to anyone in Germany that he could think of to try to get a message to his family that he too was still alive.

At that time, I could not imagine the emptiness and loss of self that Bob must have suffered throughout those dehumanizing events. Moments, hours and days had turned to years. Nothing but a boy thrust into a completely alien world and longing for his family. He must have felt very alone at the hands of these people he would never have even thought to harm. Blamed simply for the burden his nationality, abused without regard for his innocence. He had never been part of the war aside from being yet another victim of its crushing, haphazard violence. His captivity must have seemed as interminable to him as it was unintelligible, and his helplessness in determining his own fate even more bleak as he pondered his ailing father and a mother and sister all left with the terrible memory of witnessing his brother lose his life.

There were times when I would catch a glimpse of him in our home, alone and staring out into space with a sad, faraway look in his eyes. Despite it all, he always remained a gentle and caring young man who seemed only to be thinking of others. Ever-polite, even-tempered and good humoured, it was only in his wistful expression when unaware he was being observed that his lovely nature was at all betrayed. My heart broke in those moments I caught him looking into that impossible distance; one travelled in the desperate act of trying to vanish into a forest floor; one which must have felt to him as if he were digging his own grave.

The look in his eyes at those times made it hard to imagine anything other than his wish for everything to disappear. I'm only certain that had he been taken along with his family by the SS that day, his fate and his brother's would undoubtedly have been the same. I do not know how he coped. How he held all these thoughts inside and saw the world with anything but overwhelming bitterness. How he kept himself from madness.

~~~

After Bob became an adopted member of our family, it was like having another older brother around. We so enjoyed our times together on family outings, picnics and hikes, and he readily took part in our family fun and games. He also loved to stand by the piano and sing while I played. We'd do our best to perform popular songs from the radio in English, and German songs from a European Folk Song book we had, teaching me a bit of German in the process. Cubby had given me quite a bit of music too, among which were some Strauss waltzes, a few
~~~

of which Bob knew the words. One of his favourites was, "The Lorelei," and to this day, whenever I hear its lovely melody, I hear his voice in my mind.

Like many POWs, Bob made little craft items to sell, and he often made bracelets out of colourful plastic strips. He taught me too. They were pretty and I still have one he made. Happily, he eventually received a letter from one of the parties to whom he had written in Germany and, through them, was able to trace where his remaining family members were living. His mother, father and sister had all survived and had been released from the camp. His father was the most affected by the ordeal and his health had worsened, still, he was alive.

Once he made contact, the letters between them began to flow, among them one addressed to my parents that thanked them for caring for their remaining son, and for showing him such kindness. Bob did not have the language skills to accurately translate it into English, so Daddy took it to someone who translated it for us, and we sat around the fireside in the living room with our cups of tea as he read it. It touched our hearts deeply, and we wept, humbled by both their trials and longsuffering, and their gratitude to us in caring for Bob. There had been moments during our getting to know him that had changed us all, had altered our perspectives on friend and foe and illuminated the vast differences and disparities that so many times exist between appearance and reality. I know they certainly did mine, and they weren't always painless lessons.

I remember being in the queue waiting for the bus after school one day. Just as it pulled up to the curb, Bob came around the corner to get in at the end of the line. It was an unexpected surprise, as it was mid-week and he never really came to town other than at the weekend. As the bus boarded and we were all getting seated, he saw me and grabbed the seat beside me. As it turned out, he had got a special pass and was happy to be out and about. We greeted one another as always and began one of our usual conversations.

After a bit, I suddenly realized that the bus had gone very quiet; ours seemed to be the only conversation going on. I looked around and was greeted by stony faces. When I stopped to look, I had broken the spell and then the murmuring started. "Fancy, associating with a German... Do her parents know who she's talking to?" Among other things. I was beyond appalled. I was *mortified*. In fact, I was positively white hot with *anger*! I wanted to jump up and say, "Listen, he may be German, but he is certainly not the enemy! He's a human being in a circumstance you couldn't even imagine or understand! He didn't kill your sons, brothers, or fathers, and *whatever you're thinking*, you're *wrong*!"

Well, I wanted to, but I couldn't bring myself to it. I was choking on the alternating instincts to fight or flee when Bob started to get up out of his seat, saying, "I'm sorry, Kath, I wasn't thinking. I didn't mean to put you in this position... I'll get off at the next stop. We'll talk more when I get to your house."

"NO!" I said, and rather too forcefully, and then, again—*"SIT DOWN!"*

I lowered my voice to the volume of a seething stage whisper and continued to speak, making sure I was heard by all: "I am *NOT* going to be intimidated by people who don't have any idea what they're doing, much less talking about. I'm not ashamed *of* you or to be *seen with you*. You're my friend, my brother... Just sit still. They're the ones who should be ashamed."

At my insistence, and with realization I'd probably make an even bigger scene if he did try to get off the bus, Bob sat back down and we proceeded on our journey. An awkward silence prevailed. We reached our stop, exited the bus, and the two of us walked to our house as we continued our conversation, shaken, but pretending that the whole thing had been a bad dream.

This event gave me the sudden realization that I was, in fact, blind to his being a German or his POW uniform, and that none of the rest of my family gave it a thought either. He was simply "our friend Bob," a person, and a good one, whose only "crime" was being perceived as the wrong person at the time—the very thing that ultimately led to the atrocities of Hitler's entire regime of hate being perpetrated in the first place. Labels are so very easy to affix based on nothing but ignorance and prejudice rather than knowledge, understanding, and compassionate reasoning.

At my age, I certainly understood what, at least in some ways, motivated the behaviour of the people around us, of course, and I didn't fault them the justifiable anger they held for the brutalities and injustices that had affected us all. But that was the point; we'd *all* been injured. Assessing blame based on the language Bob spoke or clothes that he wore were the very things that had got us exactly where we were. It was so very plain to see! I simply couldn't and wouldn't deny *him* because of their ignorance. I did not speak up because of my own fears.

As a young English girl in our small town at that time, I was very aware that every public action carried the potential of affecting and reflecting on my parents. But, I also knew instinctively, that I had done the right thing by not allowing them to sway me in my course of action. Anyone who's experienced such a crisis knows the gnawing feeling of helplessness it produces. Part of me still wishes I had broken that silence and declared my horror at their obvious bloody-minded and pig-headed bigotry, but, as another one of my favourite quotations aptly puts it: "You have not converted a man because you have silenced him." And that goes for young girls too.

~~~

It was not too long after this incident on the bus when it became possible for Bob to leave England and truly return home. The night before the British shipped the POWs back home, we gathered around the piano in the living room and I played as we all sang Vera Lynn's, *Now Is The Hour That We Must Say Goodbye!*, tears streaming down our cheeks. Of course, Bob wanted desperately to go home to his family, but he cried bitterly too. It was hard to say goodbye, but we were happy to know he was returning to those who also loved him, and they would all have the chance to begin picking up the pieces of their fractured lives and putting the horrors of the tortuous years of separation behind them.

Bob's presence had brought out some of our best qualities: compassion, empathy, non-judgement, and helped both Sam and I to put a human face on what was, in many ways our own distorted perception of who Germans really were. They were neither all soldiers, nor devoted to the causes of mad and genocidal nationalists. Our parents' courage in their convictions showed us that it was right to treat others as we would like to be treated ourselves, and that it is important to give back for what you have received. Mum and Dad had always been treated with warmth, compassion and friendship wherever they had travelled and lived. These were big lessons
~~~

at that age. Also, in the face of obvious ignorance it is all right—even vital—to stand up for what you know is true.

We continued to hear from Bob from time to time after he returned home. Gradually his letters became less frequent, and the last time we heard from him was the announcement of his marriage to a lovely German girl, complete with a wedding photograph of the happy couple and their families. I have always hoped and somehow trusted that he has lived happily ever after. I simply don't want to know any differently. He certainly deserved any and every happiness that ever came his way.

POW bracelet

Bob as he ran away from SS troops at age 15

Bob in his POW uniform

Bob's family, Stuttgart, Germany. L to R: Mother, Sister, older Brother Deiter (shot in front of family in prison yard of concentration camp by Nazis) and Father

Bob's wedding in Stuttgart, Germany. Bob top left, his Bride seated in front of him.

Chapter 31

Emerging from the war, my thinking simply no longer represented anything like those one equates with those of a child. I was ever so grateful we had survived in one piece as a family—intact, together. The things important to a child prior to the onset of war, the immature self-centered and myopic tendencies childhood encourages, had been almost entirely suppressed by our circumstances. Toys, new clothes, possessions were really no longer as important as family, and the belonging and security they provided during the tough times. My dad was fond of saying throughout his life, "My riches lay not in the extent of my possessions, but in the fewness of my wants." How true that seemed when coming out of the darkness of war into the light and relief of freedom. It really didn't matter about shortages and things we didn't have, we were together and moving unfettered toward new beginnings.

With the absence of daily fear to which we had become accustomed, Sam and his friend Ronnie were even freer to venture farther afield and roam the moors and dales to find places to explore. Of course, now that I was a bit older and wiser, I made it clear that I wasn't going to be left out in tagging along. While I was "only a girl," I would thus have to prove myself worthy of accompanying such rugged explorers, and it really took them no time at all before they set some daring tasks for yours truly to perform.

Not far away from the house there was another of the seemingly endless supply of old Midland quarries that had outlived their usefulness, one that, through an irresistible combination of imminent proximity and its promise of real danger, seemed to invite adventurous children like us. Sam and Ronnie decided this was just to place to see what "our nipper" was made of. Loving a challenge and with absolutely *no* idea of what I was getting myself into, I blindly followed along, trudging off with them one sunny day in August, equipped, tellingly, with one of my mother's rotten old clotheslines.

Sam took the lead and hiked 'round the bluff to the top of the quarry face, taking the looping clothesline with him. Ronnie stayed with me at the bottom. Reaching the top, Sam tossed an end down, and Ronnie knotted it firmly around my waist.

"She's ready! I'll get her started!"

Looking up the fairly sheer quarry face, Sam looked an awfully long way off. I was… apprehensive. I *hate* heights! But, I knew the respect I would earn if I accomplished this task so far outweighed any danger or uncertainty I was feeling, and that my complete and utter panic would be well subsumed by the accolades I received when I made it. Taking a deep breath, I called up to Sam with instructions to keep the rope taut as I began my ascent. Sir Edmund Hillary would certainly have done well to have me on one of his expeditions. Slowly, painstakingly, and with a caution equalled only by my sheer terror (I assure you) I inched my way up the rocks, loose stones and gravel falling away beneath my feet as I tested each foothold's ability to take my weight. It seemed to take ages just to progress a foot or two, but I gritted my teeth and clambered upward, while at least half the cliff face showered down on poor Ronnie at the bottom.

"Don't worry, Kath," he called, "I'll catch you if you fall!"

Big comfort, that—Ronnie was a thin and reedy young lad, and I a very sturdy little girl. If I did fall, I'd either snap him in two or flatten him like a pancake for all eternity. Meanwhile, Sam shouted encouragements: "Come on, Kath, you can do it! That's it! Test each foothold... Be careful!" If I fell, Ronnie's state would be the least of our problems—the music Sam would face arriving home with a broken sister would be the last music he'd ever hear. I got the feeling from the last refrain he was wishing he'd never got us into this one.

After what seemed an eternity watching the ground getting farther and farther away, and the feeling I couldn't or shouldn't go another foot, I reached the quarry rim. Sam grasped hold of my wrists like he was pulling the last survivor of the Titanic out of the frozen Atlantic, as he praised my brave ascent. I think he was scared to not say anything on my way up that might instill panic and cause me to lose my nerve or grip, and now nearly ready to collapse from nervous exhaustion. I was certainly never so glad to see him as he pulled me, rigid and exhausted, onto gravity affirming, horizontal ground.

The boys hoorayed and hurrahed and it was clear I had proven my worth. I had "spunk!" That's what they told me. Guinea Pig or not, Sam was proud, and that's all that really mattered to me. Well, that and me not ending up a shadow of my former self and the instrument of Ronnie Dixon's sure demise.

Of course, once you've done something, there's always

something else. My next test to join the club would involve navigating the long, smooth tunnels and sluice-ways at the reservoir that supplied Buxton's public water supply. Sure enough, the three of us set off to accomplish just that, and all-told it was a fairly uneventful test. It was more of an experiment in the psychological suggestion of terror on the uninitiated.

The thrill came about halfway through, when I turned to Sam and asked what would happen if they opened the sluice gates, as, if he remembered, I couldn't swim. He intimated that not having that particular skill would make little difference; we'd simply be swept away in a huge and overpowering tide of water that would make it less a matter of swimming than of holding one's breath while praying for dear life. That information relayed, I simply redoubled my effort to reach the end of the tunnel fastest, long before either they or any deluge could catch me.

Afterward, I decided that I had taken enough risks, and that if they weren't satisfied with my performances thus far they could keep their silly old club. I'd start my own. I was not interested in impressing anyone, much less those two, anymore. Whenever these things were mentioned years later in conversation with our parents, they were somewhat shocked and dismayed we had done such foolish things. Mum was especially beside herself.

In tamer pursuits, that summer, I played soccer and cricket with the boys. I enjoyed both games immensely, although by summer's end I had fully decided that, all things considered, what I really enjoyed was being a girl, and, what I would really rather prefer to play was something more civilized and elegant, tennis—which I had become obsessed with at age eight and, along with my girlfriends, had begun to spend a good deal of my free time playing on the clay courts on the other side of Buxton, at Ashwood Dale.

Time was also coming when some decisions would have to be made about future schooling. The way the British system was set up at the time, I had only about another year before I would have to move on to another school.

There were two levels of secondary schools after grade (primary) school. One required no further action, it was automatic, and one passed on to the next level to continue there until you were fourteen years old. The other was higher level education, a college preparatory school, only attainable by winning a scholarship through examinations and one's proven ability to reach standards of entry.

Practically all my young life, I had observed the girls from Cavendish High School at a distance. Hoards of them would board the buses in Buxton when Mum and I had been out on our shopping trips into town. They scrambled on laughing and talking excitedly, their navy and white uniforms worn with pride and impeccably completed by identical brown leather satchels laden with books and homework. When they unbuckled them, I would peek in at the hardcover exercise books I longed to examine just to know what sort of things they were learning. While neither loud nor boisterous, Cavendish girls were so obviously full of fun and youthful exuberance, and, besides being not only well-dressed, were well-spoken and beautifully mannered. If anyone their senior on the bus did not have a seat, male or female, they would jump up and give up theirs. The offer refused, they would positively insist. They were a cut above, exuding a pride and a dignity I had never observed anywhere else, and it became my burning desire to be one of them!

Of course, I had to pass the examination to be worthy

to wear the navy blue and white of Cavendish. Only the scholastically worthy entered those gates. But I was bound and determined to wear that uniform, and not be relegated to the brown and gold of Silverlands, the girls' secondary school.

I was ten years old when I sat for the exam. I remember taking it with what seemed like my heart in my mouth and absolutely no idea at all as to how I had performed when it was over. Anxiously, I awaited my results. Days turned into weeks with no word. My class had thirty-three students, and each day we all checked in with one another:

"Have you heard?"

"No. You?"

"No."

Then the day finally arrived. When I walked into my classroom, two girls were already jumping up and down, ecstatically waving their letters of acceptance. Two out of thirty-three, I thought... My heart sank into my shoes. I had not received one. I had not passed. Throughout morning classes I struggled to hold back my emotions. On the verge of tears, the disappointment of anything I could remember in my life thus far had never been so hard to hide.

When it was time for lunch, I went home, on the way imagining what it would be like to tell Mum and Dad. How to tell them I failed? I was not going to my beloved Cavendish after all. I had let all of us down. My feet dragged as I approached the house. I walked slower and slower, trying to delay my inevitable speech of conciliation and failure as long as possible.

Dad always came home for lunch from the Electricity Works whenever possible. On that day I could tell he was already there, his company vehicle parked outside the house. Ever so sheepishly I entered the front door, my visage, I knew, radiating intense disappointment. I entered the dining room. Mum and Dad were there. Simply unable to hold back the torrent of abject hurt and frustration any longer, I burst into tears and wailed, "Oh, Mum! Dad! I *didn't pass*! I didn't *pass*! All the others were notified... I'm *SO* sorry... Please, please forgive me!"

Mum jumped up from her seat to console me, enveloping me in her tight embrace. Dad, right behind her, tears in his eyes, pulled me away from Mum and took my hand to lead me, tears streaming down my face, to the kitchen table where he pulled me onto his lap and cradled me with one arm. He reached his opposite hand inside his suit jacket pocket to produce an envelope.

He said, "Yes, my lovely, you *did* pass... the postman came right after you'd left for school this morning. You, young lady, *are going to Cavendish*, and we are *so* very, *very* proud of you, *very* proud!"

I could hardly believe my ears. I was, quite simply, in that moment the happiest girl on the entire planet. Oh, what joy, and how I savoured the victory! It was the very first moment of what would be five years that I can still honestly say remain among the most fulfilling of my entire life.

Metal blue and silver badge affixed to lapel of coat or hat

Cavendish named after The Duke of Devonshire

In the garden at "Bayswater"

Cavendish badge affixed to all books, notebooks, blazers, hats

Chapter 32

Life in a British girls' school is an undertaking I wish every young girl could experience. Cavendish was both a unique school and a stalwart example of the old Grammar School system in England now largely replaced by co-ed Comprehensive Schools. There are many, I have heard, that find the newer vision inferior to the old, and the debate continues. Whether there will ever be a real trend to bring back the older but, to my mind, superior educational method will probably be determined to varying degrees by developments and interests in privatized "prep schools" in England, and perhaps even the twenty-first century possibility of independence from the European Union. We shall see...

Cavendish was located on the Corbar Road at the edge of Buxton's Corbar Woods. The building was originally the Wye House Asylum, a mansion designed by the Duke of Devonshire's architect Henry Currey during the Georgian era. Quoting an old advertisement for that establishment, it was: "Erected in 1861 by His Grace the Duke of Devonshire... as an establishment for the care and treatment of the insane of the higher and middle classes." In this guise, it was run for three generations under doctors with the surname Dickson.

Further description reveals that: "'The Pleasure Grounds,' which are very spacious, have been laid out in the most tasteful manner, the house heated throughout by means of hot-water apparatus and well and thoroughly ventilated... It is also connected by Telegraph with all parts of the kingdom."

The Wye House Asylum became Cavendish High School for Girls in 1912, when the ninth Duke of Devonshire gave the building over to the school, and we Cavendish girls always tried to keep its history as an asylum as quiet as possible. Some people, boys in general and brothers like mine, specifically, were fond of calling it, among other things, "Cabbagedish" and would tease us by saying that we went to a "giggle house," not a school. Such sensitivity!

Truth be told, in the cellars of the school (the "nether regions" as we called them) there were actual padded cells, where they evidently used to keep those considered among the more violent inmates. They were, I can tell you, dismal and frightening indeed. My brother, true to form, often stated that he thought I should be put down there where I "truly belonged!"

Whatever its history, there it stood—a huge, stately old mansion set far back on another of Buxton's myriad *cul-de-sacs*, its dual set of stone stairs leading one up to the lower level of the property and onto what used to be sweeping lawns and adjoining gardens. These elements, upon the property's conversion into our high school, were made into tennis courts which, during the winter months, were also made over into netball (basketball) courts. In England at that time, basketball was primarily a girl's game. The park benches on the promenade in front of the school building became one of my favourite spots to sit, as they overlooked the two tennis courts and the views of lawns as green as only

English lawns can be. I used to sit on those benches to take in the serene atmosphere, the pure air, the wooded areas to the west and the north, and all the rest of the sights and sounds of the school grounds. The classrooms all had large windows from their wainscoting up to the ceiling that faced the front of the school and overlooked the promenade. The windows opened outward to let in the lovely, cool fresh air, lending an invigorating feeling to our surroundings.

Walking between the tennis courts, one climbed another level of steps that led up to the main building flanked by sloping, beautifully manicured lawns. The only male allowed on the premises was an older man we referred to as "Sergeant," or, of course, "Sarge" (it seems it was preordained I spend time with people nicknamed "Sarge"). He and his wife were the caretakers and custodians of the school and its grounds, and they lived on the very top floor of it in an apartment that occupied its own floor. Sarge and his wife also made all the "out-of-bounds" rules, and they kept chickens in a pen out in the woods beyond the other set of tennis courts on the property. All of these locations were definitely "out-of-bounds."

As I entered the hallowed grounds of Cavendish for the first time, dressed in the brand-new school uniform I had so coveted, I was filled with an immense feeling of awe and respect. I could hardly believe that *little me* was fortunate enough to actually have become a student. My heart was full, and I humbly hoped I would be able to live up to the high standards set by the institution and the students who passed through these portals with and before me.

As one well imagines, there are endless rules and regulations in British Girls' Schools, and one needed to learn them quickly. During summer before the start of school, we all received a booklet with these delineated. We were to read and learn this information thoroughly, as infractions would not be taken lightly.

Also during summer, the mothers of all the new girls were invited to a meeting with the headmistress and some of the staff, during which tea and light refreshments were served and they were acquainted with the school and grounds. During this meeting the headmistress also took the opportunity to talk earnestly and forthrightly with the mothers about their daughters' knowledge and comprehension of the "facts of life." It was essential that every girl entering Cavendish be aware of the changes to her body that were to be expected during this time in life. No student would be admitted unless this crucial talk had been accomplished. As a consequence of this, Mum returned home from her afternoon at school fully prepared for a little mother daughter chat. It seemed Cavendish was intent on controlling each detail of my admission process.

Menstruation had, in fact, been explained to me some time prior, and I had decided I wasn't going to have anything to do with it. It sounded simply awful, and I intended to put it off as long as possible. Of course, no sooner had I reiterated the point to Mum after her little trip to school than, within a few weeks, the whole dreaded event happened anyway.

Then came the next part of the talk; equally as distasteful to my mind at the time. I had heard it rumoured during my last year at council school that eventually in the course of human events certain things occurred between the male and female of the species that lead to its continuation. The few details I had heard failed to provide me with much impetus to know more. The whole thing sounded like a lot of bunk, and I went merrily on my way. My little talk with mother ended with the realisation that it was all true, and a decision not to have anything to do with that either. I did this, fairly confident that, this time, neither my unwitting body nor the seeming prescience of the Cavendish rulebook possessed any powers to prevail.

One of the first things we learned was that one never approached or entered school through the front doors. Student entrances were designated by the particular form (grade) to which one belonged, all were located at the back of the school and led directly into the cloakroom. Of the two entrances in the front of the school, one was for staff and the other solely for the headmistress and her invited guests. When we entered the cloakroom we were to take off our outer coats and outside shoes to don our indoor shoes. Shoes for outdoors were lace-ups, shoes for indoors were soft-soled with strap-and-button fasteners, allowing staff to tell quickly if we were wearing the correct ones. One of the first things I noticed when I entered the school proper was the exquisite, highly polished wood parquet floors—a primary reason for indoor shoes. Cavendish floors were sacred and not to be scuffed. We were not allowed to run on them, or to behave in a rowdy manner in general. We were to walk and talk calmly and sedately, and to behave like young ladies.

Cavendish was a gracious environment and its aims crystal clear: building an education based on wide academic achievement, courtesy, good manners and service to others. "Each for All"—our school motto—was emblazoned on all badges, hats, stationary, the books we carried, as well as inevitably and indelibly, our brains!

But, never mind brains, back for a moment to shoes: "plimsolls" (sneakers or gym shoes to Americans) were to be worn only in the gymnasium or to play tennis. These were kept in our lockers in the locker room in the gym with the field hockey boots and pads. Physical fitness and education were an absolute must at Cavendish, and we had a gym period every day. It was considered equally as important as any academic endeavour.

Getting completely outfitted for Cavendish was actually a great deal of fun, and I entered into the spirit of it with glee. Clothes were still rationed, so the very thought of a whole new wardrobe excited me immensely! Mother was instructed where the school outfitter was located downtown, and when there I was instructed what to wear and how.

Within the various pieces of the school uniform there were certain mix and match choices. For instance: I could choose from straight, box-pleated or a full pleated skirts. I could also choose the style of collar on my white shirts, a couple most compatible with a tie. One also had the option of sweaters—a cardigan, pullover, or, even (and why not?), one of each. A nametag also had to be sewn on every single item of clothing we wore, and we ordered those too.

When the huge roll of white cloth labels embroidered in red with my full name was delivered to our home, the real fun began—you may well guess how I spent the last weeks of the summer holidays before school... sewing, sewing, sewing and then sewing some more. I learned later that the reason for this was because after changing into gym dresses (along the lines of short tennis dresses with elastic waistbands) and showering afterward, nametags guaranteed everyone got the right undies; a school uniform means identical clothing down to one's skin.

I know that to many the idea of wearing a uniform to school sounds like the ultimate in disciplinarian stuffiness and an institutionalized attempt to squash individuality and stifle personality. While I understand the argument, I can tell you that, in fact, uniforms can also be quite liberating. For one, it is impossible to be better-dressed than your classmates, which means no one can ever play the, "I've got the latest fashion and it's expensive, you don't" game. While a fashionable, stylish, and singular appearance all one's own is a fantastic thing, dressed alike, one learns that really being distinctive is an achievement that ultimately comes from within, not through consumer-driven modes of ever-changing fashion accessories or the socio-economic abilities to acquire them. I am still, unapologetically, a true believer in school uniforms.

Winter uniforms consisted of navy blue tunics (I believe called jumpers at the time in America) with pleated skirts or navy knee-length skirts, and long-sleeve collared white blouses with plain navy-blue ties (for undergraduates), or navy blue ties with white diagonal stripes for graduate students studying for entrance into university. The outfit was finished with knee socks with the school colours around the tops, and black, lace-up outdoor shoes. The school blazer was a year-round garment—a navy blue blazer edged in white braid with the school crest (badge) stitched onto the besom pocket. Outerwear consisted of a navy-blue trench coat with a long alternately striped navy blue and white wool scarf, with headware being either a navy blue beret, or a velour brimmed hat with navy blue ribbon. Both carried the school badge on the front. Hats were to be worn outdoors at all times unless playing games, and always in the street while in uniform.

Summer uniforms consisted of sky-blue dresses with tiny white dots, white collared with short sleeves cuffed in white, blouses and white ankle socks and black lace-up shoes. Hats were brimmed, cream-coloured straw Panama-style with a navy blue band and, of course, the Cavendish badge affixed to the front. The traditional white tennis dress was worn while on the courts. No one in England at that time ever played tennis in anything but tennis whites—it was tradition. Immutable. At Wimbeldon, I believe, the tradition still holds fast, but, in a nutshell, everyone looked the same without exception, and we were a snappy looking bunch!

Of course there was one other crucial accessory—the beautiful brown leather book satchel I had envied whenever I'd seen them—complete with pockets and shoulder strap. No one was allowed to carry any other satchel, bag or case. With it accounted for, one then moved onto the more truly personal elements of hair, for instance—worn short and above the collar, or, if shoulder-length, tied back in two even bunches. If your hair was longer still (which, truth be told, was frowned upon) it was to be plaited into two identical pigtails and tied at the ends with navy-blue ribbons.

Failure to comply with these school uniform requirements would see one sent home with a note to your parents of the infraction—which was to be dealt with immediately and before you could return to class. I knew several girls sent home for *light blue* hair-ribbons they thought a better match for summer uniform dresses, or for wearing any ankle socks other than white.

If all of this wasn't enough attention to personal detail, it will either surprise you (or not) to learn that even our underwear needed to fulfil Cavendish regulatory standards too. To be clear, and again as an advocate of the uniform, even I—we *all*— rebelled at the deep navy blue, almost black "knickers" we were forced to wear—and *flannel*! Horrible! Ghastly, gigantic, ill fitting, and a hideous bane to any decent, fashion-conscious young woman of any class, upbringing, background, or way of life, and which we were all obligated to wear! We hated them with a purple passion, and, at every given opportunity, would try to wear our own panties instead.

Understanding that these things were of diabolical nature herself, our gym teacher always knew we could be caught out, and how to well-confirm her suspicions we were cheating.

Beforeclasswouldstartshewouldaskusalltodohandstands against the wall bars, causing our short gym dresses to, of course, ride up and reveal a whole line of different-coloured panties; white, blue, pink, green—anything but the navy blues we were supposed to wear. There were days when there was not a pair of regulation knickers in sight! Of course, after writing five hundred lines of, "I must wear regulation school uniform at all times," one learned one's lesson—at least for a bit. But, it wouldn't be long before we tried again, followed by a cycle of reverting to the dreaded ugly knickers, cheating, being sent home to comply, writing lines, fervour dying down, back and then, caught again...

Of course, after multiple infractions, the guilty were eventually marched down to the headmistresses study to have a chat. Knickers were the cause of my first trip to that inner sanctum, along with a number of my cohorts, all lined up in front of her imposing desk in rows of fours and fives. All I could think of was that this would go on our school records and not bode well for the future. Insubordination is an ugly word, and universities always looked at behaviour and one's ability to follow the rules. Oh well, at least I wasn't alone!

We waited for a few minutes and Miss Mansell, our headmistress, entered. She was clearly not amused.

"Good afternoon girls."

In chorus: "Good afternoon, Miss Mansell."

"First row step forward and lift your skirts, please," she commanded, curtly.

We complied, and there they were in full view—skivvies in every colour of the rainbow. The drill continued for the next row and the next... We all got yet another five hundred lines of writing *and* detention for a week—one hour a day after school in a special room where we could either write our lines or study—as well as a rather terse note from Miss Mansell sent home with us to our mothers. Order restored. For a little while.

~~~

Another thing we learned entering Cavendish was the school song. It was, naturally, tied to the school motto and appropriately entitled, "Each for All." Ingrained in minds and hearts it remains a worthy motto by which to live, stressing the importance of putting others before oneself, and being ever-conscious of others needs before one's own. It has stayed with me over the years and I still find myself humming it. I shall always love it:

Oh, list, listen, the birds are singing,
Ah, how sweet is the blackbird's call.
Softly the notes of the thrush are ringing,
Proclaiming God's secret
Each for All

Yes, 'tis our motto
Nature has taught us
Oh, let it ring
Through humanities halls
Come let the world know
This message has caught us
Shout! Sing aloud, SHOUT –
EACH FOR ALL
~~~

The occasion of writing has put me in touch with a former school chum, a Cavendish "Old Girl," as we called ourselves upon leaving. Barbara still resides in Buxton. Married with several children and numerous grandchildren, she is now retired, having once been a headmistress and schoolteacher herself.

I was touched that, in spite of ongoing illness and her many familial responsibilities, she has found the time to give of herself with great compassion, instrumental in bringing children to England from Chernobyl, Russia, after they were severely affected by the catastrophic radiation leak there in the spring of 1986. Barbara raised funds and assisted in finding them new homes, medical and psychological help. A true humanitarian, she, along with so many others, has lived the Cavendish motto, a motto I, too, have tried to live by. I had the privilege of being the primary caregiver to both of my late parents. If, in some small way I repaid their dedication, love, and sacrifice for us during those dark years of the war through the application of our simple but unselfish motto, I will know I have done something right and in which I profoundly believe.

~~~

Clothes, rules, mottos and songs, as important as they may have been in centering us in our responsibilities to school and the world around us, what Cavendish really offered was a thorough and well-rounded intellectual education; a firm foundation for lives of purpose. For the first four years, we studied twenty-six different major subjects each school year. During the last, before taking final exams, we dropped down to six majors. Besides English, two foreign languages were compulsory for two consecutive years. Mine were Latin and French, the latter which I took for four years. Latin was
~~~

compulsory because the English language has roots in it, and the British school system at that time declared that no one could truly master the full depth and breadth of English without it. I agree with that perspective too and find it of great use to this day. With it, English usage and vocabulary becomes so much more interesting, easier to understand and rich in nuance; a vital key to understanding etymologies and core definitions. I believe every school should still offer Latin as a choice. When my son reached High School I encouraged him to study it—to the point of insistence—and he has never regretted it.

Another subject required was diction. This was a separate English class, and if you've ever had an opportunity to take it, you know how immediately you are transported to a mock rehearsal for the stage production of *My Fair Lady*. In diction class, one learns to speak the "King's English," in order to shed colloquial tinges and local accents. In my case, this was the Derbyshire accent. The process relies on one's ability to speak slowly, measuring one's words and using them correctly and distinctly. While, along with Latin, this is just the kind of institutionalized training some would see as the absolute pinnacle of unnecessary or "dead" linguistic effort without practicality in contemporary life, it too offers benefits to those taught English as a spoken language.

At the time, we all felt a little silly repeating such sentences as, "The lark flew past the barn at half past eight" (which, phonetically, came out sounding something like: "The lahk floo pahrst the bahn at harf parst ate), in order to find its individual pronunciations and cadences, rankled by the tediousness of attaining the instructors own tones, but with results well worth the effort when attained. By the time we were ready to take next steps in our lives, our teachers had made sure we would be understood wherever we were bound, confident and never judged by any regional inflections that might thwart our efforts.

These principles also followed within studies of cultural matters—music and the arts. We all studied music appreciation, listening for hours to works of different composers of European classical music to learn their structures, forms, and historical styles, and learning to develop recognition, appreciation and a knowledge of instrumental voices through exposure to symphonies, operas, and all manner and matters associated with them. A well-rounded education and literacy in these enabled us to speak intelligently on their forms and structures, as well as on their content. Music also included voice lessons, and it was from this particular endeavour that the Cavendish school choir was formed.

The same approach was applied to visual art. We took easels to the museum in Buxton and the woods and countryside around us to sketch and paint both from copies and life respectively. We learned basic art history, from the European and Old Masters to the masterworks of English landscape and portraiture, and, by the time we were through, had attained a working knowledge of a range of historical artworks, and basic abilities in holding our own in conversations about them.

Another offshoot in the curriculum that had bearing was "Deportment." This included lessons in both manners and demeanour, down to detailed examination of and training in such basic social skills as to how to "present oneself" when walking into a room, introducing oneself or being introduced. And, yes, since you're wondering, we learned how to walk across a room with books balanced on our heads. In other words, we learned what society might expect of dignified and gracious young ladies. I am tempted to offer some thoughts on what I believe is the modicum of value these long lost "arts" might alleviate in contemporary society, but will simply leave it there. Again, in my opinion, we could do worse than reviving its study.

All in all, our teachers were outstanding, and we were very much awed. We held them in great esteem and with great respect, and always addressed them as "Miss or Mrs. so-and-so." Most were middle-aged women or older, and every feature of our educational lives made us very aware that we were nowhere near their same societal level. In the classroom they sat on a raised *dais*, which you did not step onto unless invited. Each wore their uniform—a gown, black and full rather like a judge's robe—over their street clothes, and they wore these when not in the staff room. One often saw them veritably sailing down the hallways, gowns billowing.

The younger teachers often wore their university blazers under their gowns, striped vertically with the colours indicating their "houses" these blazers all had dark backgrounds usually replete with the crests of the university in question. To answer the next obvious question, no, they did not wear mortarboards to class, but certainly did on more formal occasions such as "Speech Day."

As one might well guess, our instructors were not very approachable unless you had a question on the class, a specific instruction, or on an assignment. Years later, when I had occasion to visit my son's school in the United States, I was amazed at how chatty and friendly teachers were with students, and how there seemed an open path to discussing or even disputing some element of curriculum. To approach a teacher to state that you were unhappy with a grade in my day and experience was completely unheard of. It would never have entered our minds. It staggered me that, being given whatever grade the instructor felt was deserved under the circumstances, any further discussion was unwarranted, much less encouraged.

The Staff Room was where teachers gathered and officed. One would walk past and sometimes hear them laughing, which in some cases was the only time you thought of them as humans possessing a full range of emotions. The headmistress's office was separate from these and, as touched on before, the one place to which you did not want to be summoned or laughter ever emanated. If you were, you knew you were without speculation in terrible if not mortal trouble. On the few occasions I was, or came face-to-face with Miss Mansell in the halls, I was rendered speechless—capable only of stuttering and mumbling unintelligibly at a nearly inaudible volume. I would prattle away until she walked on, collapsing after against the nearest wall to collect my wits and take a few deep breaths. In all seriousness though, while Miss Mansell was much feared, she too was equally loved and respected. She was a firm-yet-fair and just lady; democratic and willing to give students the chance to be heard, even vote, on certain issues.

In my last year at Cavendish, Miss Mansell taught me in the one class she always taught, English—she tried to teach each and every student at least once during their sojourn, and knew each by name. We truly were her girls, and I knew that she really believed in our talents and ambitions, just as I'm sure that she knew she was the one responsible for Cavendish and its reputation for excellence.

Although I was not there during the war years, I'd heard tell how she would ride up to school on a motorbike, speeding past the students as they walked to morning classes! Undoubtedly, her car was up on blocks just like the rest, and a motorbike was more economical. How completely out of character for one's headmistress to come zipping by on such a conveyance, especially one imagines so stern, prim and proper. I loved the image it conjured in my mind... it has always allowed me to see her in an entirely human way and inspired my love for her for having provided it.

~~~

The tone of the average Cavendish school day was set with the entire student body assembling in the gymnasium for morning prayer. Used for all general assemblies, the gym was a freestanding building occupying a separate wing built at an adjacent right angle to the long school building, connected to it by stairways and long corridors. After meeting in individual home rooms and calling roll for the day, we'd march by class down the hallways, two by two, "crocodile style," to get there; lowest class first. No talking or horsing around along the way, each class walked quietly with their Mistress alongside, eagle eye upon us. The bell would then summon us to begin.

England, as most know, is a largely Protestant country, and the only ones exempt from Cavendish morning prayers were Catholic and Jewish students, of which we had three or four of the former, and one of the latter. This somewhat ceremonial gathering started the day off in an atmosphere of respectful reverence. Again I actually think that it's a great pity that so many children are deprived today of aspects of spiritual awareness like these, regardless of what they believe or church they attend. It is also my humble opinion that this missing element is part reason for the violence and civil disrespect that seems so prevalent in our culture.
~~~

Without shared guiding principles that foster fellow feeling and regard for, if not necessarily a higher authority, then, at least, the discipline to occupy a peaceable communal space with others, there is little sense instilled of one's role in the cultivation of a societal whole. While I'm certainly not advocating some totalitarian or monolithic mentality (look where that got us!) gathering and fellowship has the benefit of reminding us of the presence of others, and the levelling feeling that we are always part of a larger picture. Amen (or Ah-men, as our pronunciation would have it in "English!").

Assembled in the gym, a Prefect (upperclassman awaiting entrance to University) would read a passage from the *King James Bible*, followed by the entire school body repeating "The Lord's Prayer," and our singing of a traditional Church of England Hymn accompanied on piano by a Prefect matriculating in the study of music. Miss Mansell would then read out pertinent school announcements, including special commendations and awards, as well as her general comments. We were then dismissed to attend our respective classes for the day, leaving the gym through reversal of the process in which we had entered.

Arriving in our classrooms for our first class, the class's designated door monitor would stand in the corridor holding the door handle and, when the class Mistress was in sight, alert us in a softly audible voice to rise to stand at attention by our desks. When the Mistress entered, she would mount the *dais* and say, "Good morning, girls." We would all reply in kind, using "Miss" and then surname. Looking us over for a moment, she would finally say, "You may be seated." Then and only then were we permitted to sit down.

When the bell rang to herald the end of the period, we

would go right on working until the Mistress said, "Good morning, girls (or afternoon, as determined by the hour), you are dismissed." We would rise again to stand alongside our desks, murmuring the appropriate response, and awaiting her exit from the room, door held open once again by the monitor. When she had left, we were free to collect our books and papers to proceed in orderly fashion to our next class.

Ritualistically repeated throughout the school day, our routine demanded that whenever a grownup—Mistress, parent, or even custodial or office staff— entered a room we occupied, we were to rise and stop talking. This habit became so ingrained it followed me for much of my early adult life. I still do very much like the polite English way of, if not standing of course or stopping one's conversation, the acknowledgement of another's entry into the room: it establishes a baseline of respect and sets the tone for whatever following exchanges are to come. While respect is ever earned and not simply given without reason, respectfulness should be expected nearly without fault. Though subtle, there is a difference.

During the course of morning classes we had mid-morning milk break. As observed earlier, it was served warm in little capped glass bottles as there was no refrigeration. After morning classes we returned to the gym for our midday hot lunch—an activity I dreaded. From our parents' perspectives, school lunches were a real godsend—a hot meal for a small weekly fee that didn't come out of home rations. From ours, it was a bit less ideal. There were no choices and we took what was there or we went hungry. Rationing, still so much a way of life, meant that while some food shortages eased, some actually worsened.

Meat rations, for instance, were cut in half, leaving only ones more readily available like horse and whale. Both were dark in colour and, at least where my taste buds were concerned, generally unpalatable. Mum would not even buy horsemeat for us at home. I tried my level best to avoid eating either meat, it was largely because of them that school lunches were among the worst experiences *ever*, but, there was one *other* thing besides the meat that really got me: having to face up to... peas.

England has only in just the past few decades begun to shed the reputation as a nation incapable of producing brilliant cuisine, and this largely through the influence of trade and more diverse international culinary traditions and ingredients. Beyond this general assessment, they do have a long history of having a way with the preparation of peas that does not, in my estimation, deserve encouragement any more than now than at the time. In England, peas are often served mashed, or "mushed," as they say—resulting in a lumpen, green glob on one's plate that just dares you to enjoy them. I wish you *bon chance et bon appetite*. I abhorred them then and have ever since.

Other options, shepherd's pie: gravy, crust and a few things all mixed up, not too hideous and among the better options. Bubble and squeak: *all* vegetables scrambled into something that looks much like quiche and is yet devoid of either eggs or cheese, and (did I mention) all vegetable. Toad in the hole: a traditional dish made with sausage in a Yorkshire pudding crust with onion gravy—this tastes better than the name suggests, ideally or in theory, but, not so much in the school preparation. Indeed, the Cavendish versions of each and all (perhaps mercifully so), had very little meat and far too many vegetables to suit my taste. As a result, I ate little of any Cavendish-prepared lunches, managing to get by until going home for family dinner.

Speaking of food... there was another important school rule that actually followed us well beyond school grounds, and it was: We were *never, EVER,* to eat food in public or in the street. This fell under a general rule about manners. Young ladies *did not eat in the street like street* urchins or navvies. It was especially true if one happened to be wearing a Cavendish uniform. Eating was to be enjoyed in the dining room, in a restaurant or a train dining car as appropriate. To eat outside, in uniform, was another infraction.

My best friend Rose and I came out of school one warm and sunny afternoon and headed for the bus stop to go home. Having a good twenty minutes before our bus arrived, we decided we were simply ravenous and must eat something immediately. Just down the hill, a few buildings away from the stop, there was a greengrocer, the sidewalk outside featuring boxes of fruits and vegetables. We walked toward it and spied among these a big box of rosy, scrumptious-looking apples. Eying them longingly, we entered the shop to ask the price—"Penny ha'penny" (one and a half pennies). Digging in our pockets, we handed over and made off with our edible treasures.

We just couldn't wait. We sank our teeth into the apples—so crisp and fleshy, sweet and good. We savoured the apples' juice with glee and drew in their exquisite smell with each greedy bite, standing there silently enraptured, a million miles away in intoxicated revelry. I looked down for a moment, fixing my eyes on our shoes, and, suddenly, became aware of two other pairs of shoes in my field of vision; grownup shoes. Rose and I raised our eyes slowly. Hovering over us, practically standing on top of us, were the two most dreaded teachers on the entire Cavendish staff. One, Miss Saunders, was vice-headmistress; the other her close friend and our Latin teacher, Miss Abbott.

They both had reputations as the strictest disciplinarians on campus. Oh, my...

Miss Saunders, tall, white-haired, forbidding looked down her aristocratic and aquiline nose at us both and said in a chilly tone: "Are you... *eating*, girls?"

"Yes, Miss Saunders," we replied sheepishly, holding up tooth-marked apples for her scrutiny.

"Is that *all* you have? Miss Abbott asked.

"Yes, Miss Abbott," we replied again.

"Report to my office in the morning before prayers," she ordered curtly.

"Yes, Miss," we intoned again in dazed and resigned chorus. As they turned to leave, something akin to the sensation of swallowing an apple whole crept over me. We each went home with our collective shame equal only to the dread of the next morning.

After stewing all night, we reported obediently before prayers for sentencing: Five-hundred miserable lines of, "we must not eat in the street whilst in school uniform or any other time," *and* an hour a night detention for a whole week. A bit stiff, I thought, and it really messed up our schedules. But, still, we both knew what we were doing when we did it, and realized that we'd pay a price if caught—as the old British'ism puts it: "It's a fair cop." Maybe, if Cavendish would have had better food, Rose and I better memories, or, at the very least a modicum of self-control, things would then have been different. Alas, we did not, and sure enough...

Later, that same summer, on a searing hot eighty-degree day in the middle of a heatwave, Rose and I were once again simply dying, and, this time, as you'd imagine, for something *really cold*. During the war, ice cream—called "ices" or ice lollies," like American popsicles—had been non-existent.

We were only then beginning to see them in stores. Off we went…

Of course, we were smarter, wiser now thanks to our previous tribulations, so, before we even exited the shop, we glanced up the hill. The coast was clear. Stepping out into the bright sunshine we began tearing the wrappers off our refreshingly delicious ice-lollies. Still nervous, I took a lick as I glanced up the road again. There they were! Miss Saunders and Miss Abbott! Didn't they have *anything* else to do but walk up and down this road?

"What'll we do?" hissed Rose in a rapidly escalating panic.

"Pocket!" I barked back under my breath.

We both shoved our lollies into our uniform pockets and acted as innocent as we possibly could just as the "terrible two" were about to pass by. A moment later, they did, nodding as they glared at us down their noses on the way by. We nodded back. "Good afternoon, Miss Saunders, Miss Abbott," we greeted them politely through gritted teeth and forced smiles. Not exactly caught again, we weren't going to have to write lines, but—it was a pyrrhic victory if ever there were one. What a mess! It was incredible. We had a great deal of explaining to do to our mothers.

After that incident, Rose and I decided it just wasn't worth trying to get away with these things anymore. We were on the straight and narrow and would stray no more. Some lessons don't come easily. Tempted by an apple and ending up in a real mess… that sounds familiar. Again, somebody should write a book. I'd probably believe it.

~~~

Another phase of Cavendish education consisted of courses in so-called, "domestic science"— which translated
~~~

into the more common parlance of the time meant needlework and cookery. Needlework was not then, nor has it become since, my forte, but, I did come through with a few skills that have served me well: Stitching, seaming, measuring, learning how to follow as well as make one's own patterns, cutting material, sewing both by hand and using a machine, embroidery, knitting, darning, patching, piping, crocheting, needlepoint... you name it. If it involved some kind of needle and thread we probably learned it. I never cared much for it, and have tried to avoid its practice, although I once did make a pretty decent looking camisole and pair of knickers, if I do say so myself.

Cooking was a different thing altogether. I enjoyed that immensely! There were even more things to learn about it than needlework! We cooked our way through countless dishes, planned menus and shopping lists, ordered food, and studied cooking it for both everyday purposes as well as learning it for entertaining. During the semester as part of our training, we even cooked dinner for our own families once a week, transporting the dishes from school to our homes on the bus in covered baskets ready to dish up for the evening meal. Everyone seemed to enjoy that, especially Mum, who got out of kitchen duties those nights. We made stews and roasts, baked cakes, scones, and biscuits (cookies to Americans) and countless other dishes for which the school provided ingredients so they didn't eat too much into our own. It was a little bit extra and very appreciated. The course, coupled with my mother's excellent instruction on cooking and other domestic subjects, helped me ready for the world of having my own family in the years to come.

~~~
~~~

My years at Cavendish passed so quickly; all too quickly. So many happy hours… But, truth be told, there was one other time I managed to become embroiled in a spot of trouble—and this one was a bit more of a doozy. And, of course, it involved my best friend, Rose.

We were taking a class in Statistics, a subject that honestly intrigued me, learning to plot graphs using information we were assigned to gather outside class. After a vote, we decided we would examine and plot the school's daily consumption of electricity, charting peak hours and so forth.

Breaking into smaller groups of six, each was assigned a time in the day to go down beneath the school's main corridors into the "nether regions" that ran the length of the building. Of course, we obtained permission from "Sarge" to go forward with the task, as these parts of the school were normally very out of bounds, and he agreed to help us, but, cautioned that the room in which we would take our daily readings contained not only the electric meters, but also the master clock that synchronized every clock in the school. Each team had a leader, and I was appointed leader of my group. As team leaders, Sarge took us down to explain which meters we would be concerned with, and showed us the master clock. We were welcome to go in to get our readings as needed, but under no condition were we to touch anything else.

It was all a bit Old Testament—we must not touch, because if anything went wrong, we would be in very serious trouble and it would affect everyone else ("But of the tree of good and evil you must not eat!") We all stood in awe and vowed to obey. "Oh, Sarge, we wouldn't even *THINK* of such a thing—would we? No, of course not!" Each team leader instructed their individual group, showing them around and pointing out "the clock of good and evil."

On we went, very excited about the project—not that reading meters was such a big thrill, but because it would take us into the normally forbidden and mysterious regions that housed the padded cells that we had heard all about. We could almost hear within our vivid imaginations the bloodcurdling screams of those former inhabitants as they threw themselves against the padded walls, mad and madder still in their hopeless attempts to escape. Lost souls with no way out! Hideous images flashed through morbidly overdeveloped imaginations like in some tale by Edgar Allan Poe, each of us prickling with the sense of the cellar's macabre history.

As mentioned prior, the main corridor on the ground level of the school above us ran the entire length of the building, the classrooms and labs off to the side facing the front of the school, and the utility rooms, staircases, and cloakrooms situated facing the rear of the building. The long, dimly lit corridor we descended into was eerie and damp, and there was a distinct chill in the fetid air that made us shiver and move along huddled close together. Each of us carried a flashlight and looked over our shoulders at intervals, expecting fully, each time, to find some spectre following. As we approached a point almost halfway along the corridor, we aimed our lights into the padded cells perpendicular to our path. Each had a large glass window facing the corridor backed with thick vertical iron bars. I had only ever read about such spaces in books and had Jane Eyre and her Thornfield Hall on my mind specifically, as well as Grace Poole and her mad woman in the attic character; her maniacal laugh and wailing screams causing chills to run down the spine. The walls were quite literally padded with what looked like thick leather, crimped at intervals like the upholstery on an armchair. I shuddered. To be shut up in a place like that would have been diabolical.

We inched along gingerly until we reached our destination, a space that sat directly below the "Little Hall," one of the large classrooms on the ground floor above. This was where the master room containing the metering devices for the school was. Rose was by my side, as she seemed always to be, especially whenever potential trouble was afoot.

Rose was an unusual girl, very artistic and greatly talented in not only painting and drawing, but in writing poetry and prose as well. She was, as they would characterise a girl like her at that time, or perhaps any other, a little eccentric—which is exactly why I liked her so much. Saying that she was at my side much of our time at Cavendish is very true, but even then she also always seemed to be far away in some odd way, in some other world or dimension drifting along in the zone where normal thoughts didn't exist much of the time. And, evidently, she was wherever *that place* happened to be on the day on which I explained the "clock of good and evil."

All was going according to plan. We took out our notebooks and looked at the meters, jotting down the readings of each. And then, as we were turning to leave, I heard a voice behind me I knew was Rose's: "Hmm, I wonder what this is?"

I turned toward the sound of her voice which, if memory serves, I heard the very second I became distinctly aware of a rather pronounced clicking sound; one I would determine very quickly to be the toggle of a breaker switch. And this one just happened to be on the side of the school's master clock! And there was Rose, casually (and repeatedly) flicking it up and down, up and down, over and over again...

I was momentarily frozen with shock. But, only momentarily... *"ROSE! DON'T TOUCH THAT!"* we all chimed incredulously, as the adrenaline started pumping and my temples began to throb. I then hissed at her in a frantic stage whisper: "Sergeant told us... THAT is the master clock for the whole school—the one *all the clocks are set by*! If it stops, they all stop! The whole school stops! *We went over this, remember!?* We promised we *would not touch it*. Did you *NOT hear that*, Rose? Didn't you *hear*!?!?"

"Oh, that's what you were on about?" my absent-minded classmate answered back.

"OH? OH!? Is that ALL you have to say? *Of COURSE* that's what I was *'on about*!'" I was *beyond* upset. I was frantic. I tried to calm myself and hoped there was a way of mitigating this and all wasn't lost. Perhaps if we just collected ourselves and thought this through for a moment... I asked Rose, attempting to be as calm as possible: "Now, Rose, think... what *position* was the switch *in* when you *first* touched it? Was it *up*, or *down*?"

"Well, I don't know. I think it was up... Or was it *down*?"

Through clenched teeth, I seethed back, "*Well*, which *was IT? UP*, or *DOWN*!?!"

She gawped back, wide-eyed, denoting the realisation that she knew she was running out of rope pretty fast, but also with that seeming Rose-like detachment that made it very clear that she simply had no idea of the chain of events she may have just set in motion—or, stopped, as the case clearly was.

"I really do think it was up, so I'm sure it's all right... I put it back up," she said matter-of-factly and without any real attempt to defend a clearly held viewpoint, then, again adding a positively Rose-like, "Kath, really, what *are* you getting so upset about?"

Upset!? I was positively apoplectic. Hoping that luck had intervened to protect us from utter disaster we trundled back upstairs and went outside to finish what was now left of our lunchtime break.

In a school that ran by the bell for every single solitary activity under the sun, and in the bosom of an empire on which it was said the sun never set, our lunch break that day at Cavendish simply went on, and on, and on, and on. And a slow and horrible realisation crept up on me that all was not well. It had seemed a very long time since I'd heard a bell—any bell. The light in the sky didn't look right either. It was obviously late. I had avoided looking at my watch for a while, but steeled myself and looked down at it to confirm my worst expectations—almost two-thirty in the afternoon! We were one whole hour past the usual bell that signalled afternoon classes. Everyone else, preoccupied evidently, hadn't even noticed.

Slowly, it crept over me. Rose had left the switch in the wrong position. She'd had a 50/50 chance of getting it right, and, somewhat predictably, had guessed wrong. The clocks had all stopped and *my* group had stopped them. It was on my watch. *I was responsible!* Great Scott, we were in trouble.

I should have just checked in with Sergeant immediately, and now, not only had we done something wrong, I had compounded the whole thing by not owning up to it! It was really all my fault. Unknown to any of us and as the worst of luck would have it, on top of all this catastrophic nonsense, Miss Mansell was due at the Town Hall for a meeting with Buxton's Mayor and town Aldermen—an important meeting, obviously. She, along with everything else, was now well over an hour late. My life was simply over… the late Kathleen Audrey James.

Back in class, the six of us on my team looked at one other as terror flooded our hearts and fear shone in our eyes. We held a quick meeting of the minds, feeble as they obviously were. We agreed—we would take the collective blame. We wouldn't give Rose up. Rose, ditzy but still honourable, said no, *she* did it and she would take the blame and its consequences. We all countered, she was risking too much; we knew she could, and almost undoubtedly would, be expelled for such a gross infraction. If we all took the burden on, they might go easier on us. We'd no doubt end up writing lines the rest of our born days, or be banished to the padded cells downstairs. Maybe even burned at the stake but surely they would never expel all six of us.

My life flashed before my eyes. I would have to go down with the ship. It was the only honourable thing. "Each for All," the motto rang in my ears and filled my heart. It was my last, my final, my only defence.

We were summoned to Miss Mansell's study. We stood before her desk, sick with contrition, utterly terrified, ready to throw ourselves on the veritable mercy of the court. We were doomed and we knew it.

It began. There was much confessing, and it seemed everyone kept overruling me, claiming that *they* were responsible. I countered and claimed responsibility due to being in charge. I added that I should have contacted Sergeant immediately upon knowing we had broken our vow, but having thought everything was all right. Rose too made a dramatic plea—she alone that was responsible because she threw the breaker. I was no longer angry, just sorry for her. The poor girl, throwing herself on the pyre, her horn-rimmed glasses cockeyed on her face and smeared with the tears that ran down her cheeks.

Miss Mansell was a wise woman and knew exactly what we were doing. She also knew only one of us was truly responsible for throwing the switch on the clock, but heard us out. I like to think that she admired our resolve not to "rat" on each other. With a glint of a smile in her eyes—only a glint mind you—she meted out our punishment. She said we were to apologize to Sergeant; write a letter to Buxton's Mayor and Aldermen admitting our guilt and offering apologies for wasting their valuable time; spend the rest of the term in detention; and that we tend to any jobs Sergeant wanted done for the rest of the term on our own time outside of school... Oh, and, yes, of course, there were the lines—I believe it was two thousand. We had got off easily as far as I was concerned!

Needless to say, our meter reading project was over for that term, and we were forced to focus on another project for our statistical studies instead. I really don't remember what it was, but it should have had something to do with the probability of six schoolgirls being able to alter the course of human endeavour—at one point I'd have said the odds were about a million to one. I know better now.

Chapter 33

Outwardly, Rose seemed spacy, ditzy, disconnected, and at times downright clueless, as the previous account illustrates. She could also be the most stoic, shy and retiring girl one would ever meet. She had pale, china-blue eyes and a completely round, almost owlish, face, which appeared even more so thanks to those ever-present, horn-rimmed spectacles. Her skin was porcelaneous with a distinctly pink hue highlighting her cheeks; as if in a painting by Renoir or Bouguereau, or a doll from a factory. She was sturdy, but not at all athletic, and, as intimated, somewhat a renegade. More than a few girls thought she was just *too* different, too weird to befriend, which made me feel a bit sorry for her and led to my decision to make her mine. We had first been thrown together because we had the same schedule of Art classes.

She also had two thick dark brown plaits of hair that came down almost to the middle of her back, and I envied them. My hair, so curly and frizzy, meant I had a bad hair day from about the age of about five until I reached sixteen. When I was very little, I had no less than forty-eight cascading ringlets that made me look a bit like Shirley Temple, or Betty in *Annie Get Your Gun*, but much less flaxen. When I began attending

Cavendish, I wore my hair tied back in two bunches during the week, and loose at the weekends when not in uniform. Most of the time I wore a hat that did a great job of hiding most of its tendencies to resist what little control I had over it. When I got older and moved to America, I had it straightened regularly—what a relief!

Rose was a late-in-life baby. Her parents were older, her father well into his sixties when she entered Cavendish. The other girls used to make fun of her because her mother made her wear a red flannel petticoat in the winter to keep her from catching cold, a very old-fashioned practice indeed; practically "from the stone age," as she put it. After a few trips home with a few terse notes from the powers that be to her mother, her mum finally got the message that this was unacceptable attire.

Of course, it should be noted, if not completely obvious, that all the girls had pretty much the same opinion of their own parents—I thought mine were old-fashioned too, as I think children inevitably do. English parents, at least at that time, also tended not to "pal around" with their children, or feel much need to keep them constantly entertained in quite the way I have always noticed American parents seem to do with their children. There was no confusion between one's children and one's best friends. Parents were parents and we were children—that was that.

I'm always constantly amazed too how in America parents cart their children all over the place with absolutely no question or thought otherwise—to their extracurricular sporting events and related practices, lessons, friends' houses, camps and what-have-you. Mothers in the U.S. have seemed to me at various times to spend their entire lives as part time taxi drivers and full-time agony aunts. Once we were pretty much old enough to get anywhere, we had to make our own way to everything—even the dentist.

Rose actually lived *in* Buxton, whereas I, technically, lived in a nearby village a bus ride away. After we would part company at the bus stop after school on Fridays, we seldom saw one another, our paths just didn't cross at weekends. During the week, we each had three periods of homework each night. We had four on weekends. Each took forty-five minutes. On top of that, I practiced the piano at least an hour per day. There wasn't a lot of time for much else, and what extra I did have, I spent on the tennis court. Rose was, as one might imagine, not a tennis player, expressing the same disinterest in it as she did any other sport. "You're always playing tennis," she would complain, and, she was pretty much right.

We both did belong to the Debating Society, and we also attended a compulsory after school dance class together as well, which was wonderful! We covered beginning ballet, European folk dancing (including Scottish and Irish dances and jigs), ballroom, even square dancing—complete with a violinist dressed in Western American garb sawing away in traditional "fiddle" style. On one occasion the class took a field trip to the Playhouse at the Pavilion Gardens to see Royal Ballet Prima Ballerina Dame Margot Fonteyn perform in a production of *The Red Shoes*. We also saw a performance of *Swan Lake* there too. I, like about every other girl I knew, wanted to be a Prima Ballerina in those days, and I telegraphed my desire by painting a watercolour frieze of ballerinas in tutus and red ballet slippers en pointe up high on my bedroom walls. It was a long and laborious task painting all those ballerinas, but it was a labour of love.

At the end of the term we gave a dance performance for our parents, and at the end of the school year we had a formal dance in the gym where we dressed up in long gowns to the test the airs and graces of our formally learned ballroom skills. In a slight stroke of misfortune, I was the third tallest in our class, which meant that I had always to be "the boy," in these things, leading my partner and dancing forward as they would dance backward in "the girl's" role. As a result, I really never learned to follow and had an awfully hard time learning to dance backwards when finally in the arms of some poor young man or another. This led to years of having constantly and silently to remind myself in my head while whirling around out on the dance floor: "Just shut up and follow, Kath!"

Rose had little patience with any of these things. She didn't really want to dance or play tennis, and at times her disinterest meant that beyond a mutual interest in visual art, we had very little in common. Sometimes we'd get cross with one another, but, somehow managed to stay friends all the way through school.

The one thing Rose did like and did a lot was "fall in love." She fell in love about every other week. She first fell in love with David, a cute little chap who used to live next door to me when we lived at Cubby's Tanderra. David, once, when I was very little, coerced me into eating worms off his mother's best china or else he would not play with me; probably the precursor to every other incident involving me doing silly things to please Sam and his friends... boys. Rose followed David around all over the place and made up all sorts of excuses to go to the pharmacy his father owned in hopes he'd be there. He seldom was. Shortly after her hopeless crush on David, Rose then discovered a private boys' boarding school not far from the hockey field where we played in the autumn. Rose, utterly disinterested in hockey, certainly feigned interest when it came to young gentlemen at posh, boys' prep schools, though. Sons of the rich and famous... I think Rose fell in love first with their handsome grey and red uniforms and then worked backwards.

The boys' school in question was an old mansion surrounded by six-foot-high hedges and walls that Rose was absolutely determined to breach. Through observations of its schedule, she knew the boys had prep time in a room on the street side of the school every evening. She would arrive shortly after they settled at their desks to peek in at them through the school's large front windows.

This was Rose all over... she really should have sought out a career in espionage, as she was always following or peeping in on some unsuspecting young man. I often thought it was too bad she'd been too young for the French Resistance, they could have used her. Most would have considered her behaviour as a young lady really very *risqué*. It was definitely against the rules, but, then again, Rose didn't much care for rules (as I'm fairly sure you've concluded). She continued with her clandestine spying for some time, debriefing me on following days with great glee. I'll admit I always loved the stories, but warned her that one day she was going to get caught, and she'd better be ready with a jolly good excuse. She pooh-poohed me, saying, she'd never get caught as she was "far too careful." Careful. That's our Rose.

Finally, of course, it happened. She got hauled off by a school grounds monitor who'd caught her skulking around in the bushes. But, it turned out that she'd taken my advice and came up with a pretty good alibi—well, for a one-time pass. She said she was looking for a ball that she'd accidentally thrown over the wall—probably about the only time Rose had use for at least the pretence of athletic activity. She was more careful after, but, it was also Rose to a tee, she finally just got bored. She hadn't been able to make contact with the boy she really liked and moved on to other things. But she also always definitely remained a bit "boy crazy." Looking at her you never would have known that lurking beneath that calm and seemingly uninterested exterior, there beat the heart of a very red-blooded young lady just raring to stir things up.

As time and tide and youth and friendship often have it, we gradually drifted apart and lost contact. Years later, I did receive a letter and photograph of her and her new husband outside a church located right behind the police station where my grandparents had lived and worked. In the photo she wore a beautiful white gown and carried a huge bouquet of red roses. Attended by several young flower girls and bridesmaids, there Rose stood, and by her side, a beaming, handsome young groom who looked very pleased with himself. She looked very pretty and very, very happy. Evidently she'd finally caught the boy she really liked, and that's all that really mattered to me.

Chapter 34

As I moved along in school, the piano Cubby bought me still stood in the corner of the living room. From the age of eight on I had been taking lessons, and was beginning to improve. It was a hard-won thing at times, but love isn't always an easy road and this one, like any other, had its share of bumpy stops and starts along the way. At first, I thought I had bitten off more than I could chew. I found it quite daunting, overwhelming at times. I realized that without effort nothing is accomplished, but even I hadn't realized how much effort its serious study would take. I learned to read music the European way, learning the names and values of notes step by step, as well as the crochets, quavers, semi-quavers, and other unusual names for them. I was told years later in America they didn't know to what I even referred when using those terms. The method in the U.S. is the naming of notes by their value (whole notes, half-notes, quarter-notes, and so on), a whole different world. I also learned beginning theory, as well as ear-training and lessons in the writing of music on staff paper.

My first teacher was Miss Broadmeadow. Middle-aged and of slight build, she was very quiet but had an excellent reputation among those who taught beginning students. She lived in a bungalow down a pleasant street that wound from Burbage into town. In the middle of her front lawn she had a silver gazing ball that always fascinated me as I walked up the path to her front door, the sun reflecting on its silvery skin, dazzling me with bright shards of shimmering light as I passed by.

Miss Broadmeadow was a thorough teacher, and as far as I was concerned, she had the patience of Job. How I struggled to comprehend at first, testing her patience repeatedly. Yet, she never became exasperated or sharp with me, for which I remain eternally grateful. I persevered, eventually reaching the stage where I fully absorbed the lessons her level of training could offer, ready to go onto my next with a new teacher and to embrace even bigger challenges. I hated to leave her. We had really come to understand one another and had a good rapport. Reluctantly, even tearfully we said goodbye.

I should mention that there were not exactly a wealth of piano teachers in Buxton at the time. Dad knew a gentleman who was a musician and had some piano students, but he mostly taught violin and cello. He took me to see him. He was a formidable looking older man with longish white hair and a beard, but who was really rather gentle when he spoke. He explained that most of his students were learning string instruments and that the few piano students he was teaching were much more advanced than I, and he thought I needed a more intermediate teacher. We continued our search. Miss Broadmeadow told Mum that in the past she passed on many of her students to a Miss Watts and had contacted her on my behalf. She'd agreed to meet me.

Miss Watts's reputation actually preceded her. *Everyone*

pretty much knew who she was and, if it had been a popularity contest with all the votes in and counted, she would have lost by a nearly unanimous landslide. Every student I spoke to at school absolutely hated her, and relayed that she was not only mean, but mean to the point of cruelty. I was warned repeatedly and told Mother. Mum said that perhaps the stories were exaggerated and that we should at least go along and see to give her the benefit of the doubt. Good old "have-faith-and-don't-judge-others-lest-you-be-judged" Mum. Also, again, we didn't have much choice. Mum made an appointment, and, with the horror stories mounting in my brain and the butterflies multiplying in my stomach a full two days before our appointment, it would be an understatement to say that I was intimidated. But the day came, and off we went.

After catching a bus to Higher Buxton we then had a long walk across a commons to another road lined with large and impressive stone houses with well-kept gardens. Miss Watts lived at the end house with its large bay windows facing the road. We were directed to approach its side entrance where we were admitted by an older woman whom we later learned was Miss Watts's mother. We entered the house and ended up in a small vestibule. We then went through an inner door into a hallway where a highly polished wooden staircase with beautifully carpeted treads led upward to the second floor. To the right of the stairs was a door through which we were ushered along with an announcement of our presence: "Mrs. Alice James and Miss Kathleen James..." I shuddered with apprehension, silently trying to calm myself and thinking, surely, she couldn't be as bad as all that. Surely...

A thin, waspish lady stood near the centre of the room. The room was definitely "lived in," its furniture expensive but rather worn, even faintly shabby, its oriental carpet showing its age. It was obviously used for piano lessons, with music stacked on occasional tables and music books filling the bookshelves. It seemed comfortable; its owner seemed not to be. She was older than Miss Broadmeadow, with very dark brown, nearly black hair worn just above the collar. Coldly and unsmilingly she looked Mum and I up and down, seeming to take stock of our every detail with dark, penetrating eyes. She finally spoke, saying, "I'm Miss Watts," evenly, flatly.

"How do you do?" replied Mum. "I'm Mrs. James, and this is my daughter, Kathleen."

"How do you do, Miss Watts," I murmured, tentatively.

She responded without further pleasantries. "Sit at the piano," she intoned, gesturing toward it with a sweep of her hand and adding, "Play something, anything you've learned lately. Let's see what you can do."

My knees suddenly seemed rather unlike my own, and began to buckle as I made my way numbly toward the piano bench. Her grand piano sat in front of the bay windows facing the street, next to it a chair that she obviously preferred while teaching. First impressions, as we all know, are usually lasting ones. Mum used to tell me that all the time, and I was already not getting a very good one from Miss Watts. I already didn't want to take lessons from this woman. I just wanted to go home.

Timidly, I put my hands on the piano keys and began to play—all thumbs! After a minute or so of struggling, she stopped me to deliver a verdict which surprised me. "Well, I suppose I can do *something* with her," she said to Mother, then, turning to me, "Come Mondays at 4:30 and *don't ring the bell*. I'll have a student, so just wait outside until *I* come for *you*. And, remember, if you *are* going to be my student, you will do *exactly* as I say. You will come to your lessons practiced. You *will* be ready. If you are *not* ready, I shall *not teach you*. I'll turn you *out*. Do you understand?"

"Yes, I understand, Miss Watts," I said meekly.

With that, I was, reluctantly, on my way to the next exciting episode in my musical career. I will mention that I did object strenuously to Mum after we left Miss Watts's house that I was against taking lessons from her, but she said, "Miss Watts has a good reputation for getting students into the Royal Schools of Music," and I should "persevere," because she was very well known in town.

I took lessons from her for about a year, and it was *NOT*, to say the very least, a pleasant experience. It got to the point that on Sundays, the day before my Monday lessons I would start feeling unwell. My stomach knotted. I couldn't eat. I felt sick, with awful bouts of nausea. These symptoms would continue until after my music lesson and then subside until the next Sunday. That was the constant, but, I also remember one terribly rainy Monday when it was pouring down buckets, as it seems it can only in England.

I got off the bus and did my usual walk across the common in a real downpour, about a half-mile journey. When I arrived at Miss Watts's house the rain was still teeming down, and I went around to the side entrance as always as instructed. I could hear the piano inside, so I knew she was still occupied with the student before me. I waited. There was no portico or overhang, so the rain just poured down on me as I did. I was soaking wet and could feel my clothes getting colder and colder against my skin, the rain penetrating every layer I had on. My shoes were sopping wet and squished when I moved.

I knew I wasn't supposed to knock or ring the bell, but I was *SO* cold... surely she would make an exception on a day like this. Perhaps if I knocked, her mother would come and let me stand inside the vestibule until she was ready for me. Her mother appeared to be nice enough. Gingerly, I knocked at the door. No one came. I waited for a minute and knocked again, this time a bit more firmly. Suddenly, the door was flung back on its hinges and there, furious, stood Miss Watts: "Don't you remember you're *not supposed to knock* at this door!?"

"I'm sorry," I said, "It's just very wet and cold… may I please stay in the vestibule until you're finished?"

"No, you may *not*!" She yelled. "I'm not finished, and you will stay right there until I call you," she hissed, slamming the door in my face.

There does come a point when you just can't get any wetter than you are, and you really can't get any colder, either, and so I just stood there, resigned to my fate and trying to think of something, anything, else. Something pleasant. Warm. Dry. Finally, I heard her coming again. She stood for a moment inside the vestibule talking to the student she had been teaching and whom I had heard playing a Chopin Etude; beautifully I might add. From what I could divine from the conversation, the student was ready to take her examination to the Royal School of Music and was practicing her performance. She was older than me by several years. I sincerely hoped that one day I could play like that, so flawlessly and with such feeling.

This, of course, was my critique of what I'd heard, and was, evidently, in stark contrast to our teacher's opinion. I simply couldn't believe what Miss Watts was saying, which was something like: "You will *NEVER* pass this exam! You will *NEVER* make it—you have *NO talent* whatsoever and simply don't have the wherewithal or the technique to make the grade and, *mark my words*, you simply will *NOT* pass!"

I could see just enough through the glass in the door to

tell that the poor girl was in tears, sobbing as she stuffed her sheet music into her music case. A moment later she bolted out the door and began running away from the house in the pouring rain as fast as she could. I was no longer thinking about being soaked. I simply wanted to barge right into the house and paste Miss Watts right in the mouth. What kind of a person was this? How dare she destroy someone's confidence like that!

I went inside now with a boiling, seething hatred for this woman I could barely contain. I remember I was studying a piece by Bach that, I'm sorry to say, I hate to this very day because of my experiences with it then, or more accurately, my experience with *her* over it. I was so upset, and there was simply no way I was going to make it through this particular lesson perfectly. Sure enough, I made a mistake. I played a wrong note, and, just as quickly as I had, *smack*! Miss Watts came across my right knuckles with the metal-edge of the wooden ruler she kept at the end of the piano solely for just such a purpose.

She said: "You *know better* than to come here unprepared."

"I am prepared," I said flatly, not even looking up from the piano keys.

The retort threw her into an immediate and incendiary rage, and she yelled out, "How *dare* you argue with me! You are *NOT* prepared! Now go home, and don't bother coming back until you *are*!"

I grabbed my things, put on my sodden coat, and left in a near fugue state, trudging blindly back to the bus through the continuing downpour across the common and to the station, crying all the while out of helpless frustration and anger and then most of the way home. When I arrived, I told Mother what had happened. I also told her I would never, ever go back. I wasn't even sure that I liked music anymore. I didn't want to take piano lessons or play. Miss Watts had warned me once "not to go crying to my mother," because it wouldn't help. I didn't want to be a crybaby, but I had tried as long and hard as I possibly could, and I could no longer hold it in. I was through! No more. *No more!*

Mother was, understandably, very upset by all this. She said she couldn't believe Miss Watts would act that way. I told Mum that it was like studying piano with Hitler (and we all knew how I felt about him!) and I wasn't having any of it. Sensing I was in no way amenable to altering my position, she acquiesced: "You don't have to go there anymore if you don't want to. I will see her and explain."

And she did. And, as I understand it, gave Miss Watts a pretty good taste of her own medicine while she was at it.

~~~

Just before the choice was made to send me to Miss Watts, Mother had inquired about another teacher, one whom, as it turned out, had an absolutely super reputation in town—and her husband was the current maestro for the Buxton Symphony Orchestra with whom she performed on occasion! They were a musical family held in high esteem. So why, oh why we hadn't started there in the first place is as lost on me now as it was then but, nevertheless... her name was Mrs. Lockett.

The real answer to that conundrum was undoubtedly because it was so very difficult to become her pupil. She was so popular that she rarely took new students and had a long waiting list on which there was rarely any opening and one could languish for some time; the only way one might have any real luck was if someone moved away, and this seldom
~~~

happened. Mum had known about the Locketts before she married Dad, as she used to go to Trinity Church with Mr. Lockett's sister, Lucy. They used to pal around and go to church "Bring & Buy" sales together, and they belonged to the choir too. Mum used to tell a silly story about that part of their relationship that always made me laugh.

When Mum and Lucy would go to choir practice they would always finish after it was dark outside. Lucy said that she didn't want Mum to walk home alone to Cubby's house in the dark, so she would walk her home. It was quite a distance, and when they got there, Lucy too had to get home and was now afraid to walk *there* alone and unaccompanied. She asked Mum if she would mind walking with her ... one quickly sees the problem. They agreed finally that they would return a distance of about halfway and then split up; that way there was at least some hope of them getting some sleep before dawn. I always thought, based on this tale, that Mum and Lucy's relationship seemed just like the one Rose and I had. I could definitely sympathize.

One afternoon Mum met me outside the gates at Cavendish after school. Mrs. Lockett lived right around the corner and, in fact, the street leading to her house bordered the Cavendish grounds. It was a beautiful and secluded, set back from the lane and, as everything seemed to, sat behind high stone walls and hedges. I was, at that particular point, not all that excited about another new teacher and had even told Mum just to save her money—things were still tough, and the family needed every penny. They certainly didn't need to waste money on my piano lessons. Miss Watts, I'm afraid, had truly broken my spirit and I was deeply discouraged. Mum was insistent.

The musical sound of the door chimes seemed to reverberate deeply within the house, mellow and substantial, fading just as the shadow of a person approaching the door could be seen through its frosted, cut glass windows. I remember thinking what a beautiful door it was. When it opened, there stood Mrs. Lockett, a lovely smile lighting up her pretty face.

She was about 5'6", with soft, wavy auburn hair that curled around her face. She seemed to exude sweetness and gentility. We said our hellos, and she led us through a beautifully furnished large entry hall and into her music room. It was like walking into a picture in a magazine. The room was huge, and, instead of noticing what was within it, one's eyes seemed naturally led to large floor-to-ceiling windows that looked beyond and out over the picture-perfect gardens beyond; pristine green lawns spreading out to flank beds of blooming flowers and plants. Just beyond the windows was a flagstone patio with potted plants and flowers everywhere, an atmosphere completed by comfortable chairs and a few occasional tables. Benches were placed at intervals, inviting the chance to sit and take it all in, a birdbath on the lawn was its central feature.

Finally, my eyes turned from the outside to take in a piano placed just to the right of centre in the room—a black ebony Bechstein concert grand that was absolutely magnificent. I was completely awed. Mrs. Lockett seated Mum and I near the piano and began asking me a lot of questions about my musical background and my tastes and interests, and, finally where and with whom I had taken lessons. I mentioned Miss Broadmeadow, whom she knew, but was then reluctant to mention Miss Watts, much less my experiences with her.

Mother, sensing my reticence, rescued me, saying that I'd had an "unfortunate experience" which had ended my relationship with my most recent instructor and that, in fact, I was having a difficult time even wanting to play, much less take lessons again. Mrs. Lockett said she thought that she knew what I'd been through, suggesting that this experience was well over and that we need not think or speak of it anymore. The way she said it, I believed she really did know, and I was as impressed with her intuition as I was relieved that I didn't have to relive the whole thing again by telling her. Then she said, "Well, Kathleen, play for me."

I froze. I really didn't want to play for anyone, but I stood up and approached that beautiful instrument, knees and hands shaking. As I began to play, my hands seemed to sink into the keys, and I heard the sweetest sounds I had ever heard coming from a piano. SO beautiful, in fact, I couldn't believe that I was creating them. All Mrs. Locket said at that point were the words I really needed to hear—that I had a, "very sweet and soft touch," and, "I'll take you as my student."

Years later Mum told me that the two of them had a talk outside the room that day during which Mrs. Lockett offered that she had never seen anyone so terrified of a piano in her life. She'd picked up on the fact that I was literally scared out of my mind to make a mistake. Mum confirmed that I was, and it had all started with my studies with Miss Watts. Mrs. Lockett said she knew what she did to her students, naming her before Mum did and adding that she would, "Take Kathleen, even if my roster was full and I hadn't another minute left in my week" to eliminate what *she* feared most—that upon losing my confidence, I would develop a hatred of not only the piano, but of music itself. She wanted, Mum said, to restore my joy for music and confidence. She certainly did just that.

Mrs. Lockett was very thorough in each aspect of music, especially theory. Her guidance, along with the educational experiences in musical appreciation and history that I was learning at Cavendish rounded out the practical aspects, giving me a better than average command of the subject. As far as performing was concerned, however, my playing was limited strictly to the classical side of things. Growing up I was very naturally attracted to modern music and the hits of the day and bought sheet music to so many of those songs—haunting the music shop in Buxton every time a new one came out. My training very much locked me into a classical mode that meant for many years it was very difficult for me to play anything that wasn't *completely* notated.

It wasn't until meeting my son's piano teachers that I began to break free of this reliance. I took lessons from them too, each contributing missing links I longed for, and setting me on the road to the wonderful world of improvising. I found then I could just sit down with only the melody line of a song and the suggestions of chord harmony and add my own personal touches on a whim. One never knows it all, and there are always so many roads to travel, but these were tremendous discoveries that took my playing into a whole other dimension—a new world of modern music.

Of course, I still love the classics. The last time I took piano lessons, I was introduced to Mozart's piano works for four hands—duets—that provided much enjoyment. At times my instructor and I almost laughed ourselves off the piano bench when one of us would get ahead or behind in the music and some very interesting combinations of notes Mozart definitely never intended emerged. With all these experiences, music has remained one of my favourite and relaxing hobbies, one that, at times, from which I can hardly tear myself away.

Beyond her duties as my instructor, Mrs. Lockett also guided me through my ongoing series of examinations with the Royal Schools of Music. Each year I sat for the next level, and shortly before I left Cavendish (and England too for that matter), I sat for the last of these that I would ever take. I remember that bitterly cold and snowy day well, rising very early and setting out for my test a bundle of nerves.

The examiner had come from London to see local students at a hall in Lower Buxton where he sat, alone, in a room with a grand piano awaiting us. We were not given any opportunity to acquaint ourselves with him or the piano beforehand. The only things we were given were the assigned music as set by the Royal Schools in London, which we'd had time to learn to play (hopefully) well enough to pass, and the specific date and approximate time we were to present ourselves for our individual tests. Mrs. Lockett's students tested the same day, and we met at the appointed time. The only thing we took into the examination room was our music. There was no audience, and no one else allowed in the room but the student and examiner who directed the proceedings.

To give you an idea... first, the examiner had me to turn my back as he played notes in intervals for me to name. He then asked a few other things to "test my ears." This was always fairly easy for me, and I did well. Next, he asked me to play certain scales: major, minor (harmonic and melodic) at random. These too were pretty straightforward. He then played a piece of music and asked me to identify the time signature, and then put a piece of music I'd never seen before on the music stand and asked me to play it. Sight-reading has never been my favourite thing in the world and, truthfully, this part rattled me a bit, but I managed to get through it.

And then, it was time—he asked me to play the first of three pieces in the book I carried with me. I knew them all by heart, but it wasn't just a matter of remembering or playing the notes correctly, it was also about one's expression and technique; feeling was also so important.

I played the first, and then went on to breeze through the other pieces fairly well too—I breathed a sigh of relief. He then thanked me for coming and I thanked him, and it was over. Of course, I had done this several times before over the past couple years or so, the only difference being that each time the material and scope became more advanced and difficult.

When I finally opened the door between the exam room and the corridor, Mrs. Lockett nearly fell over into it! She'd been listening with her ear pressed to it to see how I'd been doing. She did it with all her students. We were "her girls!" And, speaking of—she had two daughters, one older than me, and the younger one had entered Cavendish the year after I'd begun taking lessons from her. They were, as one would expect, both excellent pianists. They were also taking exams that day, and she was obviously very eager to hear them. She had no reason in the world to worry, they always passed and, again, as one might expect, "with distinction"—the highest honour one could receive.

She hugged me gleefully when I emerged and told me I had done marvellously; she knew I had passed. And she was right: confirmed, via mail and by an article cut out of the newspaper several weeks later announcing the names of the passing students. There was mine, and, accompanying it, the words "passed with distinction," alongside a sweet little note from Mrs. Lockett saying how pleased and proud of me she was, and that she couldn't wait for my next lesson. I had, "come a long way."

It meant so much. As far as I was concerned the accolades belonged more to her. It was *all* thanks to her. How much easier it would have been to quit and never touch a piano again, but she wouldn't let me. I have always hoped that in passing with distinction I had, in some small way, repaid her for rescuing the timid, frightened little girl who sat at her beautiful piano on that lovely afternoon; one so afraid of making mistakes. I hope so. I have been grateful to her all my life for not giving up on me and encouraging me the way she did. She was the sweetest and best teacher I ever had, helped open musical doors I didn't know were there, and, in the end, brought me to life again.

Little did I know that upon leaving Buxton that I would not play, much less own a piano again for seven years! A huge gap in my life and one in which I often felt lost and disconnected. I had not realized how much playing had meant to me until separated from its therapeutic and cathartic value. There would be many times when I would close my eyes to imagine the keyboard in front of me, playing the music running through my head like a ticker tape. I even discovered that I could practice without a piano and, with some pieces, without even a score. I owed that to Mrs. Lockett, and she was the one person who, when we left Buxton behind, it truly broke my heart to leave.

Chapter 35

The war had interrupted and changed many things, but Buxton remained a town for the arts—for music, opera, theatre and stage performances of all kinds. Our town orchestra, The Buxton Symphony Orchestra, was a collection of fine musicians who hailed from all over England. In summer 1946, it resumed its concerts and my Uncle Joe was its First Trombonist. He called the instrument the "Mother shift the teapot" due to its long slide and, as he often brought it out in our home to play, one could readily see why.

Uncle Joe was a real character, and he kept us laughing constantly with his wonderful sense of humour. During the summer season he stayed at our home on weekends, always arriving on Friday evenings. He then attended rehearsals Saturday mornings and performed that evening and at a matinee performance on Sunday. Because of my interest in music and my piano studies, he took a special interest in me, taking me along with him to rehearsals in the huge, glass Symphony Hall in Pavilion Gardens.

There I sat all by myself, a few rows back in the very centre, to watch and listen as the Concert Master put the orchestra through its paces. It was so very exciting, and I felt—in a way, rightly so—they were playing just to and for me. It must have been a strange sight that open and empty auditorium with just one little girl in it, following along intently. What a privilege! I heard every performance first absolutely free, *and* I got to watch the Concert Master direct the orchestra in how to play the music. I learned much about the different composers, the phrasing of their compositions, and the style and execution of orchestral music… it spurred me on to practice my piano ever more diligently and to study even harder.

Another thing about Uncle Joe, he was somewhat of a dead ringer for the silent film star Oliver Hardy (of the comic duo Laurel and Hardy)—the resemblance at times was almost uncanny. This was especially handy at the end of the summer season when the orchestra, laying formalities aside, gave a sort of whimsical tongue-in-cheek performance, a kind of musical spoof. The orchestra members were always dressed in black tie anyway and, for this special night, Uncle Joe simply needed only a bowler hat to add to the ensemble in order to transform himself into the plump and jolly "Ollie" Hardy.

One day Uncle Joe arrived at our house with a beautiful golden cornet he proceeded to teach me how to play. I fell immediately in love with its mellow tone and was quite taken with the idea of taking it up seriously. He taught me to play the lovely and tender piece, "Bless This House," a well-known hymn my mother always loved. It sounded absolutely beautiful on the cornet, its clear and almost heavenly sound affecting me deeply and bringing tears to my eyes. But although Mother liked the sound as well, she had a different opinion about my study of the cornet. She was firmly convinced that within learning correct *embouchure*—the fitting of the lips to the mouthpiece—I would spoil my lip and the shape of my mouth.

In the end, she vetoed the cornet lessons, much to the dual disappointment of both Uncle Joe and yours truly. It was with great reluctance that I obeyed, but, in the long run, I thought she might have a point. What if she was right and I ended up with calloused lips. I wanted to play, but I also wanted boys to think I was pretty. These were days of very different appraisals for girls (women) and, I guess I just didn't love it quite enough to invite such possible sacrifice. I still wondered for a long while after if I could have become a really good musician and played in the brass section of an orchestra... It still seems more of a man's world and, personally, I've never actually seen a woman in that orchestral role, although, I know for a fact that a few now do occupy it. I still have a piano—first, last, and always my favourite instrument—but, every once in a while when I hear a cornet, I have such a desire to know just one more time what it's like to raise it to my lips and play, "Bless This House" with all my heart.

Uncle George & Auntie Gertie, The Owners of "The Star Inn" in Staffordshire

Uncle Joe shoveling snow in his tuxedo dressed for an evening symphony performance

"The Star Inn" in Staffordshire. Name changed to "The Lord Nelson" when Uncle George & Auntie Gertie sold it.

Mom & Dad weekending in Shrewsbury

Chapter 36

Sometimes on weekends Dad had enough free time to continue our car trips into the countryside to explore. One of the little villages nearby, steeped in history, was the quaint little town of Eyam (pronounced E-am), whose entire population had been wiped out in the plague of 1665—we visited the actual cottage where it started; its source a bolt of cloth transported from London! It was sobering to think of this picturesque little house being the tinder for such a cataclysmic event. We also visited the villages of Taddington, and Tideswell with its beautiful medieval church; Bakewell, famous for its delicious dessert, "Bakewell Tart," which I still make from an original recipe handed down from my mother, *and* which still gets raves at dinner parties. We visited nearby Chatsworth, stately home of kings and famous the world over for its breath-taking grounds, herd of deer, as well as its miles of lush countryside so beloved by hikers. The mansion at Chatsworth also contains millions of pounds worth of art treasures and famous paintings.

We tooled around country lanes drinking in the beauty and exploring such places as Manifold and Goyt Valleys, and Miller's Dale, clad in its profound atmosphere of peace and contentment, and raising feelings I'd never experienced before, and have seldom since. We went to Chesterfield to see its famous cathedral's "Crooked Spire"—twisted by weather and the natural elements—as well as to Shrewsbury in Shropshire, with its famous abbey and castle. We enjoyed a luxurious night there at a very regal looking bed and breakfast called "Broom Hall," waking to a scrumptious full English breakfast before setting out again.

Soon after, the grey, stacked stone north country walls piled atop one another in no particular pattern gave way to the soft hedgerows of Staffordshire. Those walls, indigenous to Derbyshire, wind over the fields, farms, and dales, separating pastures and properties for miles and miles. Sometimes I would rearrange a few stones for fun, to leave my mark on the countryside, wondering how many other people did so too as they passed through. Growing among the winding hedgerows were wild raspberries and blackberries as big as your thumb. We would stop to pick them for breakfast, but so often they never even had a chance to make it to the table.

Around this time, another of my mother's relatives surfaced after what had been a long time to make their presence known. My Uncle George and his wife were living in a tiny village outside the little market town of Uttoxeter—just south of Buxton and about halfway between where we lived and Birmingham.

Uncle George was Mum's senior by about two years. He and my Auntie Gertie had purchased a lovely little inn and public house (pub) called "The Star Inn" at Leigh, Staffordshire. The inn was located adjacent to a church dated back to 900 A.D., and on maps the little village is simply called "Church Leigh." A more charming little roadside accommodation, with its stone flagstone floors and low beamed ceilings, would be hard to find, and it's still a popular spot frequented by locals who love to play skittles, have a pint, or just hang out.

The summer they acquired the inn, they invited us to come and spend a couple of weeks there and we jumped at the chance! They were an unlikely pair to own such an establishment, at least Uncle George was... he had trained for the priesthood, one of Mother's eleven siblings whose turn it was to be brought up Catholic, and about the last person in the world you would ever have expected to find in an English country inn, let alone a public house (pub). He was a very quiet man, almost withdrawn, and always very fastidious and impeccably dressed; paying attention to the most minute detail of his appearance.

The larger issue, the thing that really didn't quite add up was that—due to his father's vicious addiction to liquor, he was also passionately opposed to drinking! It came as a huge shock to my mother, his daughters, and, in fact the whole family, that they had purchased the inn, because it was so completely alien to his character. Mother always ventured the notion that perhaps Uncle George wasn't more aware of all the goings-on in the pub as he was also quite hard of hearing. But, he cheerfully bartended—instructed by none other than Auntie Gertie herself, who did a tremendous job of training him—often until eleven o'clock closing time, when he was heard to call out, "Time, Gentlemen, please!" I would hear him from the room upstairs where I was staying. The obvious conclusion, to me at least, was that he did it all for Auntie Gertie, who was completely in love with the place. In short, he loved her and knew simply that it would make her happy.

Auntie Gertie was a natural, a long-time barmaid, the inn was right up her alley; she was just happily now running her own establishment, not someone else's. She had been doing housework for Uncle George's grandmother when the two of them met. Suddenly, the calling of priesthood seemed to wane for Uncle George. He was in love and set his calling aside in favour of marriage and children. They had two girls much older than me.

During the war, Uncle George and family had lived in Stoke-on-Trent, Staffordshire, where beautiful English china had been manufactured for centuries. They had owned a Mom-&-Pop store which supplied afternoon tea. Across the alley in back of their house was the famous Wedgewood factory, and, every day at four o'clock, Auntie Gertie would make up trays of tea and scones, little salmon and cucumber sandwiches, and biscuits to deliver to the factory's executive suite. It was in this house during the summers where I had originally visited them as a child, becoming acquainted too with my cousins Gladys and Margaret. We visited each summer until the girls went off to college. Not too long after matriculation, they too were married with children of their own.

Uncle George also had a spectacular collection of world-renowned Royal Doulton bone china figurines: ladies reclining on sofas in ball gowns, couples dancing in period costumes, carriages drawn by white horses, animals of all sorts, and, perhaps the most recognizable of all, the detailed and colourful "Toby" Jugs. All were accented with real gold leaf, and I loved them. He had spent a lifetime collecting these treasures, housing them in a lighted and locked antique cabinet so little fingers (my cousins and their children) could not touch them. When we stayed at the holidays, we learned to tread very softly when in that room so as not to shake the cabinet and cause any to fall over.

When the war came and the bombing started, Uncle George, very concerned for the safety of this precious collection and not knowing quite what else to do, packed them up carefully in heavy trunks, dug a deep hole at the back of his garden, and buried them for the war's duration. When it ended, he dug them back up and returned them to their cabinet. Not one was damaged in even the slightest way. It's amazing to think of the many inventive things that people did to protect their valuables and, indeed, themselves during that time.

The Star Inn itself, a very old structure, is two-stories tall, its stone exterior painted stark white. The inside, quaint and charming with oak-beamed ceilings and flagstone floors, has always held a sort of mysterious feeling for me. The very first time my brother and I wandered into the bar, Uncle George sat us up on the bar stools and made us our very first "Shandy"—mixing half and half portions of draft beer and ginger ale.

Mum found out and about hit the ceiling! She was *livid* (to put it mildly), and gave Uncle George real what-for for giving us alcohol. He'd definitely softened his approach to drinking, at least on that day, and it was my mother's remembrance of what it did to their family that came to the fore—not to mention that it was illegal at our tender age. Knowledge of the effects of alcohol on children were a bit less authoritative at that historical time, and he had truly meant no harm. Mum finally stopped fuming, and he certainly never made that mistake again.

We loved Uncle George and our "hols" in Church Leigh. Sam and I would go down the lanes among the hedgerows to pick berries for Auntie Gertie to serve for breakfast with fresh cream and newly laid eggs from the farm. Uncle George would play games with us, chasing me around while doing the vacuuming while saying he was going to "suck me up the pipe" like he did with "the monsters that lived in the pub" until I screamed and ran away. At night I would lie in my bed upstairs above the bar parlour and hear the clink of glasses and laughter down below. What luxury! It all seemed a very special hideaway.

Further supplementing my education in the ways of adult behaviours, was on one of these summer journeys that I first heard about "lovers." Sam and I would go off romping through the wheat fields beyond the inn and churchyard and come across places where the wheat had been flattened out. I asked Auntie Gertie about this and she said, "Oh, it's just lovers." Not wanting her to think that I didn't know what that was, I said, "Of course," and then went and asked my mother. Mum said they were simply people who liked to rest in the wheat fields, and when they lay down on the ground it flattened it out. Well, how boring, I thought. Who on earth would want to lie down to rest in a wheat field? You couldn't even see anything doing that... Just another one of the silly things grown-ups seemed to do, I thought dismissively.

During the bitter winter, 1947, when the whole of Europe was locked in the grip of a cruel and seemingly never-ending deep freeze, Uncle George sent us a photograph of the inn with snow piled up around it all the way up to the second story and just a narrow path carved through it to the front door. We were fairing little better in Buxton. I remember the snow was so deep at our house that Dad had to carry me even beyond the main road to reach a point snowploughed enough to allow me to walk to school. Girls who lived in the outlying areas could not get to school at all because the buses weren't running. Towns were cut off with no foodstuffs or supplies, huge drifts blocking the roads. Classes were sparse and everything seemed surreal. Animals froze in the fields.

Having no central heating, too, we were all often on the verge of colds and other illnesses during the wintertime, and that particular one I had a lingering case of tonsillitis that lasted throughout and causing me to miss a great deal of school. Mother too became ill and it turned to pneumonia. Planes were sent to drop food and medical supplies to some of the villages that were cut off from the outside world. Everyone breathed a sigh of relief when the sun finally came through. I have lived in a few climates considered snowy and cold in my lifetime since, but I've still never experienced a winter like that.

Chapter 37

One summer after the war, one of Dad's friends invited all four of us to go and stay with his family for two weeks. He had recently been appointed caretaker of a huge estate, covering upwards of forty acres, just a few miles over the moors on the road to Manchester called Whitehall. During the war, the house had been repurposed to the government as a school for boys evacuated from London and other areas in the south of England during the Blitz. Afterward, it became a private school for a while, then abandoned and since left unoccupied. Dad's friend and his family lived in the estate's groundskeeper's "cottage" that was, in fact, a bit less so that and more so fairly spacious and comfortable house. Sam and I were quite excited at the prospect of staying there for two whole weeks. Equipped with tennis racquets and as much gear as the car could carry, we set off.

It seemed no sooner had we left Buxton than we were rounding the curve to the ornamental gates of the Whitehall grounds. We drove through, past the empty gatehouse and another unoccupied estate cottage to continue up a broad, winding driveway lined on each side by rhododendrons ablaze in purple, pink, and white blossoms, and thick plantings of daffodils that must have been multiplying for years and years. It was a spectacular sight in full bloom, and some lines from my favourite Wordsworth poem popped into my head: "I wondered lonely as a cloud... Hosts of golden daffodils..."

The driveway turned to the left and, as we rounded the next curve, we caught our first glimpse of the mansion—a stately half-timbered structure right out of a picture postcard. My girlish imagination immediately began working overtime, as it looked for all the world as if it had been plucked out of a nineteenth century novel.

Once we entered it, it became clear how enormous the house really was—an expanse of all the appropriate spaces and rooms one imagines of an English country estate from its immense entrance hall and reception room to a cavernous kitchen, multiple libraries, and beautifully panelled staircases that wound their way to the floors above. Exploring each of the rooms, it was as if the house's inhabitants had simply gone out for the day and left everything just the way it was, never to return. There were books piled everywhere—on the library tables and in the ground floor rooms, on the desks in the second-floor rooms, which had apparently been used as classrooms. The only thing missing were the sounds of student's voices, and I could almost hear them as it was.

Rambling around Whitehall promised enormous fun, and my brother and I were in our element imagining it as it had been in its heyday a century or more before. We played hide and seek throughout, and, at one point, I even turned around to find Sam had disappeared completely and I was suddenly alone... He had been there just a second before, and we were nowhere near a door. As it turned out, Sam had leaned against a panelled wall to find that it swung inward, depositing him into a secret passageway. Naturally, when he suddenly appeared again out of nowhere, it frightened me to death, but it was a pure accident that turned out to be a great find! We soon discovered we could go all over the house behind the walls in numerous secret passageways, entering different rooms from behind the walls instead of through the doors We wondered if any of the students had ever found them, as there was no evidence that anyone had been in them in a long, long time.

There were French doors that led outside from the lounge, the dining room and the salons located at the side of the mansion. They led out onto a wide flagstone terrace surrounded by stone balustrades with steps leading down to the croquet lawns and exquisite grounds. Flashes of ladies in long flowing gowns entered my head, and in my mind's eye I watched them as they strolled around the lawns with croquet mallets, their big, floppy hats shielding delicate complexions from the sun.

Down the path leading to the right of the croquet lawns was a maze. The high clipped hedges made us all feel like the Lilliputians in *Gulliver's Travels* and, of course, we became thoroughly lost. There were little alcoves here and there within the maze complete with ornate stone benches or even statuary. At a couple of points I thought we would never get out, but with a bit of strategizing we finally figured it out. I could see how it might not be the smartest thing to go in there alone or at dusk, at least without a flashlight. Sam warned me not to without telling anyone, as he knew I was liable to try.

Farther along the path lay tennis courts of red clay. They were in great shape, and we spent many an hour playing on them, thankful we had our racquets and gear with us. I really never went very far without my racquet in those days, that's how mad about tennis I was. Scattered around the grounds too were summerhouses (gazebos) and grottoes, some complete with fountains. Whoever had planned the gardens did a spectacular job. There were so many, and each a different mood. We also found a stone tower with a spiral staircase that led up to a lookout point. We climbed to the top of it to see the countryside spread out for miles and miles around us. It was magical, and we revisited it often on the trip.

At the rear of the groundskeeper's cottage were the estate's carriage houses and stables. There was even a generating plant to supply electricity so there was no danger of being without power even in the bleakest of winters. I tried to imagine the estate as it was when fully staffed and its own self-contained little paradise. To the side of the stables was a huge kitchen garden with all kinds of vegetables and bushes laden with gooseberries. We literally made ourselves sick gorging on those, losing almost a full day with the fiercest stomach aches you can imagine.

Chapter 38

So often sitting on my favourite bench on the promenade at Cavendish I surveyed it all and thought ahead. No matter how happy I was, how much I wished it would never end, I also knew that soon enough I would have to venture into the world beyond this safe haven where I felt both content and protected.

I was indeed becoming a young lady, but still very much in that awkward stage between child and grown-up. Leave it to Uncle Joe, who teased me unmercifully on his visits, to jolly me along. He would say: "Come on, Kath, put your 'Cabbagedish' hat on and let's go out!"

I loved our outings to the Pavilion Gardens. We would walk from Burbage to Buxton down the St. John's Road as he explained the current symphony performance, bursting, as always, into unabashed explanations of arrangements and singing parts of the melody without any concern for those sharing the path: "Pom, *POM*, pom, pom *POM POM POM*!" I was so shy and self-conscious, so easily embarrassed in that way that those in their teens are, that I always seemed to be looking around to see if anyone was near—all the while thinking he was going on as if he was "not all there;" and always relieved when we'd reached our destination and he could go and put his "pom, pom, *POMS*" into practice. He bought me the first ice cream soda I ever tasted in my life on one of those afternoons, and, despite my twinges of self-consciousness, I still felt so very special being escorted by him into his wonderful world of music.

Uncle Joe's son, David, was two years older than I, and, at this point I should clarify, was not really my cousin. Even though I called Uncle Joe "my uncle" and his wife, "Auntie Vinie," they were not actually blood relations. Like Cubby, they were an adopted part of my "family"—closer than my own relatives to be sure—and I loved them. Sometimes during the orchestral season, Uncle Joe would bring Auntie Vinie and David along for Sunday afternoon matinees. Mum and Dad would go too, and we'd make a long afternoon of it.

David couldn't have cared less about the symphony, and always made it clear that he'd much rather do something else. So, while the older ones went to the performance, I, who had already been to rehearsal the day before, would often accompany him around the Gardens to take a turn on the putting greens or to paddleboat around the lake, with its ducks and beautiful white swans.

I liked David. A lot. In fact, he was my first crush. To my embarrassment, this fact was also extremely noticeable. Sam teased me about that, I can tell you. Whereas Rose's crushes and schoolgirl fantasies were lavished from afar on unsuspecting strangers, mine tended to be boys I actually knew through my family, and, therefore, less mysterious quantities.

Another boy I liked was named Peter, and he, also, was the son of family friends who lived just outside Manchester. I seldom saw him. He was handsome and funny, and we had some good times together. Both David and Peter were more friends who happened to be boys, rather than "boyfriends," and, although these were idyllic times in my first blush of romantic feelings, there were no big storybook romances of the kind I had read about in books.

My friend at school, Evelyn (name pronounced like my aunt's), had a "real" boyfriend who was somewhat of a surprise to us. His name was Raymond, and he was a student at Kent Bank Road School for Boys, the equivalent of another local non-scholarship school, Silverlands. Usually, students from schools like Kent Bank or Silverlands did not mix easily or well with those from Cavendish or Buxton College, where my brother went. As non-scholarship schools, their students' paths didn't cross naturally or inevitably with the others. If I'm remembering correctly, I believe Ray was a neighbour of Evelyn's and that is how they would meet, but, no matter the case, theirs was a romance with a capital "R." They were positively inseparable, and, needless to say, the absolute envy of all us girls.

As we were separated from the boys at school, eventually these things became a big deal, but, truthfully, the segregation of the sexes never really bothered most of us, and, I think, many times, it was for the best. On the whole, we felt more focused on our studies and more completely self-sufficient without the constant distractions boys would have presented. Grade school had been co-ed, and it was much more troublesome; brimming with the constant shenanigans and teasing that always seemed to accompany boys wherever they went. We, or at least a lot of the girls I knew, myself included, truly didn't miss them when we got to Cavendish.

It wasn't until our senior years in school that we really gave much thought at all to the opposite sex—well, except of course for "our Rose"—and, of course, I had my brother at home with his constant influx of friends from Buxton College to remind me what it meant to have boys around. They certainly filled in a gap between the "silly little lads" and real crushes in ways that meant I was perfectly comfortable around boys, and boys were just, well... boys—a fairly un-mysterious lot on the whole.

Rose, the only child of very strict and old-fashioned parents, probably (well, if behaviour was any indication) had a much different point of view than I did—which helped explain her early boy-craziness. Evelyn too was an only child, so she, like Rose, seemed enthralled with boys as she (like Rose) was never really around them growing up. At best, I just took them for granted, and, if asked to concede anything at the time, it would most likely have been that they were a pain in the neck. Somehow though, my feelings about these things even seemed to be changing... I was actually becoming just a little bit intrigued.

In my senior year at Cavendish, when the subjects dropped to six majors, most of my classes were art classes. Rose and I had a whopping eleven art classes per week, most of which coincided. We all but occupied a study room at the top of the school and had it all to ourselves most of the time. There we worked on projects and had plenty of time and privacy to talk about everything, and usually that everything started out something like: "Well, what did you do last night, Rose?"

"Oh, I went round to Normanton School looking for boys, *and* to the chemist shop to see if I could find *David*."

This last pronouncement some day or another gave me some purview as to how those two met. As mentioned earlier, David was the son of the pharmacist whose shop was located kitty corner from Rose's parent's house... our little spy had observed him going in and out to see his father. David had indeed grown up to be a rather tall, handsome lad with dark hair, piercing deep blue eyes and a fine physique, so, let's face it, Rose, as usual, had good taste in crushes. Truth be told, I enjoyed Rose's fantasizing about all those boys as, in a way, it saved me from having to do much work on my own, and she could always be counted on to provide plenty of fodder for those afternoon discussions about her "relationships"—fantasies, nearly one and all—to obsess her until she had a real boy to call her own.

Chapter 39

Our youngest teacher at Cavendish was a woman named Miss Knight, who was in her late twenties to early thirties and very pretty. She taught history, was lots of fun, and, unlike many (most) of our other teachers, had a very light-hearted relationship with us girls. She was a whole different generation than most of her colleagues and even allowed us to crack jokes and to laugh during class... unheard of!

Then, during the last two years at Cavendish, we actually got a young male teacher! He arrived at school shortly after Miss Knight and had the distinction of being the only male on the entire school grounds (poor chap) with the exception of Sergeant. He was about thirty years old, tall and slender, fair-haired with a constant twinkle in his blue eyes. To top of it all off, his name happened to be Mr. Trees. We girls immediately nicknamed him, "Twiggy." Twiggy, like Miss Knight, was also light-hearted and lots of fun, and you can well imagine... our schoolgirl minds were suddenly awhirl in true romantic schoolgirl fashion with the idea that with the arrival of Mr. Trees *and* Miss Knight, that this must be much more than coincidence— it was *kismet*! A match made in heaven!

We watched them closely, observing how they seemed to

enjoy each other's company. They laughed and joked. They strolled the grounds together. As we looked on, we were certain that true romance was in the air, and that our favourite teachers were becoming our favourite couple; falling, so obviously, so hopelessly in love. It would, we were sure, just be a matter of a short time before they would announce to us and the whole world that they were engaged and intended to marry. It was all so right!

We watched and waited until the day came that, just as we'd predicted, Miss Knight stood up and announced to all in her class that she was going to be married! Oh, this was just wonderful! How very romantic! She then announced that thereafter she would be called by her married name—Mrs. Turnley.

We sat there, stupefied. Our bubble burst. "Mrs. Turnley?" Who was *that*? It was supposed to be Mrs. Trees, or at the very least, Mrs. Twiggy (if one were referring to her informally)! This new name—was simply not acceptable! How *could* she marry someone else after all she and Mr. Trees had so obviously meant to one another? Someone we didn't know a whit and, almost assuredly, would not like even like if we had. Poor Mr. Trees...

Funnily, he didn't seem at all perturbed by the news. Never mind what was wrong with *her*, just what was wrong with *him*? How could it all have gone *so very wrong*?

Of course, we had completely overlooked the fact that our prematurely betrothed couple were the only people on campus who happened to be of the same age and simply had more in common than with any of the other faculty members. They understood one another. Resigned to learning the valuable lesson that, "all's fair in love and war," not to mention, "things aren't always what they seem," we conceded right then and there that any ideas we might have had of testing our matchmaking skills further would best be shelved.

Before Miss Knight officially became Mrs. Turnley, she promised that she was going to devote a term to American History. We were very excited! Up until then we had studied only British and European history and had never ventured into the Americas. Then, despite her promise, somehow it was decided that the curriculum would take another turn and the Americas were once again swept from the map in front of us, relegated to just another distant colonial enterprise with which we were not to be bothered.

It was disappointing but did not deter my insatiable curiosity about the USA. The only thing I definitely knew, was during the war our country had been inhabited by those thousands of American soldiers who brought us strength and with it the impetus to know more. It was decidedly not a lot to go on in investigating a nation's history or understanding its people, but it was the start I had. Well, that and a few other clues.

Throughout the preceding years I'd very carefully observed magazine advertisements I saw with their photographs of American movie stars... shampoo, toothpaste, cigarettes... Radio ads did not exist in England, and, of course, television not yet invented, so I made scrapbooks out of the ads, cutting out the most beautiful and most handsome film stars I could find and pasting them into the pages. I knew my movie stars, as, whenever possible, Mum would take Sam and I to the pictures (movies) and, if on offer, I would always vote for American films.

Much fascinated by depictions of American life, my estimation was that the USA looked glamorous—filled with smiling families living on tree-lined streets in big, two-story (detached!) homes surrounded by beautifully landscaped gardens with their flowers growing in (what I imagined) bright colours (black-and-white film) around perfectly manicured lawns. In every American driveway there was always one if not two, huge, polished and shiny American cars. And what a shine—the sun seemed always shining—everything about it looked just perfect.

As one entered these stylish American "movie homes," there would always be an entrance hall with a staircase leading to the upper floor, and at the bottom an alcove with a comfortable chair, a small table, and, on it, a *white* telephone. Lolling on the comfortable chair always seemed to be a pretty teenage American girl dressed in jeans, cuffs rolled up to reveal the white bobby socks at the end of legs propped up on the staircase treads—and, talking on that white phone. The ladies of these onscreen houses seemed always too to be languishing in huge bathtubs filled with foamy bubbles, yet, again, talking on a white phone. One could almost feel the steam, smell the expensive perfume, but, for me the key was, yes, you guessed it, that phone...

Strange to most, I'm sure, this fascination with white phones, but to me, it was this singular object that somehow represented the epitome of American life in all its glorious sunshine, freedom, liberty, and egalitarian promise. A white telephone shone like a beacon of happiness and success—an unequivocal symbol one had truly and without reservation arrived in this world.

Years later, in America, married and ensconced in our very first apartment, I called from a relative's house to schedule our telephone installation. They asked me, "Ma'am, what colour telephone would you like?"

"What colour?" I answered breathlessly. I can choose? Was

there any colour *other* than..."Oh, please, may I have a *white* one?" I ventured the question breathlessly, hoping silently that these were neither a mythic invention of moviemaking props departments, nor out of stock due to popular demand.

"Sure," the service technician said, nonchalantly. "We'll be there this Thursday to install it."

"Oh, thank you, *thank you*!" I replied, with undoubtedly a bit more gratitude than warranted, and certainly exceeding the usual reception the technician on the line received under such everyday circumstances. Well, never mind, I was getting my very own white American telephone. I had arrived. America—a chicken in every pot, a car in every garage, a white telephone in every entryway. I still have one to this day.

Chapter 40

Looking at the world near and far from my favourite vantage point overlooking the Cavendish tennis courts, I would run through all the things I had learned during my sojourn in my mind.

Throughout my life I had heard how important it was to be "an accomplished young lady," and to be very sure, Cavendish had given me a head start on many of those things required in fulfilling the role. What my parents had not instilled, it had done well in preparing me to face, and I felt I had done well in all these respects too. I had studied languages and diction; the sciences including chemistry, physics, biology, and botany; I'd studied the arts, literature and poetry, art appreciation and history, drama and theatre, dance and music; and I had studied the domestic sciences, social graces, and aspects of deportment through debating and sports (especially my beloved tennis). I knew how to speak, behave, and interact appropriately, as well as how to have compassion and empathy for others with humility, dignity and strength. I had been sincerely fortunate to be served all of this knowledge on a proverbial platter and had eaten it up. I felt I could hold my own with the best. I was ready to step out into the world, confident. Truly prepared for the future.

I also had the very clear suspicion that, whatever I'd learned or experienced thus far, or how well I thought I had done, the easy part was now behind me. It would be the application of it that would truly be the test to come, and it would be a lifelong one. I was also aware that to be fully "accomplished" also meant to be able to appeal to the right sort of man too, and, of course, that meant "a husband." These were the times. These were the standards by which we lived and which we were measured, and by which we measured ourselves.

Beyond appraisals of my next phase of life, it was clear too as I pondered that my family's lives were moving toward a crossroads too. My parents' lives and my brother's too were changing just as surely as my own, and, on top of all this, there was Cubby; as timeless and, to my mind ageless, as she was, she was also almost 88 years old. She had, it seemed, never changed, and, if she had, it was indiscernible to me. She was and would forever be there, ever Cubby: sweet, kind, feisty at times… but always there.

We saw Cubby several times a week. On Saturday mornings I would ride my bicycle down to "Belgrave" to visit her and would drop by many times when out running errands for Mum to the butcher shop in Higher Buxton, or what have you. I'd just pop by to enjoy a little time with her and eat the fairy cakes she always seemed to have ready for tea.

One Saturday morning, Mum and I were home, Dad having gone to see a friend in town. I was (imagine) looking out the living room window when I saw a very tall lady walking up the street at good pace. As she got closer, it became clear that it was Miss Owen, an older maiden lady who was a tenant in Belgrave's upstairs flat. We knew very little about Miss Owen, as she kept very much to herself; very prim, very quiet, very English. She often looked in on, and out for, Cubby, always a good neighbour. While Cubby had a telephone, our family, as most people in Buxton at the time, did not (it's no wonder my fixation with those things had become so!).

The minute I saw her coming, I knew something was somehow wrong. I called out: "Mum. Come quick—Miss Owen is coming up the road."

Mum hurried into the room and looked out, a worried look coming over her face.

"Oh dear, something must be wrong at Belgrave. I hope Cubby's all right."

She met Miss Owen at the door, grim-faced and quite out of breath. Mum quickly invited her in. She got right to the point: "It's Miss Shirt," she said, "She's not at all well and I am very concerned. She's had a cold the last couple of days, and today she is not herself at all. She's developed a terrible cough and won't get out of bed... She didn't want me to come and I mustn't stay. I must get back. I didn't know what else to do."

"You did the right thing," Mum said. "I've put the kettle on. You must have a cup of tea first and then I'll go back with you. Kath, you get ready and come, too. We'll stop in Burbage and call a taxi. We'll be there in no time."

Mum always knew what to do, springing into action and calming everyone down at the same time. I could tell by the expression on her face that she was worried, and I had a funny feeling this was very serious too.

After a hasty cup of tea, we set out for the village and were on route to Cubby's in a taxi as quickly as one could have been. Taxis in Buxton were very posh, they were, in fact, mostly Rolls Royce or Bentley's, not at all like the taxis even in London. In just a short time we were at Belgrave and Mum, once again, took charge. After one look at Cubby, she called the doctor and we waited on pins and needles for him to arrive. When he did, he spent a great deal of time with Cubby and Mum, as she related to him how, just the week before, Cubby had walked all the way to our house, preferring to in lieu of taking the bus. She also said that Cubby had seemed unusually exhausted when she arrived. Mum had given her some tea and lunch and got a taxi for her to go home afterward, even though Cubby had protested that she could walk home, though rather feebly. I had ridden along with her to make sure she got in and settled before returning to Burbage myself. Perhaps that trip had been too much for her and she had become overtired, and this was somehow the result.

The doctor too looked very serious. He said that she pretty clearly had pneumonia and would have to be watched very closely. Shortly after he left, Cubby fell deeply asleep.

Around noon Mum came out of Cubby's room and simply fell to pieces; I had never seen her like that before... I finally got her to tell me—Cubby was gone. It had happened so quickly. One look at her and I realized, much as I had when Grandma passed in front of Dad and I that day at the nursing home, it was now up to me to take charge. I called upstairs to Miss Owen to look after Mum; I had to go and find Dad. I then called the doctor on Cubby's phone and he came back. He said simply that nothing further could have been done, and that I should look after Mum, call my father, and then the undertaker. I left Mum in the hands of Miss Owen, called the undertaker, and then a taxi to set off for Bayswater.

As I reached Anncroft Road I saw him walking with his friend toward our house. I asked the driver to pull over, and once he had, I opened the door and blurted out, "Dad, please get in, Mum needs you."

"What's the matter, Kath?" he asked, immediately grasping that something grave had happened.

"It's Cubby, Dad, we've lost her... Oh, we've lost her."

Dad, shocked, but seeing that I had reached my limit in coping, told his friend to jump in the car took me in his arms as we sped back to Buxton. How thankful I was for the safe and gentle arms I'd sought shelter in so many times and where I felt so safe. Dad's friend stayed with us until we were at Cubby's, taking the car on to his home after. Dad and I went into Belgrave and he took charge, comforting Mum, who was dazed and clearly in shock.

The funeral took place a few days later. And there we were, faced with life without our Cubby. So strange. Such a sad, empty feeling.

Chapter 41

The course of life can so easily and profoundly be changed by one event. The war had done so already to some larger extent, but, as profound and sweeping as the changes were at times, it was still its collective and global reality that allowed us to deal with the shocks and losses it brought. As the course of a nation can be changed in the twinkling of an eye, in scale and with a swift, personal specificity, it was Cubby's loss that would ultimately represent the event that would truly and suddenly change my family's lives forever, the turning point with the most intimate and deeply felt effects on our sense of selves and as a family unit.

Although there was no way of fully comprehending this within that moment, much less being able to articulate our awareness of it, I think we all recognized in our own ways that the life that we had known, life as we had defined and even tricked ourselves into believing it irrevocably to be, was gone. To find things anew, some path that would allow us to recognize what we must do next, would take both acts of looking inside and heavenward. We would need to find our bearings and steer in the darkness toward the brightest star we might find.

Slowly, Mum came to grips with Cubby's loss, but, as she was the Executrix of Cubby's estate couldn't really put it to rest easily or quickly. She cast herself forward with the business of it all. In some way, it was probably the best thing—allowing her, as it did, the chance to at least to act rather than being left in a state of silent and helpless grief. She became occupied with the solicitor, the estate agents, the paperwork, and all the other things necessary to accomplish the task at hand, knowing all the while that she was doing whatever she still could for Cubby. It took a while to tie up all those loose ends, and when it was finally done, she was spent.

How I wished I could have eased her pain somehow, but there is nothing one can do in these moments but wish and wait. They remain singular moments for each, and in ways so infinite and far beyond one's reach. In the presence of death one very surely understands what is alive in those closest to you.

I too busied myself. At the time I was preparing for final exams, my mind thoroughly occupied with swotting and worrying about how I would do. I hated exams, and if the word "test" was ever mentioned, a strange wave of panic has always washed over me. I was completely overwhelmed. The effort to study, coupled with the loss of dear Cubby, was almost too much. But, somehow, knowing, or at least trying to understand the depth of Mum's loss, I just couldn't worry her with my concerns. But the questions still loomed: What would be my next step? Where and how far would this all take me?

On top of these shifts—as always seems the case when the clouds turn a darker grey on the horizon—Mum and Dad's lease on Anncroft Road was nearing an end too, and this, I knew, was also of concern. We would need to find a new place to live. And that decision was in turn impacted this time by father's work, which had also changed.

All over England, industries were being nationalized, Dad's among them. The electrical metering facility in Buxton for which he had been nearly solely responsible in building, staffing, and painstakingly put together in all its intricacies, had been moved lock, stock, and barrel to Stockport, closer to Manchester. This too had recently meant a huge undertaking, and Dad had been increasingly involved in putting together a completely new installation that combined those of his old staff with those from a new one in place for some time.

They needed to be merged, which meant that he would now be responsible for the supervision of staff of sixty people metering the entire Northwestern Electricity Board and with a new supervisor watching over the lot. Considering these logistics alone, Mum voiced her preference for wanting to buy a house in the suburbs of Stockport, so Dad could lessen his commute and have as much time for the family as possible. And then there was Sam...

Sam had finished Buxton College three years before, moved away, and was living in another county. He visited, of course, often bringing along his new roommate, David, a divinity student. It seemed that every young man I was to meet at this point in my life was named David, but I remember this David very well, as he represented another of the last memories of life I would have before things *really* changed; and because of the trouble young men can bring no matter what name they are called.

David was intriguing, but not exactly in the ways the David with whom I was quite taken was. Nevertheless, he seemed to like me and had even started writing me letters after tagging along home with Sam at the weekends. I was flattered. He was older, and I guess I was first impressed that an older boy would take notice of me, but, actually, he was not the kind of boy I tended to like. Nevertheless, it was fun to have the attention, as well as a boy pen pal.

Our correspondence continued for some time. Being a divinity student, David always ended his letters with a Biblical scripture, which I would look up. One day, I received one with a few Xs after his signature, the usual scripture (book, chapter and verse), but, for some reason I didn't bother to look it up right away, choosing instead to leave it until later. I also left the letter out of its envelope on the end table in our living room, the last page on top.

That evening, when Dad came along to sit in his chair to read his newspaper, he happened upon the letter sitting there and picked it up. The kisses on the bottom of the page were pretty obvious and, undoubtedly, must have piqued his interest, but it was evidently, when turning his attention to the scripture that he really took special interest and got out his Bible to look it up. It read, in part: "... I will multiply your seed as the sands on the seashore..."

I actually don't know the reference to this day, and never really read the rest of it that I remember, but regarding its immediate prophecy as to its meaning where yours truly was concerned, it was interpreted as swiftly as it was deemed inappropriate, and, apparently, life as I knew it, was over. I really didn't understand, but Dad seemed to have an insight into its veiled contents that caused him to exit his chair with a roar, and the next thing I knew he was yelling in a way very unlike him for me—"KATHLEEEEEEEEEEEEN!"

Nobody called me Kathleen, except Mother—and only then when I was in very big trouble. And oh, was I in trouble this time; though for the life of me I couldn't figure out why. I came running nonetheless, and upon my appearance before him, Dad made one thing immediately clear —I was strictly forbidden to communicate with David *ever* again, divinity student or not.

After a couple minutes of assuring him that I would comply with this request (the best way of handling these things is to always, and I mean always, agree) and with *whatever* else needed be done to address whatever he was yelling about ("Yes, dad. Yes, dad. Yes...") he finally came to the realization that I had absolutely *no earthly idea* what the scripture in letter even said, and had done nothing at all to provoke its use in the letter's closing. Then, and only then, did he calm down.

The end result was simply the end of yet another budding romance, and I never really lingered on the subject to find out what Father's interpretation of it all was. I can only well imagine... I do know that soon afterward Dad had a little heart-to-heart with David, which, if I also had to guess, almost assuredly scared at least half the life out of him.

What I learned from the whole thing for certain—and it was a lesson you'd think I would have learned from the tales of Auntie Evelyn's trials and tribulations over a letter in vase years earlier—above all, never, ever, *ever* leave your personal correspondences scattered around for others to read. I will say this: at least Evelyn knew what she was in trouble for. I'm obviously still a bit foggy on my own count.

So many times in life you just can't predict what's going to happen, though we all try to mitigate our uncertainty by pretending we can. When mine seemed to present all its changes at once, I simply couldn't have realized that if I'd just allowed everything to settle, the way would become clear. I say this as there was certainly no way, at least in looking at the information available at that time, to predict what happened next, and, in my wildest dreams I could not have foretold it. It still remains quite unbelievable to me even now.

Chapter 42

Not long after Mum settled Cubby's affairs, my parents were presented with a wonderful opportunity. Dad, it turned out, had six weeks of holiday just as I approached my summer break. Sam too was at a point at which he too was free to get away, and, Mum, grieving Cubby but finally free of the responsibility of her estate, was much needing a change of scenery too. Assessing all these factors, the two of them decided it a good time for us to go on a family trip—a real break from post-wartime England and a balm to soothe Cubby's loss. And they went all in—purchasing tickets on a Trans-Canada Airlines charter flight to (drum roll if you please)... New York City! I was beyond incredulous! Before I could even say the words, "Empire State Building," it seemed we were setting off by car, in the wee hours of a Thursday morning toward the end of July 1950, to London to fly to the U.S.A.

It took all day, and we arrived at the designated spot for dropping off the car in the late afternoon, continuing on to Heathrow by a chartered bus. We'd no sooner arrived and checked in with the gate agents when it was time to board our plane, and at around 8 p.m., our scheduled flight took off—first stop, Montreal, with the final destination being New York's LaGuardia Airport.

It was obviously my first experience flying, and, as we sat on the tarmac awaiting take-off, I thought of Grandmother James, who, at least in my memories of her, always seemed to deliver advice in the form of simple edict. Replacing "learn to play the piano" with thoughts on opportunities for flight one gets: "Kathleen, if you ever get a chance to fly on an aeroplane, you simply must take it."

"Well, Granny," I thought, "Here I am on your aeroplane, ready for off to see America!" How I'd wished she were there to make one of *her* dreams come true, too.

The thing about great adventures is that they often begin in ways one least expects and just as often, much less so than one desires. For instance, shortly after clearing the shores of Scotland, we were informed by the plane's captain that we had "lost" an engine, which, I learned, meant it had ceased to function. Surely, I thought, that is bad. Quickly reassured that the plane could actually fly perfectly well on only one of its four engines if necessary (a fact I'm sure meant to inspire confidence) it remained news that actually didn't do too much for me.

In order to address the issue we made an unscheduled stop in Keflavik, Iceland, where we spent the four or five hours in the terminal waiting, as well as in eating what are known as Icelandic buns—an evidently traditional sweet snack that most cultures call a creampuff—which were both as good as they were unfamiliar.

Iceland, land of the midnight sun, was, at three o'clock in the morning, bathed in a permanent twilight that allowed us a clear view out the huge floor-to-ceiling windows of the airport lounge. So we watched, as air mechanics clad in sand-coloured overalls crawled all over our plane's afflicted engine until it appeared that all that could had been done, and announced that we would board once more. I still hadn't somehow really come to terms with this glitch, and honestly wasn't enjoying this flying business all that much thus far.

Among other truths plainly told, just before our emergency had been announced, I'd been sitting in my seat reading a story in a magazine discovered in the pocket attached to the seat in front of me about an airplane's *en route* failure that ultimately resulted in it crashing into the ocean (so much for "light travel reading!"). Shortly thereafter, this potential reality was introduced by our "stewardess" (in the parlance of those times) along with a prescribed drill we would enact in the unlikely event that such "ditching" became necessary. Questions remaining could be addressed by consulting the literature available "in the pocket of the seat in front of us." I somewhat assumed she did *not* mean the magazine article I'd been reading previously, which seemed in fact to present the exact "how-not-to handle" scenario of the event in question. Shortly thereafter, at a perfect moment to really set the delicate wheels of possibility fully in motion in my mind's eye, the engine loss was announced.

As a result of this overload of unwanted information, I now felt the need to stay awake just in case something really did happen—though what I would have done about it other than dissolve into a completely useless state of panic is anyone's guess. I think I'd decided that my consciousness might somehow help the pilot to get this thing across the ocean safely; the strength of my will alone keeping us aloft in some silent osmosis between the cockpit and myself.

After our brief, Icelandic sojourn, we took off from Keflavik bound for Montreal (about nine or ten hours, give or take), and soon thereafter were served a hot meal with all the trimmings. This did help distract me for a bit, but I ate less out of hunger than anxiety.

When we reached Montreal, we had been en route for a full thirty-six hours, and I, as the psychic co-pilot of the entire enterprise, was now completely exhausted and running on sheer nerves and adrenaline alone. Whose brilliant idea was it to go away, again? Now I just wanted to go home. Nevertheless, we'd made it to the other side of the ocean, and whatever I was doing to help the situation seemed to be working!

On the ground in Montreal, it was announced that we would be changing planes. "About time," I remember thinking. We would have about two hours to wait as our next plane was readied and its crew boarded. With all that time, I decided what we needed was a bit of a pick-me-up, so Sam and I both downed double-dip ice cream cones; huge, rich, and delicious things the likes of which we'd never seen before. It seemed that things were definitely taking a turn for the better!

Boarding our new plane, we were now really ready for the last lap of what was beginning to seem an endless journey, reassured too that it would be a relatively short hop to New York. According to those in the know—we'd "be there soon!"

Of course a brand new flight meant a brand new crew, and that meant that we started all over again... Announcements, safety instructions, resettling, and, as if food alone might just be the only thing to keep us aloft, not long after getting airborne we were offered yet *another* dinner with all the trimmings. We were already stuffed! I was certainly feeling so. But, in true English fashion, we all agreed that it would be rude to refuse or to leave the food we'd been offered untouched.

Not long after this repast, the soothing and silvery tones

of the flight attendant once again came over the plane's P.A.: "Ladies and Gentlemen, we ask that you please fasten your seat belts, as we are expecting some moderate to heavy turbulence between here and our final destination. We also remind you to please use the airsickness bags located in the pocket of the seat in front of you should you find it necessary."

It seemed that every tiding, glad or not (and thus far they had very much been the latter), pointed to the seat pockets in front of us. "*Marveilleux!*" I thought. And, then, no sooner had the announcement begun to sink in when it began not only to sink in but to rise up. With no prior flight experience with which to gauge "moderate to heavy turbulence," we had no preconceived ideas about its effects. Suddenly, we lost altitude, plummeting for a few seconds like an express lift from the 104th floor to street level, and then, bouncing back up again with as much reverse g-force as a second earlier! Now I really wanted to go home!

As a few more rounds of buffeting, plunging, dipping, correcting, tossing, bumping, and other quite violent acts of swanning about up there, all the meals and snacks I had consumed in order to comfort myself began to discomfort me instead. The ice cream and two scheduled dinners we'd eaten were now about to make quite unscheduled appearances—and soon.

We were all in the same boat, or, plane, (not that the distinction mattered in the moment), and proceeded not only to use the airsick bags in the seatbacks in front of us "as appropriate" but also, as if to use up every ounce of hospitality the airline might have left in them, by offering our meals back in the most abject and disappointing way; and then asking for more... airsick bags that is. They obliged, if not exactly happily, then, at least with dignity and measured but sympathetic gratitude.

Somehow we persevered, arriving none too soon in one piece at LaGuardia, a delicate but decidedly unflattering shade of green. From the time we had left home until the time we landed, it had taken forty-eight long and, variously, harrowing, tedious, exhausting (any and every adjective applies) hours of travel. And, on top of it, I had slept none of it. I no longer had anything left in me—either literally or figuratively. I was, as the saying goes, dog tired, and could barely stand up anymore.

We de-planed, and after going through U.S. customs waited for our arranged contact to meet us in the main terminal. I was, at this point, barely conscious and literally falling asleep on my feet, finally coming to horizontal rest in a heap atop one of the big suitcases we had. As we waited, some nearby Americans took pity on me and asked Dad if they could bring me "a Coke" to settle my stomach. Dad asked what that was, and they said, "It's our national drink!" Adding, "She'll like it," and, "it'll make her feel better." Dad thanked them for their kindness and accepted. Upon its arrival, he coaxed me in trying it. I took a sip. It was just *awful*! I mean I knew I was tired and even perhaps a bit more than out of sorts, but if *this* was their national drink, the poor Yanks were in deep trouble! Nevertheless, I took a few more sips and, lo and behold, after a little bit, the man was right—my stomach indeed began to settle down, and I began to feel better. I closed my eyes and fell back into a deep sleep again on top of the suitcase.

I awakened to the sight of two beautiful American girls standing nearby. I looked them over, groggily. *So, this is what they really look like in colour*, I thought… absolutely stunning! Wearing sundresses with spaghetti straps over their tanned, bare shoulders they were the picture of all those glossy magazine ads full of American teenagers and movie stars. The absolute pictures of health; hair coiffed, faces carefully made up… I had never even seen a sundress before. I was wearing a sensible two-piece tan suit with a high-necked blouse, with matching and equally sensible Cuban-heeled shoes, and, of course, gloves for travelling. They turned to look at us, and I heard one of them say, in rather cruel but undoubtedly honest assessment: "Wow, look at them… Wonder where they're from? They look kind of funny."

However honest, however true, that rude little remark made me feel even worse. I'm sure we looked "funny," not to mention completely overdressed for July in New York with our drab clothes and pale-as-ghosts-from-the-long-journey-and-years-of-limited-diet-and-sunshine pallor. We must have looked an absolutely miserable lot. All I knew was that I wanted to crawl into the nearest hole and sleep, and sleep, and sleep… Luckily, before I collapsed completely from exhaustion *and* embarrassment our contact arrived, and, at last, I thought, rest was in sight.

But, it would not be so simple. Instead, thinking we would be hungry after such a long trip, and operating on the knowledge that we came from still-rationed Europe, the dear, sweet, thoughtful man got us into his car and took us immediately into Manhattan to a place called "The Automat," where he sat us all at a table in the corner and said, enthusiastically, as he turned on his heel—"Wait here. I'll be right back!"

He returned at the helm of a rolling cart with three full tiers overflowing with plates of food. Everything, from sandwiches to meat and potatoes, vegetables to various kinds of salad and fruit, desserts of every kind; everything you could imagine and all for us. I had never seen so much food in one place! Oh, dear...

My first thought was that it must have cost him a fortune, and, how do you tell someone who, out of the goodness of their heart, wants to feed you because you look so pale and starved?

With a warning look from Mum and Dad that implied that our graciousness must outweigh any overriding feelings of any other kind, we again quietly started to eat to show it. Periodically, in fact what seemed about every few minutes, I would, still largely suffering from airsickness and lack of sleep, excuse myself to go to the ladies room, where I quietly yet so very appreciatively threw up. I would then, as cheerfully as possible, return to the table to smile and eat some more. I did this a few times and until I thought I really was going to pass out. Eventually, our host, realizing we simply couldn't eat any more and with most of the food gone, offered to take us to our lodgings.

We had done our bit. We'd held up the side. It was quite a welcome to America... the land of plenty, and then some. He packed us back into his car and we left The Automat, finally on our way to our destination for the next six weeks. And what a six weeks it would be!

Chapter 43

America. Everything we saw and everywhere we went overwhelmed us with its sheer size and energy; its *extravaganza* of sensation. An explosion of lights, sounds, and an exuberant overabundance of everything and, seemingly, anything one could imagine all at the same time! The life I had lived in our blacked-out world with its drab and scarce food, rationed make-do fashions, and practically none of what seemed the "luxuries" in life, was suddenly thrown into a stark and blinding light.

To say it was an extreme culture shock is to make one of the grandest understatements imaginable. Standing in the centre of Times Square with its flashing, pulsating bands of light I just stood rooted, looking up until my neck ached and almost requiring I be physically pushed to keep up with the rest of the group. I couldn't take my eyes off the moving neon signs with their up-to-the-minute news bulletins of what was happening all over the world circling around them, and the infamous Camel cigarette sign with its smoking man puffing out rings of smoke overhead... All the traffic, car horns blaring and crowds moving busily and purposefully through the streets... what sights... what sounds. How awed I was of this spectacular scene, and how I quickly fell in love with this amazing place. I was completely dazzled.

Our hosts too were wonderful, generous, kind, and giving of themselves as they enjoyed showing us around New York: The Empire State Building, The Statue of Liberty, Central Park, Radio City Music Hall (with its incredible Rockettes), from Wall Street and up to St. Patrick's Cathedral, the Circle Line boat ride around Manhattan, The Metropolitan Museum of Art... What adventures!

The restaurants and delicatessens with their incredible sandwiches piled up with two inches of meat alone on each; more meat on one sandwich than a ration back home would provide a family for a whole week. This was Utopia!

I even rode on the back of a brand new Harley Davidson motorcycle wearing a Harley Davidson peaked cap—just like Marlon Brando in *The Wild One*, but a few years ahead of even that! We rode across the George Washington Bridge and up the Palisades to follow the Hudson River to the parking lot of a nightclub called "The Riviera," just to stop and gaze back at New York's monumental skyline.

Then, finally, we rode back to New Jersey and the house where we were staying about eight miles outside the city. We also travelled by car to northern New Jersey, with its acres of beautiful wooded scenery and the place where three states met—New Jersey, New York, and Pennsylvania. We began to realize how vast America really was compared to our little island.

The six weeks sped by like a rollercoaster, and, before we even knew it were getting ready to go back to England. As we prepared ourselves, very much in the thrall of this completely overwhelming experience, it was then that my brother Sam suddenly announced he had made a momentous decision.

Unbeknownst to us while this whirlwind sightseeing trip had been taking place and we were all deep in a haze of all things "America," Sam had been making inquiries about attending a college located in a place called Ithaca, in upstate New York! He had done the legwork and even arranged an interview (really just a formality)—he was all but accepted as a student already! There was only one hitch—the U.S. Immigration and Naturalization Service (INS) would not let him extend his visitor's visa, and he would have to return to his country of origin.

As Sam had been born in Canada and was officially a *Canadian* citizen, he would have to return *there* to apply for a visa extension to enter the U.S. legally again. Sam hadn't been in Canada since he was barely three years old, yet, he would now have to take up residence for at least six months before he was even eligible to apply. Nevertheless, he had made up his mind and a plan went into place that resulted in him leaving us behind just as we got ready to leave and heading for Toronto with a school-chum-to-be.

We were positively floored... on our heels, with only questions and speculation to carry on with. When we would even see each other again was anybody's guess, and for all of us, especially me, this was a somewhat devastating end to our otherwise joyful and carefree holiday. I felt like my right arm had been removed—torn off! Dad, surprised by the immediacy of the decision, was still somewhat stoic about the whole thing. If anybody understood up and jumping at a chance to explore points unknown he certainly did, and fathers, in general, seem to deal with children leaving much better than mothers. Ultimately, he understood Sam's decision having done much the same thing in his earlier years. But Mum was stunned. Not wanting to stand in the way of either his future or his wishes, she put on her brave face. But I could tell, and I knew better. Having said that, it would still take me many years to fully realize how very deeply that separation had affected her.

Adversity brings people closer together like nothing else. We were a team, a blood team. The four of us had endured the war together and it had still not been so long prior to forget about that. My mother seemed absolutely stricken for a while; the golden-haired little boy she had nurtured through thick and thin, though now tall, handsome, and a charming young man who could reduce her to putty with a smile or kiss on the cheek, was hard to let go. I watched her face as we boarded our plane to return to England. Her eyes misted with tears as she looked back. I knew what she was thinking, and, even more so, feeling. Would he be all right? How would he fare in these strange places? I don't think Sam ever realized how she felt at that moment, how very worried and sad she was to see him go and her little brood broken up.

It was a long and quiet trip home for me minus one. My seat companion, not there, even his constant teasing was missed. Everything had happened so fast it was hard to grasp, and I knew that when we were finally home an even colder reality would settle in. It was a much bigger distraction from the long journey back home than I needed to be sure, and I think I would've taken "moderate to severe turbulence" over missing my brother; maybe only barely, but still.

~~~

Back in Buxton, everything did indeed seem a bit empty without my big brother. Sam, my confidante, my pal… I felt more alone then, and the house was no longer alive with his laugh and perverse, yet wonderful, sense of humour. I would
~~~

walk past his room and look. All his things were there just as he had left them as though he would be coming in the front door any moment, to yell, "Hey, Nipper, where are you?" I tried not to show my sadness if only for the sake of Mum not needing my own on top of hers. All we had now were the letters and snapshots he sent along and, mercifully, he was diligent about those and they did flow with some regularity.

I returned to Cavendish for my final months and somehow missing a spark. I knew shortly I too would be moving on with my life, but just couldn't quite envision its path. The impact made by our time in America was still in the forefront of my mind, and the impression it made had changed my perspective, coloured my thinking—vividly.

Mum and Dad too seemed always to be having a host of serious discussions about what to do about everything too. The lease was now really ready to expire at Bayswater, and Dad was doing a lot of commuting for work every day already. They were definitely thinking more than ever about buying a house that would put him closer to it. It was a turning point, all right, but I had no earthly idea how big the turn could really be. I was about to find out.

On holiday in New York

Sam and I outside host's home in New Jersey 1950

Chapter 44

I simply couldn't believe my ears—moving, I expected, but… to the *U.S.A.?!* You *must be joking!* My parents had actually said it out loud! They were thinking about it and wondered what I thought… What did I think?!?! Well, I thought it would be "a great new beginning," no, it—*the greatest new beginning ever!*

That shining land across the ocean with all its glitz and glamour, light and colour, a million things to do all the time, had somehow seduced us all, and my parents were actually considering moving there. My job, as I saw it, was now to influence them in any, and as many ways, as possible to do just that! But, at the end of the day, I didn't really need to do too much at all... They were already sold and the decision all but made.

As it was, we were all still blinded by the illusion we carried from our brief but jam-packed visit. In addition, beyond the shiny or superficial aspects that clearly held us in their sway, was the fact that Sam was now there too. It was really nearly a foregone conclusion the second the idea popped up, and, once again, before anyone even knew it, arrangements were being made and the momentum building.

Beyond the logistics of moving house, those arrangements included the long and laborious task of the paperwork involved in emigrating. The preliminary application itself was an extraordinary thing, so long, in fact, that when Dad stood with it in his hand raised as far above his head as he could reach, it cascaded down to drag on the floor—and he was 6' 3"! This completed, we all then had to go to Manchester to meet with a representative from the American Consul to be sworn in. As he did with everyone, he asked Dad and Mum why they wanted to move to America. They answered that they simply felt there was more opportunity for us all in the U.S. than in either England or anywhere in Europe at the present time. They were right.

While we hadn't been to the continent, everything in England certainly still felt like it had been flattened in one way or another, so much so that, in many parts of our island, it was hard to imagine how long it would take to restore the basics. Having seen "the plenty" America represented first-hand, they wanted that the most for me and for Sam—much more I think than themselves. They were approaching a time in their lives when, if anything, they wanted things to slow down a bit. Emigrating across the Atlantic was probably no remedy for that particular desire, and, while we had all taken to it easily on our trip, America was still a vastly different culture.

This was a *very* major decision to say the least. It was also another example of their truly unselfish nature—uprooting themselves once again to start all over; had it been me in their shoes I sincerely doubt I would have even done it. They'd far more to lose than I did as a teenager. But, fortunately, I was the beneficiary of such a bold move, and in spurring them on I applied myself to the task indeed and with gusto.

I have, occasionally, and in more retrospective times,

wondered if I did the right thing. I've wondered, as nearly everyone does at some point their lives, what our lives might've held had I not been so supportive and dug my heels in to stay in England. But, truthfully, besides my lobbying, Sam had already nearly done his six months in Canada and was about to return to the U.S. to begin his schooling in Ithaca. The thought that we could be going to the same place he would be, and meeting up with him at the same time we were resettling, reconnecting with him and eventually attending his graduation was so encouraging and compelling. It carried a lot of weight beyond what I'm sure were my particular contributions to the discussion.

And so the move began. The monumental task of disposing of household goods and going through all the things connected with just plain living completely took over our lives. We whittled possessions down to those things we could take with us on a Cunard liner, Mum packing as much as she could into large trunks. I went through my things, emerging with a few bits and pieces I just couldn't bear to part with—my treasured and worn copy of the literary triumvirate *Jane Eyre, Wuthering Heights,* and *Shirley*, and a few other things like sheet music, sketches, some relatively new clothing items that had been bought for our first trip to America the prior year.

As you might well imagine, my one real sadness was that my beloved piano would not make the journey. It was a sombre moment watching the rear doors of the furniture van that came for it close and watching it pull away to go back to the saleroom. Beyond the fact that I loved it, of course, it also brought back my many memories of its history in our home, and the happy day of its delivery… and Cubby…

As we were packing up, exams and Speech Day loomed at

Cavendish, and it seemed that the life I knew was all being sorted out and no going back. The twinges of sadness I had too in leaving my safe cocoon there were only made bearable by my anticipation of the brightly exploding fireworks that I envisioned ahead of us in America.

It was that prospect that kept me going through all the tearful goodbyes and heartfelt wishes of relatives and close friends whom I loved so very much. Uncle Joe and Aunt Vinie, Uncle George and Auntie Gertie, David, Mum and Dad's closest friend, Stan, and countless others who had been there for us, for me, over the years. Rose and Mrs. Lockett were very hard to leave behind, but then they, my teachers, and, notably and especially my headmistress, Miss Mansell, were all so encouraging and reassuring in speculating on all the wonderful opportunities they knew lay ahead—urging me to go on with my education in America because they believed I could, and would, do great things in my life.

When we sang our school song for the final ceremony that would separate me from Cavendish forever, I knew I would never hear or feel those words in the same way again, and I nearly came apart. But with each tearful goodbye there was also the promise of a new greeting, and I focused my mind's eye there—ahead.

Chapter 45

The day came. We spent our last night in Buxton, once again setting out early in the morning hours one day in March 1951, but this time to Liverpool. No flying this time to New York, we were booked instead aboard the Cunard line's *R.M.S. Scythia*.

We stayed overnight at a very English hotel near the docks in Liverpool, and with an iconic and fitting maritime name—*The Lord Nelson*. Our luggage had already been transported to the ship, and so, upon rising the following morning, we spent a little time looking around the port before we boarded at three o'clock. We said goodbye to some of Mum and Dad's friends who came to see us off.

Soon after 3 p.m., March 10, 1951, we stood at the rail on Scythia's deck, watching as we unmoored from the Liverpool dock. A tugboat manoeuvred the ship from its slip to accompany us out to the open seas. We waved to our friends gathered below, emotions a jumble as we navigated our own courses in our minds, each beginning to embrace futures full of whatever we imagined them to hold. Traveling great distances like these was neither as easy nor affordable as it is now, and people didn't just pop over the Atlantic at the drop of a hat like today. I stood on that deck and wondered silently if I would ever see England again, and then, if I looked back, if I'd turn into a pillar of salt like in the Biblical tale of Lot's wife. I laughed at the thought—we weren't exactly leaving Sodom and Gomorrah. But we were leaving the only home I'd known. I turned to watch as England's shores receded and darkened until there was nothing left to see but a line on the horizon.

Eventually England disappeared from view, and with it my past and everything I had learned and loved about life thus far. Silently, it slipped behind me, out of sight. As the realisation welled up in me, I suddenly wondered with a new and acute urgency just what in the world we were doing, and I remember, even if just for a few moments, thinking that if I could have turned the ship back I would have. Instead, I sighed and recited to myself the Latin phrase, *jacta alea est*—the die is cast. It was. We had cast it to the wide ocean between our old life and a new one, and we would see what its roll would bring. I felt ready to find out, and lucky enough to be with those I loved on the journey.

~~~

The *R.M.S. Scythia* was, by all standards of the day, a huge floating hotel and, in true Cunard fashion, a beautiful one at that. The wood in the ship's many salons was polished to its highest brilliance and its floors all shone. There was marble and brass everywhere the eye settled, its grand curved stairways thickly carpeted in rich colour. It had theatres, ballrooms, exquisite dining rooms, movie theatres, game rooms, lounges, libraries, outdoor and indoor swimming pools, even a colonnade with shops to browse and buy both useful and pretty things. There were plenty of games to play, shuffleboard being the most popular, and a throng of deck stewards ready to suggest activities and cater to one's every
~~~

wish. If you were to sit down on a deck chair, one of them would appear as if conjured, to tuck you up in a blanket and bring you whatever your heart desired: drinks, snacks, magazines.

Within a half-hour of leaving Liverpool, a bell rang (back to those familiar bells again), to summon us to the lounge on the main deck for the first afternoon tea aboard. Locking at my watch, I noted they were right on the spot, four o'clock, that magical hour when the only *civilized* thing to do is have a cup of tea and delicious scones, preferably oozing with butter or clotted cream. Yet, despite the hour and the inclination, somewhere deep in my being something had me feeling slightly dizzy and disoriented. The ship's deck kept coming up to meet my feet as I tried to walk and it made me feel as though I was staggering—clomping along with little control of my gait and giving me a very odd sensation.

It turned out that were on the Irish Sea, which, I was told after, has long been touted as among the roughest stretches of water on the planet; one that even experienced sailors would rather not cross because of its notorious reputation for causing seasickness. I was certainly no sailor, experienced or otherwise, nor was I any exception to the sea's effects, and, by the time we were an hour or so out of Liverpool was already feeling sick. Mum and Dad, who had earned their sea legs and seemed just fine, understood completely what was happening to me and how I felt. Mum took me down to our cabin, and cared for me as I spent the next two days feeling as sick as I had ever felt in my whole life. I very simply—as she herself had years before on her journey to Australia—wanted to die.

Finally, a few mornings later when it appeared that my stomach had settled down, we ventured out to the dining salon to test my tolerance for breakfast. As we approached, a handsome young steward in a white uniform with gold braid held the door to open for me, giving me a rather bemused look that made me wonder what he might be thinking. I shrugged it off as we made our way to our assigned table, set for eight. Sitting directly across from me was a lady from Canada with two children, a boy and a girl. The little boy looked to be about eighteen months old, and was seated in a high chair as his mother fed him. Doing her best to navigate each spoonful of runny soft-boiled egg into his mouth with somewhat dubious success meant that the entire lower half of his precious little face was covered with yellow, gooey yolk. I didn't really have much time to process it in my mind as my stomach lurched. I made a beeline for the door to find the bemused young steward once again holding it open, this time with a big grin on his face as he directed my exit to the appropriate destination, "Turn left, Miss, first door on your right..."

Some minutes later I emerged from the ladies room to make my way back to the dining salon, leaning weakly on the walls the whole way. The steward was still there and greeted me with the answer to my earlier question about the look on his face: "I knew the moment I saw you that you weren't going to be at breakfast long; you were a glorious shade of green." Well, I certainly felt green in every way one could.

While all this was playing out, Dad had gone up on deck to take a constitutional around the promenade. Speaking with a deck steward, he shared how sick I'd been thus far, saying that it didn't really look like I was going to be able to come out of our cabin for very long at the rate it was going. The steward assured him he would "take care of it, sir," and, with no further ado, came down to our cabin to tell Mum to deliver me to him personally on deck as soon as possible. My only thought was that he was probably (and mercifully so) planning to push me overboard for being so miserable and giving both his ship and the line a bad name. Nevertheless, I reported as requested to find that, on the contrary, he was the soul of compassion, and my demise—however compassionate I thought might be the case at the time—would not be necessary for his, Cunard's, or my own benefit.

First he tucked me up in a woolly blanket in the first available deck chair he could find, and then brought me an apple—peeled and cut into delicate slices—on a beautiful china plate. I politely declined. I couldn't possibly even think about eating anything. I was clearly dying, and, as if to illustrate this fact, got up and ran for the ships railing to demonstrate just what illness was killing me. Dad, who had been observing, was beside me in an instant, holding me back from leaning so far over it with his hands and reinforcing the gesture with his admonishments: "What are you doing, Kath, do you *want* to fall in the ocean?"

"Oh, Dad, yes, I do… just let me go, I feel so sick."

The young steward stepped in. "Nothing of the kind! Just come with me. You'll be fine in no time." He led me back to the deck chair and tucked me up once more, this time sitting with me on the edge to feed me the apple piece by piece. As he did so, he began to tell me that if I ate all of the apple, it would be the end of my sea-sickness for good and I could just simply enjoy the rest of the trip. Somehow, with his calm confidence bolstering my efforts, I managed to do just that. And then a deep tiredness crept over me. He brought me a pillow and watched over me as the sound of the waves and the rolling of the ship soothed me off to sleep in the fresh sea air.

He was so right. When I awoke, I felt like my old self again; absolutely fine. Tempted by a man with an apple, now there's a twist... and there was nothing profoundly lost in this bargain, instead I'd found something of a salvation—*my* sea legs.

It turned out his name was Jack, and he had been a steward all of his short adult life. He certainly demonstrated that he knew what he was talking about. He'd cured me, and he was right again—it was a wonderful trip from there. I was ever so grateful! From then on, he took Mum, Dad, and I on as his pet project, waiting on us hand and foot until we reached New York ten days later and, after which, I just wanted to take him with us everywhere.

Impossible of course, and besides, Jack had a sweetheart who was a stewardess—aboard *The Queen Mary*. They saw each other rarely because of their ship's schedules, but, he told me that sometimes, when the two ships were opposite one other crossing the Atlantic, they knew exactly what time it would occur and he would go to the radio operator on the bridge to radio back and forth with her, and—this was the best and most romantic part—when the ships were within both a few miles and visual distance of one another, to flash signals to each other too. Oh my, so lovely, I thought, and then how it gave a new and wholly opposite meaning to the phrase, "two ships that pass in the night." Speaking of...

There was yet another steward, a young, golden-haired boy in the salon who also came to our assistance every time we went to dine. He always made sure too that he exchanged a few words with me, enquiring about my health and fussing over me as he seated us. One day, he took me aside and asked me to meet him on the afterdeck at 10:00 p.m. at the end of his shift. He said we could dance in the moonlight—an offer that sounded so very nice, and my heart beat fast with anticipation. After all, I loved to dance, and what could be more romantic than doing so with a handsome young man in a white uniform with gold braid on his sleeves and shoulders while the moon shone down on the ocean and the ship's lanterns gleamed and swayed in the breeze. I was tremendously excited! A shipboard romance for little me!

However, it soon became apparent that there were forces conspiring to stop this little interlude. Later that same morning at eleven o'clock, the bell rang and the Deck Stewards began to serve hot soup to anyone who happened to be around. As I was being tucked up in my deck chair for "elevenses" (as much a tradition as afternoon tea), Jack, on duty that morning, stopped to bring me mine and to exchange pleasantries.

"You're looking extremely happy this morning," he began.

"Good morning! It's a lovely day. And you're right, I am happy," I beamed back.

"And why is that?" he inquired.

I answered, cryptically, "Oh, nothing really... I just have a little secret, that's all."

"Ah! A little secret... And what might *that* be? You can tell me. I won't tell a soul."

"I'm not supposed to! Besides, you'll tell Mum and Dad."

"Oh, I see! No Mum and Dad... that does sound intriguing. But, truly, I *promise* I won't tell. What *is* it? I'm dying to know."

He began to break me down, because, of course I simply wanted to tell, just *had* to tell someone!

"Well, all right," I said. "I've met someone."

"Ohhhhhh," said Jack. "And just who is this *someone*?"

"Well, we met in the dining salon...," I offered.

"Ah! A young passenger..."

"No," I countered quickly.

"A crewmember? Not a crewmember," he intoned with more than slight suspicion.

"Yes, as a matter of fact, he is a member of the crew just like you; he's a steward from the dining salon, and he's *so* nice. He's invited me to meet him on the afterdeck tonight to dance in the moonlight... Isn't that *exciting*!?"

Jack's demeanour changed slightly, uncomfortably, and he looked slightly concerned, even suspicious, and asked in a somewhat pointed tone: "Who is he? What's his name? You must tell me."

As Jack said this, he began to look even more grave and even began to frown.

"His name is Terry," I said. We're going to dance in the moonlight... What are you getting so upset about?"

Jack, suddenly very avuncular, said sharply, "Kath, I'm afraid you can't go," adding, "I'll have a word with him to tell him you won't be along."

"You will *not*!" I insisted. "It's none of your business! You're not my father."

He may not have been, but he certainly was beginning to sound like him. "Please listen, young lady..." Jack said, lowering both his voice and gaze as he spoke, "He's a sailor and you're a young lady. I simply can't let this rendezvous occur."

"Oh, don't be silly!" I said. "He isn't going to throw me overboard or anything!"

But, instead of backing down, Jack's tenacity increased. "You simply mustn't meet him, Kath. Please trust me. You just *mustn't*. I know about these things, and I'm only looking out for you," reiterating again in his plea with emphasis on the last word: "He's a *sailor*. Kath, *please*, you must trust me in this."

And I did trust him, but I was actually growing fairly indignant at being handled like this, and now, my glowing fantasy of just moments before was quickly being turned grim and decidedly less happy... I was confused and frustrated, and my retort to Jack was something like: "Well, actually, I *don't* know about these things and, I think, maybe, I'd actually like to find out for myself for a change!"

Jack's response came back swiftly, unswayed, and immediately full of admonishment: "This is neither the time nor the place *for you to find out,* Kath… *please* let me take care of this. I know you may not understand why it's necessary, but believe me when I tell you that I do and it is…"

I only dug in further: "I don't want it 'taken care of,' thank you… I wish I'd never told you in the first place!"

At this, Jack softened a bit and took a slightly different tack: "But I'm so glad you *did.*" He sighed, looked down and began slowly: "Look, Kath, you're still very young and so very innocent. I have grown fond of you and your parents in this short time, and I'm asking you to please, just trust me on this… I would never steer you wrong. What I'm saying is really and truly with your own good in mind. Please…"

Oh boy, where had I heard *that* before… Everyone seemed *always* to be "doing things for my own good." Why didn't they just let me grow up and make my own mistakes! Now, someone I hardly even knew was laying down the law and it felt positively claustrophobic.

Jack continued his campaign in no uncertain terms: "Kath, sailors are, when all's said and done and beyond pretty uniforms and gold braids, more often than not rough men, my dear. They've been around. You have not. I know he's handsome, charming, seems very sweet, and to you it's all very exciting—but, I'm telling you nearly without reservation that he's probably about as rotten to the core as they come."

Well. Terrific. Now Jack was my *mother, father,* and my uncle. He was *so*… adamant! But then, I began to soften, and Jack's message began to sink in. I knew he was a good and kind man. I knew he didn't want anything from me and only wanted for me to be happy. Maybe I *should* listen.

Strangely, the thing that truly convinced me to consider his point of view, above all, was that Jack, like my father, was a Freemason. He and my Dad had spoken about their shared membership in the longstanding fraternal order. My father had remained quite devoted to many of its tenets and principals, and, as Jack held them too, would not and, indeed could not, steer either me or my family wrong. It was duty. Bound by it, he had to take my interests to heart. It was indeed a strange element to burst my romantic bubble and to end the little movie I was starring in in my own head, but it convinced me nonetheless.

The words came out of my mouth slowly yet with utter resignation, and a fair amount of disappointment: "All right. You win. I won't go." I said, followed fairly quickly by a broadcast of my next pressing concern, "Are you going to tell my father?"

Jack smiled and shook his head. "No. I'm not. I promised I wouldn't tell anyone your secret and I won't tell him either. It'll be ours alone, and thank you for hearing me out... I know it's disappointing, and you won't have any way of knowing the consequences of not following through with your plan, but you have my word that you certainly won't regret anything in the decision afterward. And, I also do know this young Terry chap fairly well... I simply don't want you to be hurt."

And so as it came to pass, it was the beginning and the end of my beautiful romantic shipboard evening of dancing in the moonlight. Talk about "two ships passing in the night." I was still on my own and didn't even get the night! Why did I *always* seem so destined to do the right thing? Just lucky, I guess.

Despite this minor soap opera, somehow the *Scythia*

continued on its course across the vast Atlantic on schedule. We received the ship's newspaper each day with all the news of a world from which we seemed so cut off, taking it all in as we sat in our deck chairs, sipping tea, everything out there on land so very far away. It was wonderful and we wanted for nothing.

As we were travelling off-season, it was at this point in our crossing when Dad and I calculated we must be nearing the point in the Northern Atlantic where the *Titanic* had met its icy fate so many April's before—what a horror to imagine on such a vast and lonely ocean. Of course, no sooner did we have this realisation it seemed when a cry rose up from atop the huge mast above. I looked up to the crow's nest and turned to ask Jack what the man up there was shouting about. "He's on the lookout for icebergs. March and April are iceberg season, and we have a watch up there day and night." Evidently, during those months huge hunks of traveling ice began to melt and make slightly smaller chunks, which then break off into the currents that push them into the shipping lanes. I kept an eye on that chap up there from then on, and while we saw no icebergs, we did hit what turned out to be a rather violent storm, or, rather, it hit us.

Talk about learning the real meaning of another nautical phrase, "batten down the hatches!" Everything that was loose and not "battened," the storm removed swiftly and decisively from the decks—chairs, tables, you name it. If it wasn't lashed or fixed to something it washed overboard. The doors leading out to the promenade were all locked and everyone had to stay indoors. Below decks in our cabins, we were told to make sure any loose items were secured as well. We could hear the luggage in the cabin above us as it slid from one side of the room to the other—shhhaathump... shhhhaa-thump—back and forth, back and forth, throughout the night. Needless to say, we had quite a sleepless one that night. I tried to sleep in the top bunk of our cabin with my arm stuck through a big loop attached to the wall to keep me from falling out of bed, the ship rolling and roiling side to side, fore to aft, and in all directions at the *same* time it seemed.

Ships in those days did not have the stabilizers affixed to them like today's do, so the rolling of which they were capable was incredible. Just walking down a ship's corridor could be a unique experience, as it tilted one way while you didn't, and made it seem as if one were on a ride in an amusement park.

When the storm finally abated, we all flocked out onto the decks to drink in the sunshine and vistas of the once again serene, vast, and beautiful ocean stretching around us in every direction. It made one feel sometimes as though you were living on your own island completely removed from reality, as its waves moved the huge liner gently up and down. By now I had even begun to be able to roll along with the swells. A valuable lesson both in fact and in metaphor... by the time we hit the dock in New York after twelve days aboard, I had gained the rolling gait of a sailor and it felt strange *without* the ground coming up to meet me.

I am always amazed at how our bodies adjust to strange circumstances and, as in every aspect of our lives, we make so many oft-unnoticed or conscious adjustments to go on, to survive, adapt, change and even thrive. They used to recommend sea voyages to anyone suffering from a prolonged bout of illness or even *ennui*. I see why. Once I got over being so sick, I thoroughly enjoyed it. It was completely relaxing getting away from the world and its stresses, and I would, at that point, have been just as completely content to stay aboard ship to keep sailing around the world—maybe, I thought, *I* could be a sailor! Wouldn't that be something! It would mean always having a real destination while never really having a home, or, maybe the other way around.

Whatever the case, we were nearing our destination *and* our new home. It was time to put fantasies of moonlight dances and faraway romances away to see whether the U.S.A. was up to the very real task of being just that, our home—let's hope, I thought. It was a long way back now, and I couldn't swim.

Our last night aboard the *Scythia* I lay in my bunk with so many questions about where, when, what we would find as we made our lives in this new country. I still also wondered if or when I would ever see England again. I would of course, but it would be, sadly, far too many years. I think if I'd known that then it would've saddened me far too deeply. As the old truism goes—one never really appreciates or misses something until one no longer has it, and it reminded me of an old poem Uncle Joe would often recite that has always seemed *apropos* to this most basic foible of collective human disposition: "As a rule, man's a fool / when it's hot he wants it cool / when it's cool he wants it hot / wanting what he hasn't got." Truer words, as they say, have never been spoken.

I finally fell asleep, awakening well before dawn when the steward brought our morning tea and summoned us to breakfast. This was the day we would land. This would be our first day in America. I thought of the thousands of immigrants before us who must have shared the same feelings of excitement along with their fears of the unknown as they prepared to face this new continent.

Around five o'clock on the morning on March 23, 1951, the *Scythia* dropped anchor just outside of New York harbour to await boarding by U.S. Customs officials. We went out on deck after breakfast just as the sun rose and saw the whole harbour around us aglow. Even the water seemed to radiate an orange light from its depths to meet with the hue of the sky above.

Ellis Island lay ahead, a place I had heard much about, and where so many immigrants were either welcomed and housed or turned back. I hoped there was nothing to keep us out... I thought about the long form Dad had held out a few months before and hoped there were no anomalies, only to be distracted by something else seconds later. That's when I saw *her*—standing tall, stately, elegant and bathed in that pure orange sunrise—the Lady of the Harbour, the Statue of Liberty, in all her glory. She was simply breath-taking, awe-inspiring, extraordinarily beautiful with her beacon held high against the New York skyline. "Give me your tired, your poor, your huddled masses..."

Seeing her for the first time is a sight I will never forget. I was moved profoundly and remember even now how the hot tears welled up in my eyes as I longed for both a past now gone and a future as uncertain and obscure as anything I could—or more accurately—could not imagine. She was the symbol. She reminded me of the hope of this new beginning, this new adventure, this new history. One that had begun simply with the act of sailing away, but undoubtedly full of many simple, and not so simple, times ahead. Large, small—if indeed histories for those who must live them are ever so to them—humble or great, it didn't matter, but never simple. Mine would be one I would help write with my family. One I would write for myself too. My childhood and the life that it had contained was now and truly coming to its end.

I raised my eyes up to keep looking up at her and realized, somehow, that I was no longer looking through the eyes of a child.

On board Cunard Liner R.M.S.
Scythia en route to New York

With Canadian shipmate
& her two children

Postcard of Cunard ship

Through our cabin porthole anchored off the South coast of Ireland.

Sailing past The Statue of Liberty in New York Harbour

The "Americanization" of Kathy

Epilogue

After a half a lifetime spent pursuing my "American Dream," in November 1997 found myself sitting aboard a British Airways 777 at Colorado's Denver International Airport, bound, at last and again, for England. This was to be a pilgrimage, and as pilgrimages have been for time immemorial, an act of faith and hope for what one might find. It seemed that so many I knew had urged me not to go back ("you can't go home again!"), that I would be disillusioned and nothing would be the same. "Just leave it alone and remember it as it was..." but, I simply had to. I needed to at least try to return to my roots and was finally filled to the point of not being able to put off the desire to revisit my childhood haunts any longer.

Another adventure ahead, this time one that would, paradoxically, take me distinctly more into the past than the future. What would I find? How would it make me feel? My excitement of finding out equally mixed with the anxiety of knowing for certain. This time it was a ten-hour, non-stop flight—no more forty-hour journeys or twelve days by ship. I still hate flying, but let's face it, it was really the only way to get there and I was more afraid to not go than I was to follow through.

We got settled in and reached altitude, and after everyone was fed (some things don't change), the flight attendants pulled the shades and the cabin became quiet and felt a little warmer. I thought I would sleep a while, but sleep did not come… too excited. I reached for the magazine in the pocket of the seat back in front of me, and then thought better of it…

After the long night, we were suddenly circling London Gatwick and awaiting permission to land. It was a Friday, 7 a.m. GMT, and evidently a busy one with cloud cover complicating things as well. Everything was "stacked up." We circled a few times, our holding pattern taking us into the skies off the southern coast of England and above the English Channel. We were high up and, with the clouds, couldn't see much.

Finally, cleared for landing, we made our approach and dropped in altitude. Descending now I began to see glimpses of brilliant green landscape below. I looked down at the patchwork quilt of England's emerald green fields, lined with hedgerows and dotted with sheep. Nowhere on earth are there so many sheep—except perhaps New Zealand—but these lawnmowers of England were still keeping the landscape neat and tidy, the lush fields looked manicured and tended through their appetites.

By the time we deplaned, went through customs, and collected our luggage, it was raining cats and dogs. Ah yes, how had I somehow forgotten the rain in England? We hailed a cab to our hotel, having arranged to spend the first night on the outskirts of London, from where we were to pick up a rental van the next morning to make our trek northwest to Buxton. Taxi drivers are somehow the same everywhere and, despite the pouring rain, ours proceeded on the M-25 at breakneck speed—I could see the speedometer clocking in at 85mph, yet cars were still passing us up as if we were standing still.

After a good night's rest and a full English breakfast, we took delivery of our rental van, loaded up the luggage, and headed north on the M-1. The beauty of the English countryside now up close, still overwhelmed me and filled me with joy. After leaving the M-1 we veered to the northwest through picturesque villages on winding country lanes, and as we drove, I began to recognize names of towns I had forgotten, and the past began to flood back to me. I was *home* again, actually *here* where my life had begun; what a feeling it was.

In two-and-a-half hours' time we reached Buxton. Driving into town I knew exactly what street we were on and where it was going to take us. And, with my memories guiding us, I became joyously aware that contrary to what everyone had warned, *it hadn't really changed*! So many of the names, little pubs, hotels, businesses we drove by were the same, and I had a feeling of almost weightlessly stepping back in time to the place where I felt like *ME*... I was not a tourist, nor was I a visitor. I was a native.

And then the memories that came were even more specific... there I was, looking once again at the house where I lived during the war. I could hear my mother's voice: "Kath, hurry, you'll miss your bus!"... "Kath, button your coat, it's so cold."... "Kath, keep your mouth closed or this fog will get into your lungs." Well, "fog," in those days was really pollution from the coal fires of the potteries, (china factories) twenty miles away; heavy, yellow and thick, not really fog at all. I was struck that, here it was November and that was one thing that was a thing of the past—a welcome change, the air clear and brisk.

I also recalled Dad's voice as we would walk together: "Come on, Kath, step out, big strides..." He was so tall and I always somewhat had to trot to keep up with him. "Kath, have you got your gas mask?"... "Kath, will you get on your bike and go to the butcher?" All these things whirled and echoed in my head as we made our way. Such vivid moments, full and yet now, without Mum and Dad's presence, alternately close and lost somewhere "out there" calling me from the past where they, and I, for at least these moments still lived.

We visited a few old school chums of mine, and although we had definitely all changed, it seemed as though time vanished as we spoke, and we were taking up where we left off. The years rolled away as we spoke.

Downtown Buxton seemed unchanged, even businesses proprietors' names I knew from girlhood were the same, as I guessed family members passed the torch, and sons, daughters, grandchildren took them on through the years.

We drove out of town and saw the hills with their abandoned concrete pillboxes, once the clear signs one was approaching "McAlpine's," the moors surrounding still and quiet, save for the grouse and sheep. I realized looking around me that what I wanted most was time—more time than allotted and more than we had. And, just as quickly as I had this realization, knowing that there would never be enough, no matter how long I was there, to understand what was, and what it had meant to whom I had become.

November in the countryside, even upcountry, is an especially good month to witness the brilliant green that depicts the England of picture books and postcards. The weather is ideal for travel. We rambled around the hedgerows of Staffordshire and the stone walls of Derbyshire. We ventured farther north to the bleak and austere North

Country, each county revealing itself and its own distinct beauty. I never tire of the changes from county line to county line, neither in the variance of their landscapes nor the accents and colloquial expressions of their inhabitants.

As we spoke to those we encountered, I was struck by their warmth and intense interest in welcoming strangers, just as I was humbled by their many kindnesses, and, during the trip, it occurred to me often that you *can* go back, you just have to realize that acceptance of change need not be confused with loss—the thing we all experience but not a one of us can alter. Time moves inexorably forward, and with it one's perspectives on so many things personal and collective.

We change more than anything. Memory mediates, sometimes leading, sometimes following, sometimes both and at varying times and distances too, like the rolling deck of a ship. Each one remains, as they say, fugitive—either in flight from hostile forces or pursuit of friendly accommodation. Memory seems to close in when it conjures the horrific, just as it opens up to the joyous and the beautiful. We wrestle most with the bittersweet, with the impositions of conflicts and rewards simultaneously presented us in it. One can always find disappointment in expectations—things having not been "kept up" or as they *could* have been or *should* have been in our estimations. We are all susceptible, predisposed, to the disappointments when realities don't square with our visions of them.

During our journey, I discovered for instance, that there was no longer any Buxton Town Council—the Derbyshire County Council now calls the shots for Buxton, and, apparently, have other places in mind when preserving what, to my mind, are quintessential Buxton heritage. I could not help but miss a few of these things, but, even those missed could not change what I found, and, all in all it was still my Buxton; the place I so loved as a child and a burgeoning young woman. Many of my memories were hard to deal with, as the realization sank in that the world I knew, or thought I did in some fixed way, no longer exists if, in fact, it ever did anywhere but in my perceptions then and my recollections now. Nevertheless, Buxton is, and I call it, mine; to come from, return to—then, before, again, still, ever... always to cherish.

Standing in the same spot as I had as a child, scanning the distance as far as I could across the moors and then turning slowly back again to survey Buxton at the centre of my vantage point, it all lay before me serene and untroubled. The sheep grazed, their far-off bleating the only sound breaking the silence. The passage of time was suspended if only momentarily. I stood there in the here-and-now and the then-and-forever in the same breath. Scanning the horizon, each landmark had its place and so did I.

I felt a peace I had not since last I held this spot. It doesn't matter how far I may stray, where or what place I may live or what I do, my heart will always yearn for it. Perhaps in Wordsworth's "The Daffodils" lies the best summation of the feeling...

For oft, when on my couch I lie,
In vacant or in pensive mood,
They cross before the inward eye,
Which is the bliss of solitude,
And then my heart with pleasure fills
And dances with the daffodils

So many things transpired between that moment when I looked across a New York harbour illuminated in the bright glow of a promising future and the day on the green hillock just outside my little village in 1997. It is now the time in my life when I very often reflect and "dance with the daffodils," as each beloved time, place, and person I have known flits through my mind, vividly rendered and sharply etched both there and here in my heart.

Acknowledgements

The support and encouragement when embarking upon a journey such as writing this story, is tantamount to its success. I am thankful to the following people in my life:

To my son, Jeffrey James Murcko, my Editor in Chief, a brilliant writer in his own right, for his tireless patience, invaluable input, attention to detail, and his encouragement to keep going as I made this journey. Thank you.

To my late husband of 63 years, Joe, who never waivered in support of this project, encouraged and cheered me on to finish. His belief in this book, and in me, helped me to keep going and complete it. I wish he could have known that I finally realized my dream. My deepest thanks.

To Dr. John W. Hull, Jr., my stepson, who guided me to the right source to publish this book, and to whom I shall be ever grateful. Thank you.

To Dr. Teresa M. Hull, my stepdaughter, for her enthusiastic support and encouragement. Being here for me has meant so much. Thank you.

To Lucy Nolan, my Guardian Angel, for all your help in so many ways, together with your excitement to see this book completed. Thank you.

To my publishers, Jan & Joe McDaniel of BookCrafters, without whom you would not be holding this book in your hands. Their guidance and expertise have brought this project to fruition. I am deeply grateful to you. Thank you.

And last, but by no means least, to my incredible husband John W. Hull, Sr., (Jack), who has been an untiring support to me throughout the completion of this project. Thanks for putting up with me. You are my hero!

About the Author

The writer lives with her husband in Coloradc where she pursues her hobbies and interests in reading, writing, painting and music.

All grown up and in America

CPSIA information can be obtained
at www.ICGtesting.com
Printed in the USA
FFHW011329041019
55350928-61119FF